MATURA
Prime
Time

Upper-intermediate

Workbook

Virginia Evans – Jenny Dooley

CW00573594

Express Publishing

Published by Express Publishing

Liberty House, Greenham Business Park, Newbury,
Berkshire RG19 6HW
Tel.: (0044) 1635 817 363
Fax: (0044) 1635 817 463
e-mail: inquiries@expresspublishing.co.uk
http://www.expresspublishing.co.uk

© Virginia Evans – Jenny Dooley, 2012

Design and Illustration © Express Publishing, 2012

Colour Illustrations: Victor, Emmanuel, Angela, Simon Andrews, Kyr © Express Publishing, 2012

First published 2012

Polish edition by EGIS, 2012

Made in EU

ISBN 978-1-78098-967-9

Acknowledgements

Authors' Acknowledgements
We would like to thank all the staff at Express Publishing who have contributed their skills to producing this book. Thanks for their support and patience are due in particular to: Megan Lawton (Editor in Chief); Mary Swan and Sean Todd (senior editors); Michael Sadler and Steve Miller (editorial assistants); Richard White (senior production controller); the Express design team; Sweetspot (recording producers); and Kevin Harris, Kimberly Baker, Steven Gibbs and Christine Little. We would also like to thank those institutions and teachers who piloted the manuscript, and whose comments and feedback were invaluable in the production of the book.

Photograph Acknowledgements
Glastonbury Festival © afp/www.iml.gr on p. 34; Mireya Mayor © WENN/www.iml.gr on p. 35; Bennini © everettcollection/www.iml.gr on p. 149

Every effort has been made to trace all the copyright holders. If any have been inadvertently overlooked, the publishers will be pleased to make the necessary arrangements at the first opportunity.

Contents

1a

Vocabulary

1 a) ★ Match the words to make phrases.

1	mine	A	volcano
2	flaming hot	B	photographs
3	deafening	C	temperatures
4	stunning	D	eruption
5	freelance	E	nights
6	dormant	F	gases
7	sleepless	G	roar
8	freezing	H	photographer
9	poisonous	I	lava
10	volcanic	J	collapse

b) ★★ Use some of the phrases above to complete the sentences.

1 A(n) .... sends ash and gas flying up into the atmosphere.
2 Martin is a(n) .... who takes pictures of volcanoes all over the world.
3 Sam hiked to the top of the volcano in snow and ....
4 John spent three .... camping in the jungle. The mosquitoes kept him awake.
5 Mauna Kea in Hawaii is a(n) .... It hasn't erupted for at least 4,000 years.
6 He took some .... of the volcano erupting; they were so beautiful!

2 ★ Fill in: *shake, stay, evacuate, block, take, provide.*

1 Volcano chasers have to wear a gas mask in order to .... alive.
2 When Chile's Puyehue volcano started erupting in 2011, officials had to .... thousands of people from the area.
3 Did you just feel the ground ....? I think it was a small earthquake.
4 Volcano chasers have to .... safety precautions such as wearing a gas mask and goggles.
5 Some tall trees in the garden .... the view from my bedroom window.
6 Gloves .... volcano chasers protection from hot lava.

Grammar

3 ★ Complete the exchanges with the verbs in brackets in the *present simple*, *present continuous*, *past simple*, *past continuous*, *present perfect* or the *present perfect continuous*.

1 A: You .... **(look)** tired, Tom.
   B: Yes, I .... **(hike)** all day.
2 A: .... ever .... **(you/have)** a bad accident?
   B: Yes. I once .... **(trip)** on a rock and .... **(break)** my arm.
3 A: What .... **(you/do)** to your finger, Jane? It looks swollen.
   B: I .... **(slam)** a door on it yesterday morning.
4 A: How often .... **(you/go)** mountain climbing, Sam?
   B: I .... **(go)** about once a month. I .... **(go)** this weekend, actually.
5 A: Look at Mark and James! They .... **(dive)** from the cliff!
   B: Yes. I think they .... **(enjoy)** themselves!
6 A: What .... **(you/do)** when the earthquake happened?
   B: I .... **(do)** my homework while Tim and Sally .... **(watch)** TV.

4 ★ Underline the correct tense.

1 The plane **leaves/has left** at 9 am tomorrow.
2 The rescue workers **are searching/search** through the rubble for survivors.
3 Mark **has found/is finding** a new freelance job.
4 The photographer **has been taking/has taken** pictures for three hours.
5 They **travelled/were travelling** to Chile last year.
6 It rained while they **were hiking/hiked** through the forest.
7 He **was climbing/climbed** the mountain when he **slipped/was slipping**.
8 Tom often **is going/goes** camping at the weekend.
9 The miners **dug/have been digging** in the old copper mine all day.

Vocabulary

1 ★ **Read the story and fill in:** *rescue, desperate, struck, pain, dehydration, broke, survive, spotted, struggled, notify, remote.*

LOST IN THE AFRICAN BUSH

One day in 2003, animal conservationist Greg Rasmussen was flying low over a(n) **1)** .... area in the African savanna, when disaster **2)** .... His plane crashed, and he **3)** .... both of his legs. His radio wasn't working, so he couldn't **4)** .... the authorities. Before long, he smelled gas, so he **5)** .... to drag himself away from the plane. He was in terrible **6)** .... He was out under the midday sun, and had to fight exhaustion and **7)** .... As the sun set, wild animals approached. It was a(n) **8)** .... struggle to **9)** .... Just after daybreak, Greg heard a **10)** .... helicopter. The pilot **11)** .... him and his nightmare was finally over.

2 ★ **Fill in:** *sacrifice, credit, prosthetic, aid, delirious, motivational, disabled, troubled.*

1 Sam works as a(n) .... speaker, giving talks to teenagers about facing challenges.
2 Sophie used her .... card to pay for the camping supplies.
3 Aron Ralston had to make an incredible .... to survive; he cut off his own arm.
4 The Paralympic Games are for .... athletes.
5 Daniel helps .... teenagers who have had problems with the police.
6 Aron Ralston now has a(n) .... arm after his terrible accident.
7 The rescue worker administered first .... to the injured man.
8 Aron Ralston became .... from dehydration.

Grammar

3 ★ **Put the verbs in brackets in the *past perfect* or the *past perfect continuous*.**

1 They .... (walk) in the forest for hours before they realised they were lost.
2 Peter was upset because he .... (see) a horrible car crash.
3 How long .... (Aron/climb) before the accident happened?
4 Ann felt cold because she .... (forget) to take her coat.
5 Tom .... (wait) for two hours when the rescue helicopter finally arrived.

4 ★★ **Use the *past perfect* or the *past perfect continuous* to complete the sentences.**

1 James was exhausted because ....
2 They had already ....
3 By the time Brian arrived, ...
4 He had been .... before
  ....
5 Kelly was angry because ....

5 ★ **Put the verbs in brackets into the *past perfect* or the *past perfect continuous*.**

In 1990, two friends Robert and Barry managed to survive the harsh conditions of the Sahara desert alone for two days. The two friends **1)** .... (enrol) in the Marathon of the Sands which was a seven day foot race through the Sahara desert. Before the competition began they **2)** .... (pack) all the food, clothing and supplies they needed on their desert adventure in large rucksacks, which they carried on their backs. On the first day of the event the two friends **3)** .... (walk) in the desert for a few hours when all of a sudden a sand storm appeared out of nowhere. They had nowhere to take cover. Robert opened his rucksack only to realise that he **4)** .... (forget) to pack their compass. Terrified, the men sat in the middle of the sand storm and waited for help to arrive. They **5)** .... (wait) for two days before the organisers of the event realised that the two men were missing. The organisers sent a rescue team which eventually found them. The two men felt extremely lucky to be alive!

Vocabulary

1 ★ **Fill in:** *struggled, smashed, declared, pumped, begged.*

1 The president .... a state of emergency after the storm hit.
2 Rescue workers .... to cope with deadly floodwaters.
3 The flood victims .... for help from emergency services.
4 A crowd of youths .... shop windows during the riot.
5 People .... water out of their houses after the flood.

2 ★ **Fill in the sentences with the correct words derived from the words in brackets.**

1 Scientists fear that the storm will .... and become a major hurricane. (**STRONG**)
2 The mayor ordered the .... of New Orleans to evacuate the city immediately. (**RESIDE**)
3 The storm was so .... that it destroyed the whole village. (**POWER**)
4 There was a lot of violence and .... of department stores after Hurricane Katrina hit the city. (**LOOT**)
5 The city is making a slow .... (**RECOVER**)

3 ★ **Complete the sentences with the correct word.**

• funny • silly • relaxing • boring
• predictable • educational

1 The TV programme was so ....; I nearly fell asleep.
2 Some documentaries are very .... because you learn new things.
3 Mark told a(n) .... joke and everybody laughed.
4 They like .... and watching TV on their sofa.
5 Most horror films are .... because you can guess what will happen.
6 Janet dislikes soap operas; she finds them ....

Speaking

4 ★ **Use the sentences (A-F) to complete the dialogue. One sentence isn't necessary.**

A Isn't there anything else on?
B I like the sound of that!
C OK. That's fine with me!
D I happen to find it interesting.
E Anyway, it's nearly finished.
F Why don't you look in the TV guide?

A: Why are you watching this silly game show?
B: [1]
A: What's on later?
B: [2]
A: After this there's CSI on Channel 1 or a cooking show on Channel 3.
B: [3]
A: The Daily Show is on Channel 2. You know, it's a talk show. We can watch that.
B: OK. [4] As long as we can change the channel at 9. I want to see Grey's Anatomy.
A: [5]

5 ★★ **Write a similar dialogue to the one in Ex. 4. Use the TV guide below.**

	Channel 4	Channel 5	Channel 6
4:30	Sarah's – cooking show	Garfield – cartoon	Sportsday – sports programme
5:30	Make a deal – game show	The Penguin March – documentary	The Arnold Family – sitcom
6:00	News & Weather	The Best of Nature – wildlife programme	Simon's Meals – cooking show

Nightmare at Sea

A life on the ocean promises freedom and adventure. But the "big blue" can also be dangerous and unpredictable.
Read Tami Oldham Ashcraft's incredible story of loss and survival at sea.

In September 1983, 23-year-old Tami and her fiancé Richard Sharp, 34 years-old, were preparing to set sail from Tahiti; their task was to deliver the 44-foot luxury yacht 'Hazana' across the Pacific to its owners in San Diego. It was a task that they couldn't refuse as they would be paid a $10,000 delivery fee and they desperately needed the money. [____] Leaving Tahiti, Tami and Richard enjoyed clear blue skies. What's more, the weather forecast predicted fine conditions throughout their 31-day journey as it was past the middle of the hurricane season and it was rare for storms to occur at that time of year.

Indeed, it was smooth sailing until day 17, when the dawn broke with gray skies and rain. [____] A small land bird crash-landed onto the deck. The two sailors found it strange that the wind had carried the bird so far from shore. The next day, weather reports warned that a tropical storm – a category 4 hurricane – was developing off the shores of South America. By day 19, the storm was coming closer. During the early hours of the following day, the wind became stronger and produced a deafening roar like the sound of jet engines. The waves were dangerous with some reaching 50 feet high – about the height of a five-story building! Suddenly a huge wave hit them, and the whole boat shuddered. While Richard was steering, a large cliff of water rose behind him. [____] That's when it happened; the last thing Tami remembers is Richard's scream; suddenly, the boat fell into a huge rolling wave – spinning the yacht 360 degrees and launching it into the air.

27 hours later, Tami regained consciousness and struggled to free herself from the objects that were pinning her down. [____] The sea was calm, but there was no sign of Richard. The yacht had taken on over three feet of water. Both its mast and sails had been destroyed. The motor and all the electronics were dead. Without a radio, Tami couldn't signal for help. [____] There was one saving grace; the yacht's rudder had survived. Tami was injured and completely alone. Fighting shock, depression and fear, she somehow chartered a course to the Hawaiian Islands. [____] Deep into the journey, she spotted a ship in the distance. She grabbed her flare gun and shot off three flares but to no avail as the ship never changed its direction. She drifted for 41 days before being spotted and rescued by a passing boat near Hawaii, by this time she had travelled a total of 1,500 miles.

[7][__] Nowadays, she continues to sail and has written a book called *Red Sky in Mourning*, telling her story of 'love, loss and survival at sea.'

Reading

1 ★ **Read the text. Seven sentences are missing. Match each sentence (A-H) to a gap (1-7). There is one extra sentence.**

A Richard immediately sent Tami below deck to check the barometer while he remained at the wheel.

B And then there were the calm days.

C Both were already experienced sailors and felt confident about the job.

D She was covered in blood and she had deep cuts on her left leg and forehead.

E Hour after hour, for as long as she could, Tami steered the boat.

F Then, the wind became increasingly unpredictable.

G It's amazing that Tami survived.

H With only a small supply of canned foods and water left, things seemed hopeless.

Vocabulary

2 ★ **Fill in:** *restore, whirling, phenomena, wildfire, astonished, ignited, miracle.*

1 It was a(n) .... that she survived lost at sea for so many days.

2 Investigators have concluded that lightning .... the forest fire.

3 Meteorologists also study many strange weather ....

4 They were .... when they saw the explosion in the sky.

5 The wind grew stronger and created a .... snowstorm that blew snow everywhere.

6 After the hurricane, it took years to .... the town back to its original condition.

7 The .... has burned many acres of land.

Vocabulary

1 ★ **Fill in:** *evacuation, rubble, devastating, epicentre, shook, partial, courageous, collapse, frantic, aftershocks, stranded, triggered.*

1 The .... earthquake destroyed many houses in the area.

2 There was a(n) .... rush to escape from the burning building.

3 The building was so damaged that the police worried it would ....

4 The police officer had only a(n) .... description of the missing boy.

5 Scientists recorded a series of .... after the strong quake.

6 The underwater earthquake .... huge tsunami waves.

7 Thousands of people remained .... after losing their homes in the flood.

8 There are .... rescue workers who are ready to risk their lives to save others in need.

9 The mayor ordered a(n) .... of the area after the tsunami warning.

10 The quake was so strong that the building .... violently from side to side.

11 Rescue workers tried to pull survivors out of the ....

12 The quake's .... was in the sea, 100 kilometres from the coast.

2 ★ **Choose the correct word.**

1 The tsunami **swept/forced** away many houses.

2 The accident **ripped/hurled** the car apart.

3 The hurricane **moved/headed** for the Caribbean island.

4 An earthquake **struck/slammed** off the coast of Chile yesterday.

5 Power plants **closed/crumbled** down after the earthquake hit.

6 The injured child cried and **held/clung** to his mother.

7 The wave **floated/rolled** across the ocean and hit the coast.

8 The damaged area was **loaded/washed** with debris.

Grammar

3 ★ **Underline the correct item.**

Hurricane Hits
Southern Florida in the US

A destructive hurricane which struck Southern Florida yesterday afternoon has injured **1) many/much** residents. The hurricane caused a **2) couple/great deal** of damage when heavy rain and winds of up to 88 kilometres per hour knocked down **3) plenty/a large amount of** trees and power lines in the area.

4) Most/Too much homes across the state have lost power. The violent storm has also destroyed **5) many/much** houses and buildings and left thousands of people homeless. Emergency workers have set up **6) a few/a little** shelters for the homeless as they struggle to distribute food and water. **7) Some/Every** experts are now trying to estimate **8) how much/how many** it will cost to repair the damage due to the devastating hurricane. **9) Several/Each** forecasters at the National Hurricane Centre are worried that the storm will move along the East Coast and hit other states in its path.

4 ★ **Fill in:** *whole, both, neither, either* **or** *none.*

1 Jeff survived .... a hurricane and a flood all in the same week.

2 .... Tom or Sharon will call the emergency services.

3 .... Joe nor Paul were near the mine when it collapsed.

4 .... of my friends have ever experienced an earthquake.

5 An earthquake destroyed a .... village in Northern Chile.

Vocabulary

1 ★ Complete the crossword with the types of disasters shown in the pictures.

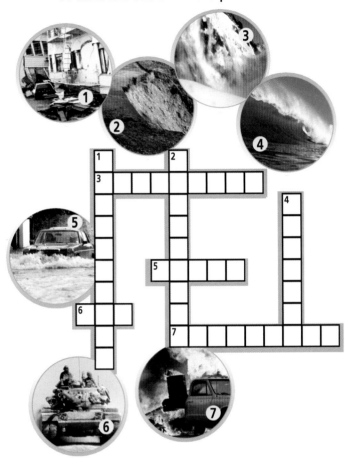

2 ★ Choose the words from the list to complete the newspaper headlines.

- DAMAGED • BLACKENS • COLLAPSES
- BLAST • RESCUE • INJURES

CLEAR BLUE SKY 1) .... **AS STORM APPROACHES**

RAIL ACCIDENT 2) .... **10 PASSENGERS**

LUCKY ESCAPE AFTER ROOF 3) ....

EMERGENCY CREWS 4) .... **PLANE CRASH SURVIVORS**

A BOMB 5) .... **SHOOK BUILDINGS IN THE CITY CENTRE**

CRUISE SHIP 6) .... **IN STORM**

Speaking

3 ★ Choose the correct exchange.

1 A: Did you hear about the plane crash?
   B: **a** Really?
      b It's awful, isn't it?

2 A: Guess what happened?
   B: **a** That's so sad.
      b What?

3 A: Look at this accident!
   B: **a** I don't believe it!
      b It's great!

4 A: There was an explosion.
   B: **a** How horrible!
      b Sure!

Listening

4 ★★ 🎧 You will hear part of an interview with a rescue worker who helped after the earthquake and tsunami in Japan in March 2011. For each question, choose the correct answer *A*, *B* or *C*.

1 Simon helped after the disaster in Japan because he was
   A a trained professional.
   B on holiday there.
   C a volunteer charity worker.

2 The most difficult aspect of the rescue effort was the
   A poor roads.   **B** lack of machinery.
   C poor weather.

3 Simon became very disappointed one time when
   A he wasn't present when a survivor was found.
   B his radio stopped working.
   C he hoped to find a survivor, but didn't.

4 Simon says it isn't common to find survivors
   A one week after a disaster.
   B after four days.
   C after such a terrible earthquake.

5 He says he found the Japanese people
   A organised.   **B** hopeless.
   C very positive.

Vocabulary

1 ★ **Fill in:** *tectonic, powerful, undersea, fault, giant, tremendous.*

1 The tsunami in Japan in 2011 caused .... damage.
2 An earthquake is a very .... natural force.
3 Tsunamis are .... waves which can wipe out areas within seconds.
4 The places in the Earth's crust where .... plates meet and move against each other are called .... lines.
5 A(n) .... earthquake 30 kilometres below sea level caused the 2004 Asian tsunami.

2 ★ **Choose the correct word.**

1 A light wind made **ripples/pebbles** on the river.
2 The large **level/scale** earthquake appears to have caused massive damage.
3 Predicting the **speed/impact** of a tsunami on coastal areas is a difficult process.
4 The tornado **flattened/slid** hundreds of homes.
5 The ship was spotted drifting toward the **inland/shore**.
6 The tornado destroyed everything in its **line/path**.
7 A natural disaster can cause **damage/loss** of life.

3 ★ **Choose the correct participle.**

1 The rescue search was called **out/off** due to bad weather conditions.
2 The police officer asked the driver to back **away/up** from his vehicle.
3 Janet refused to back **away/down** on her demands.
4 Scientists are carrying **off/out** research to predict natural disasters.
5 Back **up/down** all your computer data on a floppy disk.
6 Due to a severe injury, the athlete backed **out/away** of the competition.
7 The rescue workers carried **on/back** searching for survivors despite the darkness.

Listening

4 ★ 🎧 **You will hear an interview with a woman called Mary Stewart who is a flood safety expert. For questions 1-10, complete the sentences.**

Mary gives advice on how to reduce flood ⬛ **1** .

Mary recommends installing sealants on ⬛ **2** and doors.

Mary tells us to place important documents on ⬛ **3** .

During a flood people should stay informed by turning on the ⬛ **4** .

Mary advises homeowners to have a(n) ⬛ **5** nearby.

Mary gives the example of flooding roads and ⬛ **6** as significant dangers in a flood.

Mary tells us that evacuation ⬛ **7** must be followed.

Cars should keep away from flood waters or ⬛ **8** .

Mary cautions us not to return to our homes unless the ⬛ **9** give us permission.

Drinking contaminated water can cause ⬛ **10** .

Writing (a story)

1 ★ Read the story and answer the questions.

1 When and where did the story take place? ....
....
2 What is the climax event? ....
3 What happened in the end? ....
4 How did the characters feel in the end? ....
....

A LUCKY ESCAPE

▶ Last summer, I went on the holiday of a lifetime to the Caribbean with my friends, Tom and Sarah. It was very relaxing and beautiful there and the sun shone every day. We felt like we were in paradise!

▶ Tom is an experienced sailor and so one day, he suggested hiring a sailing yacht. We had been sailing happily around all day and having a fantastic time, when suddenly we realised that dark clouds had appeared in the sky and the wind had started to blow quite strongly. Before long, a violent storm broke out. The boat was moving up and down wildly, when it hit a huge rock!

▶ Tom tried to get control of the boat, but we soon realised that the yacht was sinking. Tom quickly got the rescue dinghy ready and we all jumped in. It was extremely windy and frightening out on the open sea. We were sure that we couldn't survive in the dinghy for long. Then, we saw a motorboat speeding towards us. It was a rescue boat!

▶ When we finally reached the shore, we were shaking with shock, but very relieved. The next day, we were even interviewed on the local radio station. We knew we had had a very lucky escape!

2 ★ Read the story again and put the events in the order they happened.

☐ the boat started to sink
☐ we went sailing
☐ a large wave threw us against a rock
☐ the local radio station interviewed us
☐ we went to the Caribbean
☐ we were rescued by a motorboat
☐ a strong wind started to blow

3 ★ Which adjectives does the writer use to describe the following?

1 .... sailor
2 .... time
3 .... clouds
4 .... storm
5 .... sea
6 .... escape

4 ★ Find the adverbs the writer uses to describe these verbs.

1 had been sailing ....
2 we .... realised
3 had started to blow quite ....
4 was moving up and down ....
5 got the rescue dinghy ready ....
6 It was .... windy

5 ★ Replace the adjectives in bold with:
dangerous, difficult, terrifying, pleased, calm, thrilling, deafening, dark.

Two years ago, my friend and I decided to go on holiday to Thailand. I had been studying hard all year, so I was **1) glad** to finally have a break. As soon as we boarded the plane, I sat back in my seat and put on my headphones. After a **2) tough** year at university, I finally felt **3) relaxed**. Soon, I would be sunbathing on a sandy beach, I thought to myself as I drifted off to sleep.
Suddenly, a **4) loud** clap of thunder ripped through the air, jolting me awake. Then, the plane started to rock violently from side to side. We were flying through the middle of a huge storm! The lights on board the plane began flickering and after a few moments, everything went **5) black**. "We're going down!" screamed one passenger. It was a truly **6) horrifying** experience!
After a few minutes, the plane finally stopped shaking and the lights came back on. Everyone on board breathed a sigh of relief. I usually find lightning storms **7) exciting**, but while I was on that plane, it felt very **8) unsafe**. I was so thankful when we arrived at the airport several hours later!

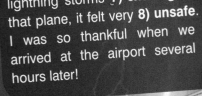

11

6 ★ **Fill in :** *carefully, violently, rapidly, slowly, anxiously, unexpectedly.*

1 The boat was .... tossed around in the storm.
2 Mark looked .... at his watch. He was going to be late.
3 The nurse .... removed his bandage so she would not hurt his injury.
4 The train stopped .... in the middle of the track.
5 Liam was frustrated as the traffic jam moved .... along the motorway.
6 The raft was moving .... along the fast-flowing river.

7 ★ **Choose the correct linking words. What linking words are used in the story in Ex. 1?**

1 We were rowing along when **suddenly/finally** we saw something moving in the river.
2 The car swerved. **Then/Later**, it turned upside down.
3 It started to rain and **finally/before long** we were soaking wet.
4 The river burst its banks. **Ten minutes later/After**, the water was rushing down the road like a river.
5 **When/As** the car rolled down the hill, it went faster and faster.

8 ★ **Link the sentences. Use the words in brackets.**

1 We arrived at the beach. We went for a swim. **(as soon as)**
....
2 He put on his bathing suit. He went swimming. **(then)**
....
3 The adults were sunbathing. The children were swimming. **(while)**
....
4 I arrived at the airport. I realised that I had forgotten my passport. **(when)**
....
5 I checked out of the hotel. I packed my suitcase. **(before)**
....

12

Setting the scene
In the first paragraph of a story, include details that set the scene e.g. describe the place **(where)**, the time **(when)**, the weather, the people involved **(who)** and what happens.

9 ★ **Read the rubric and underline the phrases/sentences in the story in Ex. 1 that set the scene.**

10 a) ★ **Read the rubric. Use the completed table to set the scene for the story. Write a first paragraph for it.**

> A magazine is asking for a story about a bad experience (200-250 words).

When:	last weekend
Where:	snowy mountain
Weather:	sunny, cold
Who:	Tim & his friends
What:	go hiking

b) **Look at the pictures and write a list of the main events in the story. Which could be the climax event?**

11 ★★ **Use your answers from Ex. 10 and the sentences from the *Useful language* box to write your story.**

Useful language

Setting the scene: One cold day Tim and ..., after they ...
Events: They were ..., all of a sudden ..., they saw ..., then ...
Ending/Feelings: Before long ..., they sighed with relief ...

English in Use
Word Formation

1 ★ Read the text and complete the gaps with the words derived from the words in bold.

On 5th August 2010, two groups of **1)** .... were digging in a gold-copper mine in San Jose, Chile. Due to a landslide, the tunnel collapsed and the men became trapped. The **2)** .... men survived 69 days deep underground before their rescue. The old mine had a long record of fines and safety **3)** .... which had resulted in a series of accidents in the past. As a result, authorities **4)** .... thought that the workers hadn't survived the collapse. **5)** ...., the men were alive and it was quite **6)** .... how they managed to survive underground for so long!

MINE

BURY

VIOLATE

INITIAL

LUCK

AMAZE

Key Word Transformations

2 ★ Complete the gapped sentences so that they have a similar meaning to the original ones, using the words given.

1 It's two weeks since Ted went camping.
   FOR   Ted .... two weeks.

2 She had never experienced an earthquake before.
   TIME   It was .... experienced an earthquake.

3 They didn't declare a state of emergency until after the storm had hit.
   BEFORE   They waited until the storm .... a state of emergency.

4 How long is it since he sprained his ankle?
   SPRAIN   When .... his ankle?

5 Kevin began rock climbing when he was 15.
   SINCE   Kevin .... he was 15.

Speaking

Choose the correct response.

1 A: What's on later?
   B: **a** I don't know.
      b I like the sound of that.

2 A: Is there anything else on?
   B: **a** A talent show.
      b We can watch that.

3 A: Did you see the oil spill on the news?
   B: **a** Yes. I don't believe it.
      b Yes. I don't think so.

4 A: Why are you watching this?
   B: **a** I'm enjoying it.
      b It's nearly finished.

5 A: What is it?
   B: **a** It's on channel nine.
      b It's a reality show.

6 A: Did you hear about the tsunami?
   B: **a** Guess what?
      b It's terrible, isn't it?

7 A: Why don't you look in the TV guide?
   B: **a** OK. A police drama is on next.
      b It's predictable.

8 A: Soap operas are a waste of time!
   B: **a** No problem.
      b I think they're interesting.

9 A: Look at this plane crash!
   B: **a** How horrible!
      b Not really!

10 A: Can we change the channel?
    B: **a** That's fine with me.
       b I can't stand game shows.

11 A: Can you pass me the remote control?
    B: **a** That's great.
       b Here you are.

12 A: There's been a major train crash.
    B: **a** That's so sad!
       b Guess what happened!

Language & Grammar Review

Choose the correct answer.

1 Bangladesh is often under ..... from flooding.
A danger   C impact
B threat   D possibility

2 The ..... buried many houses under mud.
A flood   C avalanche
B landslide   D volcano

3 He just ..... the door on his finger.
A grazed   C banged
B gashed   D slammed

4 A: Did you hear about the factory explosion?
B: .....
A Guess what!   C It's awful, isn't it?
B Look at this!   D What is it?

5 I like documentaries because they are ..... .
A predictable   C funny
B silly   D educational

6 The concert was called ..... due to the storm.
A back   B off   C out   D up

7 Volcano chasers wear a mask to protect themselves against ..... gases.
A poisonous   C flaming
B deafening   D violent

8 Tom's making a slow ..... from his accident.
A relief   C rescue
B struggle   D recovery

9 The earthquake caused the buildings to ..... .
A trigger   B smash   C strike   D shake

10 Jack likes to live his life ..... the fullest.
A from   B to   C in   D at

11 Fire-fighters ..... the floodwater out of the building.
A hurled   B swept   C slid   D pumped

12 The doctor ..... first aid to the accident victim.
A dedicated   C administered
B admitted   D mended

13 The volcano erupted with a ..... roar.
A ringing   C flaming
B deafening   D crashing

14 The village is in a ..... location that is difficult to reach.
A rare   B remote   C stable   D stranded

15 Simon ..... to Brazil next week.
A is going   C has gone
B goes   D has been going

16 Jane was cold because she ..... in the rain for an hour.
A had been walking   C has been walking
B is walking   D has walked

17 By the time they arrived at the campsite it ..... raining.
A stopped   C has stopped
B had stopped   D stops

18 ..... people were injured in the earthquake.
A Every   B Much   C Plenty   D A lot of

19 The town didn't have ..... electricity after the earthquake.
A any   B some   C none   D several

20 They ..... TV when the storm hit.
A watched   C had watched
B were watching   D have been watching

21 The rescue team ..... searching for survivors since this morning.
A has been   C were
B had been   D are

22 ..... of buildings were destroyed in the earthquake.
A Several   C Much
B A large number   D All

23 ..... Jamie nor Peter were in Mexico when the hurricane hit.
A Either   B Neither   C Both   D Nor

24 Harold ..... in this village since he was a child.
A is living   C has been living
B lives   D was living

25 Have you ..... that new sitcom on TV?
A been seeing   C saw
B seen   D see

Extreme Storm

Reading Task

Read the article. For questions 1-6, choose the correct answer A, B, C or D.

CHASING TOURS

Some people dream of sightseeing in Italy. Others fantasise about taking a cruise or lying on a tranquil beach in the hot sun, but not me. No; when I take a holiday, I want it to be something to remember. That's why I chose to go on an extreme storm
5 chasing tour!

As I arrived at the meeting point for my storm chasing adventure, I was like a dog with two tails. I simply couldn't wait to get up close and personal with my first storm! My tour guide, Roger Hill, shook my hand emphatically upon entering
10 the room. Middle-aged and dressed in run-of-the-mill clothing, Roger didn't conform to the daredevil image that I'd imagined. However, his ordinary demeanour hid the fact that he had encountered over 400 tornadoes and had lived to tell the tale!

After a brief orientation during which Roger explained what
15 we would be doing throughout our week-long tour, we jumped into the chase van and took off on our first adventure. Together with three other 'tourists', we headed across the Great Plains towards Kansas. I had hoped to see some spectacular scenery en route, but was disappointed by the flat, empty landscape
20 that seemed to stretch on forever. Now and again we would pass some grazing animals or a peculiar rock formation, but in general it was entirely desolate.

After six hours, we finally arrived at our destination. We were just in time. The clouds had started to curl into dark,
25 ominous columns that towered overhead. In the distance we could see a heavy mist approaching. I pulled out my video camera and started filming. The cloud was simply astounding. It was like a huge explosion in the sky, mushroom-shaped and swirling madly as it gathered strength. A wave of excitement
30 washed over me as the storm was finally upon us.

Suddenly, there was a loud bang. At first I thought a rock had hit the van. Then I realised what had happened: golf up hailstones had been unleashed from the sky! They pounded down on the roof threatening to break it, but since the van was reinforced we knew that we were safe. Then the lightning 35 started. It illuminated the blackened clouds, striking the ground nearby with a deafening boom. At this point, my camera ran out of batteries. I reached for the back-up, but to my frustration I had forgotten to pack it. I just hope my memory of the events will remain vivid. 40

Although our second day was almost completely uneventful, the remainder of the week was spent observing a variety of cloud formations, dust tornadoes and spectacular lightning displays. The most memorable of these was witnessed on our fourth day, when we stumbled upon an 45 intense lightning storm at sunset. It lit up the sky in stunning red and orange hues that were simply incredible. But nothing compared to our final day.

A severe thunderstorm warning had been issued in Nebraska, so we set off eagerly first thing in the morning. 50 When we arrived at our chosen viewpoint, the clouds had begun to swirl, forming the shape of a cone. They lowered slowly downwards and, before we knew it, grew into a large tornado! We gasped in awe as the twister surged across the landscape, pulling debris from the ground. Its terrifying roar 55 reminded us of its capacity for destruction. After only 10 minutes, it was all over. But witnessing first-hand the intense beauty and power of Mother Nature was an experience that will last a lifetime!

1 For the writer, the most important aspect of going on holiday is
A seeing spectacular things.
B fulfilling his dreams.
C having an unforgettable time.
D enjoying the weather.

2 The writer uses the phrase 'like a dog with two tails' (line 7) to illustrate that he felt
A content   C peculiar
B excited   D nervous

3 What had surprised the writer about Roger Hill?
A He was unusually friendly.
B He looked old for his age.
C His clothing was old-fashioned.
D He didn't seem adventurous.

4 What was the writer's attitude towards the long journey?
A He found it very relaxing.
B He grew disheartened.
C He was filled with suspense.
D He felt worried.

5 The writer uses the word 'it' (line 46) to refer to
A a lightning storm
B a dust tornado
C a cloud formation
D a sunset

6 How does the writer reflect upon his experience?
A It was too short-lived.
B He will remember it forever.
C Nature's power terrified him.
D He would like to relive it.

1

Building Up Vocabulary

1 Complete the sentences using one of the words in the box.

> • headline • tabloid • broadsheet

1 Jane buys .... newspapers because she likes to read gossip columns.
2 The bold .... on the front page of the newspaper caught Dean's attention.
3 Mark writes about complex financial issues for a respectable .... newspaper.

> • announcer • commentator • journalist

4 Maria is an experienced .... who has written many articles.
5 On the radio, the .... reads out the latest news every hour.
6 During the football game, the .... kept the audience up-to-date.

> • bulletin • newsflash • broadcast

7 Barry always watches the nightly news .... while he eats his dinner.
8 Kate glanced at the news .... to get a brief summary of the day's events.
9 While we were watching a film last night, it was interrupted by a ....

> • audience • spectator • viewer

10 The average .... of this TV show is in their early twenties.
11 John enjoys being a .... at live sporting events such as rugby.
12 The .... clapped their hands when the performance came to an end.

> • contestants • opponents • participants

13 The team shook hands with their .... before the match began.
14 Many of the .... in the marathon were raising money for charity.
15 There were ten .... on the game show who were competing to win £1 million!

> • drought • blizzard • tornado

16 Yesterday's .... left the city covered in deep snow.
17 All the crops died during the ...., leaving no food for the villagers.
18 People rummaged through the debris after the .... destroyed everything in its path.

> • breezy • cloudy • stormy

19 It looks like it might rain as it's a very grey and .... day.
20 Our flight has been cancelled due to .... weather.
21 If you hang out your washing on a .... day, it will dry quickly.

2 Complete the sentences with a word derived from the words in bold.

Mother nature is **1)** .... (CONSTANT) surprising us with new types of weather! For instance, did you know there is such a thing as a fire rainbow? This **2)** .... (NATURE) phenomenon creates a magnificent **3)** .... (EXPLODE) of colour that looks like a rainbow on fire! However, this couldn't be further from the **4)** .... (TRUE). Fire rainbows are anything but hot! In fact, they are caused by **5)** .... (FREEZE) ice crystals in thin, high-altitude clouds. When these clouds lie **6)** .... (HORIZON) against the sun, the sunlight hits the crystals at the perfect angle to produce an **7)** .... (IMPRESS) rainbow across the entire sky! They truly are a **8)** .... (MAGIC) sight to behold! Unfortunately, they only take place **9)** .... (OCCASION), and are limited to certain parts of the world. Those living in northern Europe will be **10)** .... (APPOINTED) to learn that they are almost non-existent in that region. In fact, they appear so **11)** .... (FREQUENTLY) that to witness one would be nothing short of a miracle! However, they are a fairly common **12)** .... (OCCUR) in the United States and have been spotted multiple times in a single year.

Language Knowledge – Module 1

1 Choose the correct Item.

1 The news crew arrived after they ..... the trapped miners.
   A rescued   C had rescued
   B has rescued   D were rescuing

2 ..... homes were damaged in the hurricane.
   A A large number of   C Much of
   B Little of   D A great deal of

3 Mike is exhausted; he ..... well lately.
   A doesn't sleep   C didn't sleep
   B hasn't been sleeping   D hadn't slept

4 ..... of the passengers were injured.
   A Either   C Every
   B Several   D Each

5 By the time they found the boy, rescuers ..... all day.
   A were searching
   B had been searching
   C searched
   D have been searching

6 There is ..... chance of finding survivors from the explosion.
   A little   C few
   B a small number of   D any

7 The search helicopter ..... in an hour.
   A has been leaving   C has left
   B left   D is leaving

2 Fill in the gaps. Use the appropriate form of the word in brackets when given.

1 Nicola .... (work) for ten hours before she .... (take) a break.

2 The scientist .... (go) to the laboratory every day to carry .... some tests.

3 Fiona .... (watch) TV since 10 this morning instead of .... (study).

4 Dan .... be a journalist, but now he .... (present) the news on television.

5 When Liam arrived at the airport, he .... (know) where to go because he .... (visit) the city many times before.

Key Word Transformations

3 Complete the sentences using the word in bold. Use two to five words.

1 The volcano started erupting two hours ago.
   BEEN The volcano .... two hours.

2 The last time Jo drove was when the accident happened.
   DRIVEN Jo .... the accident happened.

3 Newspapers cost the same now as they did last year.
   CHANGED Newspaper prices .... last year.

4 By the time we got to the theatre, nearly all the tickets had been sold.
   HARDLY There .... tickets left by the time we got to the theatre.

5 The hurricane destroyed our house one year ago.
   HAS It .... the hurricane destroyed our house.

6 I don't usually fly, so I was a little nervous.
   USED I am ...., ... so I was a little nervous.

7 I had never experienced an earthquake before.
   FIRST It .... I had ever experienced an earthquake.

8 A great deal has changed in our town since the hurricane.
   LOTS There .... in our town since the hurricane.

9 The emergency shelter opened a year ago.
   FOR The emergency shelter .... a year.

10 They started watching the documentary when I arrived.
   UNTIL They .... starting to watch the documentary.

11 Few people buy video cassettes these days.
   MANY There .... buy .... video casettes these days.

Vocabulary

1 ★ Match the shops (1-6) to what the speakers say (A-F).

1		chemist's	4		optician's
2		florist's	5		supermarket
3		butcher's	6		baker's

A "Could you direct me to the tinned foods aisle, please?"

B "I have an appointment for an eye test."

C "I'll take one kilo of minced beef, please."

D "Do you have any wholegrain loafs?"

E "A dozen roses, please."

F "I'd like to collect my prescription, please."

2 ★ Fill in: *invent*, *develop*, *generate*, *turn into*, *dissolve*, *on sale*, *print out*, *demonstrate* in the correct form.

1 The new technology has taken scientists years to ....

2 Stir the coffee until the sugar ....

3 Jane often .... copies of articles she finds on the Internet.

4 Many power stations burn coal to .... electricity.

5 The professor will .... his new invention at the science fair.

6 The new printer will soon go .... for about £100.

7 Alexander Graham Bell .... the telephone in 1876.

8 In the future, a window made of "smart glass" will .... a TV screen.

3 ★ Match the words to make phrases. Use a phrase to label the picture.

....

1		consumer	A	advice
2		acrylic	B	access
3		dietary	C	society
4		burn	D	victims
5		Internet	E	fibers
6		voice-activated	F	computers
7		skin	G	graft

4 ★ Fill in the correct word derived from the word in brackets.

1 The carpenter worked on the .... of the new kitchen cabinets. **(ASSEMBLE)**

2 The possibilities for 3D printers are .... **(END)**

3 Scientists have developed clothing that monitor our .... levels. **(FIT)**

4 The fully .... airbike is made of nylon. **(FUNCTION)**

5 Fabrican promises a T-shirt that you can spray on and wear almost .... **(INSTANT)**

Grammar

5 ★★ Complete the exchanges with *will*, *going to*, *present continuous*, or *future continuous* forms of the verbs in brackets.

1 A: We .... **(spend)** a weekend in Las Vegas soon. Do you want to come?

B: Sure, that sounds fantastic!

2 A: This time tomorrow, Tom and I ....
.... **(fly)** to Hawaii.

B: Wow! You must be so excited!

3 A: I .... **(go)** shopping today.

B: Oh. I think I .... **(come)** with you!

4 A: We .... **(move)** to Brenton next month.

B: I'm sure you .... **(love)** it there.

5 A: Why is Ken wearing those old clothes?

B: He .... **(paint)** the house later.

6 A: .... **(you/meet)** the others at 3 o'clock, Annie?

B: I don't think so.
I .... **(study)** at that time.

7 A: The leather handbag costs £150.

B: Wow. I'm afraid I ....
(not/take) it. It's too expensive!

8 A: What are you doing on Saturday afternoon?

B: I .... **(have)** lunch with my friends at the new shopping centre.

9 A: Can someone give me a hand with these shopping bags?

B: I .... **(help)** you!

Vocabulary

1 ⭐ Find 10 words related to supermarkets in the wordsearch grid.

P	X	U	A	I	S	L	E	C	K
R	S	R	G	J	A	E	W	U	S
E	L	A	A	G	F	F	U	S	H
P	I	R	S	J	T	E	D	T	E
A	D	Y	I	W	R	M	I	O	L
C	I	R	E	B	O	K	S	M	V
K	N	R	D	H	L	B	P	E	E
A	G	F	O	N	L	A	L	R	S
G	D	H	X	A	E	R	A	S	U
E	O	U	R	Y	Y	D	Y	O	S
D	O	S	K	N	A	H	S	K	P
F	R	C	H	E	C	K	O	U	T
O	S	F	V	G	Q	O	G	I	P
O	A	C	A	S	H	I	E	R	U
D	X	H	S	K	J	R	Z	N	U
Q	C	A	N	S	B	E	W	Y	S

2 ⭐ Fill in: *level, overflowing, grabbed, waste, treats, deal, line, coupons.*

1 Mary only went to the supermarket for a few things, but when she reached the checkout, her trolley was ....!

2 In supermarkets, products at eye .... are usually the most expensive because they're the first ones the customer sees.

3 Let's eat the leftovers, or they will go to ....

4 Mrs Baker uses the money-off .... she receives in the post when she goes to the supermarket.

5 John often returns from the supermarket with .... such as sweets and cakes.

6 Jane had to wait in .... at the supermarket checkout for ages.

7 Look! 2 pizzas for the price of 1. That's a great ....

8 Sam .... a bite to eat before he left for work

Grammar

3 ⭐ Put the adjectives in brackets into the correct forms.

1 Kroger is .... (large) supermarket in the USA.

2 .... (hungry) the customers in a supermarket are, ... (much) they buy!

3 The sandwiches here are a lot .... (expensive) than those in the supermarket across the street.

4 Eco-friendly manufacturers are trying to use .... and .... (little) packaging these days.

5 The shop's own brands are often as .... (good) the brand names.

6 This shopping centre is by far .... (big) I've ever been to.

4 ⭐ Put the verbs in brackets into the *-ing* form, *to*-infinitive or infinitive *without to*, then do the quiz by checking yes or no.

Quiz **Shop** **'till you drop!**

		YES	NO
1	I'm never too tired .... (go) shopping.		
2	I'd like .... (buy) some new clothes this Saturday.		
3	I want shops .... (be) open later at night.		
4	I often read a shop's adverts .... (find out) about special offers.		
5	I don't mind .... (walk) around the shopping centre all day.		
6	In my opinion, ... (use) a credit card is OK if you run out of money.		
7	I can't .... (stick) to a list when shopping.		
8	I never regret .... (pay) a little more for certain things.		
9	I prefer .... (spend) to .... (save).		
10	I enjoy .... (look) for bargains.		

Mostly YES: Oh dear! You might be a shopping addict!

Mostly NO: You are a careful shopper!

Vocabulary

1 ★ **Fill in**: *generation*, *goes back*, *big hit*, *durable*, *invented*, *staple*.

Sneakers

The story of sneakers **1)** .... to the late 18th century when there were basic canvas beach shoes with a(n) **2)** .... rubber sole called 'sand shoes.' Then, around 1892, the American Rubber Company **3)** .... some more comfortable rubber-soled shoes which they called 'sneakers'; their rubber soles were so quiet that a person wearing them could easily sneak up on someone! At first, sneakers were worn only for sport, but when 1950s movie stars like James Dean started wearing them, they became a(n) **4)** .... Today, sneakers are a(n) **5)** .... fashion item for a whole **6)** .... of young people!

2 ★ **Choose the correct word.**

1 Most young kids are **fussy/thrilled** eaters.
2 The components in the fragrance are currently a **manual/trade** secret.
3 What are the **servings/ingredients** in this delicious sauce?
4 The pharmaceutical company refused to reveal the **formula/medicine** for their new drug.
5 The government has **punished/banned** smoking in all public places.
6 Larry cooked a **brass/batch** of fries for dinner.

3 ★ **Fill in**: *cotton*, *wonder*, *sales*, *crispy*.

1 Her trousers are 100% ....
2 Dan loves to eat .... potato chips.
3 The shop owner noticed an increase in .... during the holiday season.
4 Do you ever .... what life was like without electricity?

Speaking

4 ★ **Read and circle the correct word.**

1 A: These jeans are on **sale / deal** at the moment, aren't they?
   B: Yes, but we've almost sold **out / off**.
2 A: What **size / item** are you?
   B: I'm a 10.
3 A: Can I **try / put** them on, please?
   B: Sure, the fitting rooms are over there.
4 A: Any good?
   B: Yes, they **suit / fit** me really well.
5 A: Can I pay **by / for** credit card?
   B: Yes, that's no problem.
6 A: Your **receipt / refund** is in the bag.
   B: Thank you very much.

5 ★ **Fill in**: *What (a/an)* or *how*.

1 .... great hat!
2 .... nice you look in that dress!
3 .... gorgeous shoes!
4 .... rude of me!

6 ★★ **Write a dialogue. Use the exchanges in Ex. 4 and the plan below.**

A	B
Ask if B needs any help.	Say what you're looking for.
Ask B for size.	Say what size.
Look for/Find item of clothing.	Ask to try it/them on.
Tell B where fitting room is. Ask if good.	Say you like the clothes & want to buy them.
Agree & say the price.	Ask to pay for them (credit card).
Ask B to sign.	Offer credit card.
Give card/receipt to B.	Respond.
Reply.	Thank A & say goodbye.

Reading

1 ★ **Read the text. Which trick (A, B, C or D) ...**

1 uses well known people? ......

2 doesn't back up what is said with facts? ......

3 wants a consumer to think they can become better than other people? ......

4 relies on saying something more than once? ......

5 tries to make people feel better about themselves? ......

6 hides important facts about a product? ......

2 ★★ **Give each advertising trick in the text an alternative name.**

A ....
B ....
C ....
D ....

Vocabulary

3 ★ **Choose the correct words.**

1 Mary bought a few second-hand **appliances/conveniences** including an old toaster from a neighbour's garage sale.

2 It was stylish in the 50s to wear pencil skirts with a **tight/wide** belt.

3 Joanne Massey **admits to/longs to** go back and live in the 1950s.

4 Beth got out her best **dishes/accessories** for her dinner party.

5 Kevin wore a **stylish/bland** suit and a trilby hat to the 50s convention.

6 In today's **fast-paced/authentic** society, technology is advancing at an incredible rate.

7 Unfortunately, the rain **spoiled/wiped** the picnic.

8 My grandparents tried to pass on to me their traditional **values/tips** as well as good manners.

Shopping Bag of Tricks

It's no secret that advertisers have many ways to encourage us to spend, spend, spend! Most of the time, we probably don't even realise they are tricking us into parting with our hard-earned cash! What's more, some of the techniques they use even have names. Here's an introduction to some of advertisers' classic tricks...

A **GLITTERING GENERALITIES** is a term for appealing words and images that make a product sound amazing even though they have no real meaning because there is no concrete evidence to support their claims. This advertising technique is all about the "feel good" factor; if you buy this amazing product, it will change your life. For example, this skin cream will make you look younger, that mobile phone will definitely make you more popular, and a certain brand of coffee will make you appear more sophisticated.

B **SNOB APPEAL** is designed to bring out the worst in us! Advertisers want us to feel that by buying their product, we will join the select few with superior taste. Examples are ads for designer clothes and accessories, luxury holidays such as cruises or a make of car which will automatically improve our image. Advertisers want us to feel that by buying the product we will be part of an exclusive club.

C Advertisers use **CARD STACKING** to emphasise the positive elements of a product and hide the negative ones. When advertisers put the focus on a positive aspect, even though it may be true, they only present a small part of the complete picture to consumers. For example, a snack bar full of sugar and calories will be advertised as low in fat. The emphasis placed on this one fact fools you into thinking the product is actually good for you! What's more, advertisers use repetition to make sure we get the message!

D Advertisers also use a technique called an **ENDORSEMENT**. They rely on the fact that the public automatically trusts a product if a celebrity or expert uses it or recommends it. The recommendations of an expert give weight and value to a product, while celebrities give the product their glamour and fame. This technique is often used in advertisements for beauty products such as hair care products and cosmetics.

2f

Vocabulary

1 ★ **Fill in:** *wonders, mankind, structure, nutrients, environmentally, lush, soared, consume, wasteland, convert.*

1 Cycling is a(n) .... friendly form of transport.
2 Vitamins and minerals are .... the body needs to function properly.
3 The Taj Mahal is one of the seven...................... of the world.
4 The building was a five-storey stone ....
5 Organic farming may prove to be beneficial for ....
6 Researchers have found a way to .... food waste into fuel.
7 Industrial pollution has turned the area into a(n) ....
8 People should try to .... less energy at home.
9 The building is surrounded by .... green gardens.
10 Petrol prices have .... recently.

2 ★ **Choose the correct word.**

1 The price of food has **risen/advanced** in recent years.
2 The design of a skyscraper is a huge **challenge/exam** for architects.
3 Supermarkets sell fresh **produce/outlet** such as fruits and vegetables.
4 Wind farms are **springing/growing** up throughout the countryside.
5 Most businesses are trying to find ways to **save/conserve** on shipping costs.
6 High levels of consumption are **draining/exhausting** the planet of its resources.
7 Solar panels are **controlled/powered** by the sun.
8 The human population is **raising/rising** every year.

Grammar

3 ★ **Underline the correct verb form.**

1 The gardener **will have mowed/will have been mowing** the lawn by noon.
2 By the end of the year, the author **will have finished/will have been finishing** his new novel.
3 Mary **will have been writing/will have written** her report by Friday.
4 By 2050, the global population **will have been increasing/will have increased** to 9 billion.
5 At 5 o'clock the mechanic **will have repaired/will have been repairing** the tractor for an hour.
6 It's no use going to the supermarket now; it **will have been closing/will have closed** by the time we get there.
7 By the time they reach the farm, they **will have travelled/will have been travelling** for two hours.

4 ★ **Put the verbs in brackets into the *future perfect* or the *future perfect continuous*.**

1 A: Have they built the vertical farm yet?
   B: No, not yet. But by the end of this year, they .... **(finish)** it.
2 A: John will be tired when he arrives.
   B: I know he .... **(drive)** for 6 hours non-stop.
3 A: How long have you been with the company, Kevin?
   B: By the end of this month I .... **(work)** here for 5 years.
4 A: Why are you upset?
   B: Because by the time the architect gets here, I .... **(wait)** for an hour.
5 A: Has Ron sold his farm equipment yet?
   B: No, but he .... **(sell)** it by next week.
6 A: Sally is doing well at work, isn't she?
   B: Oh, yes! I'm sure that by next year, she .... **(receive)** a promotion!

Reading

1 ★ Read the article. Match the paragraphs (1-6) with their correct headings (A-H). Two headings do not match.

Give me my money back!

Don't let retailers take you for a ride! Wise up and shop smart!

1 ☐ It has happened to most of us. You buy something such as a video camera. You get it home, take it out of the box and try to turn it on. It doesn't work. You take it back to the shop you bought it from, but they refuse to give you a refund. What are your consumer rights? Most people have no idea and many shops count on this to take advantage of them. So what are you waiting for? Become a smart shopper and learn your rights!

2 ☐ If you change your mind about an item and want your money back, you can get it! Under the UK Sale of Goods Act 1979, all shoppers are entitled to reject an item that is not of 'satisfactory quality'. Timing plays an important role in what you are entitled to. If you still have your receipt, you can usually get a full refund within four weeks from the date of purchase. After this timeframe however, you are not entitled to a refund unless the item is faulty or fails to last a reasonable length of time.

3 ☐ According to the Sale of Goods Act 1979, a product must not only be satisfactory in quality, but also as described. That is to say if a package or sales assistant claims something about a product then it must be true, otherwise it is considered defective. For example, if a DVD player claims to play all types of DVDs but you discover that it doesn't, then you have the right to a full refund.

4 ☐ Many shops claim they have a "no refunds policy" and will offer shop credit instead. This however has no actual legal standing and the law cancels out any shop's policy. It doesn't matter how many notices are put on display. It's up to the consumer to decide whether they want shop credit or their money back.

5 ☐ When most people buy an item abroad and it turns out to be faulty, they think that there is little they can do about it. However, if the item was purchased by credit card and cost over £100 then UK customers have the right to make a claim against their card company. This right is detailed under the Consumer Credit Act 1974, which holds the card company partially liable for any breaches of contract between the trader and consumer. So, the next time you're on holiday, bare this in mind.

6 ☐ Some shops will try to direct you to the manufacturer of an item when it turns out to be faulty. But under the law, your sales agreement is with the shop, not the manufacturer. Therefore, the shop must honour the refund. If the shop refuses, contact the manager and explain your rights. Most likely, they will return your money once they realise that you know your rights. So now that you are an informed consumer you have nothing to fear! You can shop easily knowing you are protected. Happy shopping!

A DON'T BELIEVE THE SIGN
B ORDERING ONLINE
C RAPID RETURNS
D GET TO KNOW THE LAW
E PROOF OF PURCHASE
F WHERE THE RESPONSIBILITY LIES
G FALSE ADVERTISING
H INTERNATIONAL SHOPPER

Listening

2 ★ ◎ You will hear five people talking about shopping and spending. Listen and match the sentences to the speakers. One sentence does not match.

A I'm careful with my money.
B I'm not really a fan of shopping.
C I think many people spend too much.
D I only buy the best.
E I try to be an ethical shopper.
F I often buy things I don't need.

Speaker 1	
Speaker 2	
Speaker 3	
Speaker 4	
Speaker 5	

Vocabulary

3 ★ Read the complaints and choose the correct words.

1 There's a **chip/break** in this coffee mug.
2 Don't buy that shirt; there's a **scratch/hole** in the sleeve.
3 Three buttons are **damaged/missing** from this blouse.
4 This jacket is **torn/cracked**; can I get a replacement?

23

Vocabulary

1 ★ **Fill in:** *bargain-hunting, conditions, treat, throw out, reduced.*

1 Don't .... your old items; sell them on eBay or donate them to charity.

2 This week Techfair is selling its computers at .... prices; some are £200 off!

3 The employees of that factory work long hours and don't get a break. Their working .... are very poor.

4 We love .... and trying to find the cheapest prices online.

5 Companies should .... their employees with respect.

2 ★ **Fill in the correct word derived from the word in brackets.**

1 The organisation has been working to raise .... of human rights. **(AWARE)**

2 Due to a decline in sales the company wanted to cut all .... expenses. **(NECESSARY)**

3 It's perfectly .... to inspect a product before you buy it. **(ACCEPT)**

4 It's important that adolescents learn to spend their money .... **(WISE)**

5 There are many .... charity shops in London. **(TRADITION)**

3 ★ **Choose the correct participle.**

1 Peter did **up/over** the buttons of his shirt.

2 Joan and Mary get **ahead/along** very well.

3 Robert dropped **out/by** of university after his first year.

4 He's a good spokesperson and gets his views **along/across** well.

5 Can you drop **by/out** the chemist's on your way home?

6 Joan worked long hours in order to get **along/ahead** in her job.

7 The computer crashed and I lost my work. I'll have to do it **up/over**.

Listening

4 ★ 🎧 **You will hear an interview with an online shopping expert. For questions 1-7, choose the best answer (*A*, *B* or *C*).**

1 What is the main advantage of shopping online?
A The products are cheap.
B It's a quick process.
C It isn't necessary to visit the shops.

2 What is the point of the auction websites?
A You set your own prices for an item.
B You pay a fee to use the site.
C You win the item without paying for it.

3 What is a disadvantage of shopping online?
A It is impossible to inspect the product before purchase.
B The photos of the products may be unclear.
C The return policy may not be indicated on many sites.

4 Betty advises shoppers to avoid
A sites with extra charges.
B unprotected websites.
C shops that appear unreliable.

5 What does Betty say about using debit cards online?
A They offer customers more security.
B They have higher interest rates.
C It is not the best way to pay for something.

6 Why should people check their credit card statements?
A To spot extra charges.
B To ensure they don't overspend.
C To see if a lot of money is missing.

7 Updating your computer's browser
A helps increase computer security.
B expands your online connections.
C improves your anti-virus programme.

Writing (a letter/an email of complaint)

1 ★ **Read the email and answer the questions.**

1 What is Ann's reason for writing?

....

2 What action does she want taken?

....

3 What greeting/ending does she use?

....

To: customerservice@mychoicesupermarkets.com
From: AnnRoberts@mymail.com
Subject: Customer Service

Dear Sir/Madam,

1▶ I am writing to express my dissatisfaction with the customer service I received at the Linton branch of your supermarket on January 14th.

2▶ When I got home after visiting the shop on January 13th, I realised that the item I had purchased from the clothing department was damaged. There was actually a hole in the sleeve of the shirt which I had not noticed, despite trying it on in the changing rooms at the time. When I tried to take it back to the shop the next day, the staff at the customer services desk were extremely unhelpful. In fact, they completely ignored me and carried on chatting with each other instead of dealing with my complaint. Furthermore, the clerk who did finally help me was incredibly rude. Although she replaced the shirt for me with an undamaged one, she complained loudly that I should have checked that the shirt was in good condition before I bought it!

3▶ Overall, I am extremely disappointed with the service I received. Therefore, I would appreciate an apology and an investigation into the way the customer service desk treats customers. I hope that you will look into this matter promptly.

Yours faithfully,

Ann Roberts

2 ★ **Complete the table with the complaints and their justifications in Ex. 1.**

Complaints	Justifications

3 ★ **Match the opening remarks (1-3) to the closing remarks (A-C).**

Opening remarks ...

1 ☐ I am writing to complain about a flaw with a product I recently bought from your company.

2 ☐ I feel I must complain about the inefficiency of your mail-order service.

3 ☐ I would like to express my dissatisfaction with the attitude of the staff at your shop.

Closing remarks ...

A ☐ I hope that you will look into this rude behaviour and that I will receive a written apology.

B ☐ I will have no choice but to cancel my order unless I receive the items within three working days.

C ☐ I would appreciate it if you would repair or replace the product as soon as possible.

4 ★ **Read the following extracts and say which of them are mild (m) or strong (s) complaints.**

1 ☐ I have been a regular customer at your supermarket, and have always been satisfied with your produce in the past. I hope that this matter will be resolved soon.

2 ☐ I insist upon a personal apology for the distress your staff have caused my family, and shall not be recommending your hotel to any of my friends.

3 ☐ I am writing to express my disgust at the quality of the products I recently purchased from your shop.

4 ☐ The camera I ordered from your website has arrived with a crack in the lens. I trust you will send a replacement.

5 ☐ I am writing to complain about a shirt I purchased on your website. I ordered this item three weeks ago, but it has not been delivered yet.

5 ★ Study the box, then join the sentences using the words in the brackets.

> **Clauses of Concession**
> **although/even though** + clause
> **despite/in spite of** + noun/-ing/the fact that

1 I paid for next-day delivery. The item took three days to arrive. **(despite the fact that)**

   ....

2 I had my receipt. The sales assistant wouldn't give me a refund. **(in spite of)**

   ....

3 The jacket was expensive. The quality of it was poor. **(although)**

   ....

4 I received a refund. I am still not satisfied. **(even though)**

   ....

5 The shop wouldn't replace the item. It was damaged. **(despite)**

   ....

6 a) ★ Circle the correct linking words/phrases.

1 **But / Even though** the advertisement said the laptop came with a free case, it is missing.
2 **However / Although** the DVD player had a one-year guarantee, the assistant refused to give me a new one.
3 The service in your restaurant was very slow, **but / in spite of the fact that** when I complained to the manager, he was very rude to me.
4 The shirt you sold me has a button missing. **Furthermore / But**, it has a hole in the sleeve.
5 **Despite / However** paying for four items on your website, I only received three in the post.
6 Your staff were very rude to me. **In addition / Therefore**, I demand an apology.

   b) ★ What linking words are used in the email in Ex. 1?

   ....
   ....

7 ★ Fill in: *furthermore, but, however, despite, therefore, although.*

> I have been a loyal customer at Marshall's Electronics for many years, **1)** .... yesterday I was outraged by the terrible customer service I received in you. Last week, I purchased a camera from your shop. When I brought it home, **2)** ...., I realised that the lens cover was missing. **3)** ...., the lens had been scratched. When I took it back to the shop and asked for a replacement, the shop assistant refused to supply one, **4)** .... the fact that I had my receipt. When I asked to speak to the manager, he was also extremely rude to me. **5)** .... he did exchange the camera for a new one, he accused me of damaging the lens myself! I would like to think that you value your customers' opinions. **6)** .... I would appreciate it if you could look into this matter further.

8 ★ Read the rubric and answer the questions.

> You recently bought a faulty product from a shop. When you took it back to exchange it, the sales assistant was rude to you. Write an email of complaint to the head office of the shop (200-250 words). Explain why you are unhappy.

1 Who are you writing to? ....
2 What are your opening remarks/reasons for writing? ....
3 What are you going to complain about?
   ....
4 How will you end your email? ....

9 ★★ Use your answers in Ex. 8 and the sentences from the *Useful language* box to write an email of complaint.

Useful language

Reason for writing: I am writing to complain about ... /I want to express my dissatisfaction with ...
Your complaints: I bought ..., but ..., To make matters worse ...
Your demands: I would appreciate if you ...
Closing remarks: I hope that you will; look into this matter .../I look forward to ...

English in Use
Word Formation

1 ★ **Read the text and complete the gaps with the words derived from the words in bold.**

Did you know that people in Paris, France can obtain **1)** .... baked bread 24 hours a day? Jean-Louis Hecht, an **2)** .... local baker has come up with the idea of selling baguettes in a vending machine. Unlike fresh bread these baguettes are precooked, a technique used by **3)** .... bread producers. The machine takes the **4)** .... cooked bread, bakes it and delivers it hot and crispy to customers for only €1! Mr Hecht claims that this is the bakery of the future and he foresees the **5)** .... of these vending machines in Paris and even Europe.

FRESH

ACCOMPLISH

INDUSTRY
PARTIAL

EXPAND

Key Word Transformations

2 ★ **Complete the gapped sentences so that they have a similar meaning to the original ones, using the word given.**

1 I'd rather watch TV than go shopping.
   THAN   I'd prefer ....
   .... shopping.

2 Crisps are not as nutritious as vegetables.
   LESS   Crisps ....
   .... vegetables.

3 She can't wait to go to the new mall.
   FORWARD   She's really ....
   .... the new mall.

4 He plans on getting a new flat-screen TV.
   GOING   He ....
   .... a new flat-screen TV.

5 I'd be grateful if you could help me with these bags.
   HELPING   Would ....
   .... these bags?

Speaking

Choose the correct response.

1 A: Where can I try these jeans on?
   B: **a** The fitting rooms are over there.
   b They are on sale at the moment.

2 A: What size are you?
   B: **a** I'm ten.
   b I'm a twelve.

3 A: Can I pay by credit card?
   B: **a** You're in luck.
   b Yes, that's no problem.

4 A: Are they the right size?
   B: **a** We don't have many left.
   b They fit me really well.

5 A: Your receipt is in your bag.
   B: **a** Thank you.
   b You're welcome.

6 A: Can I get a refund?
   B: **a** The goods haven't arrived.
   b Of course.

7 A: Do you need any help?
   B: **a** I'm looking for a jumper.
   b We've almost sold out.

8 A: I'd like to exchange these earphones.
   B: **a** Can you take a look at it?
   b Could I see your receipt?

9 A: What's wrong with the handbag?
   B: **a** There is a payment problem.
   b The strap is broken.

10 A: That's £24.99 then.
   B: **a** Just sign here.
   b Here you are.

11 A: They're on sale aren't they?
   B: **a** Yes, they fit me perfectly.
   b Yes, but we're almost sold out.

12 A: Could I have your ID, please?
   B: **a** Sure. No problem.
   b Yes. I'll take them.

Language & Grammar Review

Choose the correct answer.

1 Tanya likes to buy cheap ..... clothes on eBay.
   A second-hand   C hard-earned
   B throwaway   D money-off

2 Supermarkets always have ..... produce.
   A natural   C new
   B fresh   D instant

3 The heel on Jane's new shoes ..... .
   A tore   C broke
   B damaged   D scratched

4 Can you ..... some milk from the supermarket?
   A check out   C throw in
   B pick up   D get across

5 People should ..... their rooftops into gardens.
   A develop   C generate
   B consume   D convert

6 The new spray dries ..... on your skin!
   A individually   C instantly
   B possibly   D horizontally

7 Drop ..... later and see my new clothes.
   A out   B up   C by   D across

8 This computer can ..... your fitness level.
   A develop   C generate
   B monitor   D work

9 Those jeans ..... you really well. They are the right size.
   A fit   B suit   C match   D grab

10 Can I interest you in the shop's ..... card?
   A saving B loyalty C deal D bargain

11 There are always ..... of sweets at a checkout.
   A aisles   C lines
   B displays   D batches

12 The device has voice-..... controls.
   A operated   C generated
   B required   D activated

13 A: How do the trousers fit you?
   B: .....
   A No problem.   C You're in luck.
   B Really well.   D I'm a 10.

14 Sara enjoys ..... -hunting during the sales.
   A deal   C price
   B bargain   D cost

15 I've saved enough money ..... a new printer.
   A buy   C to buy
   B buying   D to be buying

16 This laptop is ..... all.
   A faster than   C the fastest of
   B as fast as   D most fast of

17 In the future most people ..... the Internet for shopping.
   A will use   C are going to use
   B are using   D have used

18 The shop will ..... my camera by the weekend.
   A be repairing   C have been repairing
   B have repaired   D repaired

19 Ellie hates ..... in a queue at the supermarket.
   A waiting   C wait
   B to wait   D to be waiting

20 By March, Sue ..... at the bakery for two years.
   A is working
   B will work
   C will have been working
   D will be working

21 Stanton's is by ..... the most expensive shop.
   A far   C the farthest
   B farther   D most far

22 Tim agreed ..... me his MP3 player.
   A selling   C sell
   B to be selling   D to sell

23 ..... fabulous outfit!
   A How   B What   C What a   D How a

24 We .... Jane at the mall at seven o'clock.
   A are meeting   C have met
   B meet   D have been meeting

25 This time tomorrow, I .... my new DVD player.
   A will enjoy   C am enjoying
   B will be enjoying D am going to enjoy

Reading Task

Read the text. Seven sentences have been removed from the article. Choose from the sentences A-H the one that fits each gap (1-7). There is one extra sentence.

Let's go shopping in the future....

The year is 2020. You are walking down the street, when you see a girl wearing a great jacket. You pull out your mobile phone, point it at her jacket and click a button. The screen on your phone instantly reveals the brand of the jacket, information about the jacket and shops where you can purchase it. **1** [ ] Sound like something out of a science fiction film? Well such 'point and click shopping' may not be that far off in the future.

Shopping habits of consumers have changed dramatically over the years with the advent of online shopping. As popular as online shopping has become, many shoppers still prefer to see products in person and go out to the shops. Shop retailers are trying to make a traditional day out shopping a high-tech and interactive experience. **2** [ ] One piece of technology that is allowing this to happen is called Radio Frequency Identification (RFID) which uses radio waves to transfer data from an electronic tag or label on an object to a reader device with the purpose of identifying the item. **3** [ ] By using RFID readers in our mobile phones, we can turn our physical world into clickable links online, providing us with useful information and purchasing options. Retailers can also send their products into the outside world. **4** [ ] Passers by can use their smart phones to point at them and click on any products they are interested in.

One area of retail which has been slow to expand into the online shopping trend is clothing. Most people want to see and try on clothing items before purchasing them. Clothing shops are bringing advanced technology to the changing room with screens instead of mirrors that provide useful information about a clothing item, suggest matching accessories and display alternative styles. **5** [ ] Afterwards, you can compare on the screen the different outfits you tried on. Tired of trying on endless amounts of clothing to find the right fit or style? Changing rooms of the future will be equipped with electronic scanners that scan your body shape and show images of you wearing the best fitting styles without having to try on anything. Furthermore, what if you want a second opinion on an outfit? A webcam in the dressing room will project an image of you wearing the outfit on a website for your friends to see. **6** [ ] Once again traditional shopping is combined with the cyber world in what retailers call "social retailing". Through online shop accounts or social networking sites shoppers can share possible purchases and receive feedback from friends or even an online community of like-minded shoppers. Retailers benefit in that shoppers spread what they like through social networking sites in a form of free advertising. **7** [ ] Thus, shoppers sharing items they like is probably the best advert of all.

All this exchange in electronic information in the future will transform a typical day out at the shops into an informative, interactive and personal shopping experience for consumers. Shopping has never been so much fun!

A A camera will take your photo or video and record everything you try on.

B These tags carry product information and can connect an item to the online marketplace.

C If you want you can buy it online right then and there.

D Research shows that 90 % of people trust recommendations of friends above any other form of advertising.

E Consumers will become more selective as more choices become available.

F They want to combine the opportunity to see and handle an item with the benefits of online shopping.

G You're inside the changing room but can interact with your friends online.

H Models will be used to walk down busy streets carrying or wearing products.

2

Building Up Vocabulary

1 **Complete the sentences using one of the words in the box.**

> • bargain • discount • offer

1 There was a special .... on apples at the supermarket.

2 Debra enjoys .... hunting in charity shops.

3 Can you give me a(n) .... on these jeans?

> • financial • economical • costly

4 My mother is very .... and only spends money when necessary.

5 Owning a car can be very .... because of the rising price of fuel.

6 Now that Robert has a job, he is in a better .... situation.

> • label • brand • trademark

7 When you see a designer ...., you know the item will be expensive.

8 The company's .... is a simple blue and white logo.

9 I always buy this .... of coffee because it has the best flavour.

> • company • business • corporation

10 The salesman handed me his .... card.

11 Rita is the manager of a .... that sells sportswear.

12 The multinational .... has over 30 branches across the world.

> • prospectus • brochure • leaflet

13 The travel .... contained photos of sandy beaches and blue skies.

14 While I was at the dental surgery, I picked up an information .... about tooth whitening.

15 Omar browsed through the university .... to find a course that was right for him.

> • profit • revenue • earnings

16 The shop assistant deposited the week's .... into the bank.

17 Eve made a large .... selling cheap jewellery for high prices.

18 The government generates .... through taxation.

> • manufactured • assembled • fabricated

19 The flat-pack furniture we bought had to be .... before use.

20 My new sports car was .... in Germany.

21 The antique clock was .... by a skilled craftsman.

2 **Complete the sentences with a word derived from the words in bold.**

Forget cleaning! A team of **1)** ....
(RESEARCH) in China have now invented a fabric that cleans itself! Laundry will become a thing of the past as this **2)** .... **(INNOVATE)** substance does all the hard work for you. It works by spraying natural fibres with a special chemical compound. This compound has the ability to remove dirt when exposed to sunlight. This means that the wearer could go for a **3)** .... **(LEISURE)** stroll in the sun in order to clean their clothes! What's more, the coating is not only good for stain **4)** .... **(REMOVE)**, but also for eliminating body odours. No longer will you have to worry about **5)** .... **(EMBARRASS)** moments on hot, humid days. Your outfit will keep you fresh and clean all day long! And if the item is **6)** .... **(HEAVY)** stained, it can be cleaned using a washing machine. So what are the **7)** .... **(ADVANTAGES)**? Well, critics warn that the spray may be **8)** .... **(POISON)** and could harm a person's health as they breathe in particles from their **9)** .... **(CLOTH)**. Moreover, it has been suggested that the substance is not **10)** .... **(ENVIRONMENT)** friendly. Further tests are being carried out to ensure the spray is not **11)** .... **(HARM)** to consumers. However, the manufacturers of the product are **12)** .... **(CONFIDE)** that it will become available on the high street soon!

Language Knowledge – Module 2

1 **Choose the correct Item.**

1 There are ..... small shops left on High Street.
A hardly any   C little
B any   D neither

2 The books at this bookshop are ..... cheaper than the other bookshops.
A a lot   B as   C more   D the

3 The shop assistant was fired after a customer ..... of poor service.
A had complained   C complain
B were complaining   D had been complaining

4 At the end of this month, she ..... at the post office for ten years.
A is going to work   C is working
B will work   D will have been working

5 Did you remember ..... the credit card bill?
A paying   C pays
B pay   D to pay

6 Sue is too tired ..... on clothes right now.
A trying   C to try
B try   D tries

7 I promise I ..... the shopping at the supermarket.
A am doing   C am going to do
B will do   D will be doing

2 **Fill in the gaps. Use the appropriate forms of the word in brackets when given.**

1 This time tomorrow, I .... **(shop)** with my best friend in .... to buy a new dress for the prom.

2 Julie .... **(finish)** studying by the time Bill drops .... later.

3 Candice regrets .... **(spend)** so much money, but couldn't resist taking advantage .... her new credit card!

4 .... quickly time passes! By the end of the month I .... **(live)** in this house for ten years!

5 I promise I .... **(try)** my .... **(good)** to get you a better deal.

Key Word Transformations

3 **Complete the sentences using the word in bold. Use two to five words.**

1 You are too young to have a credit card.
ENOUGH You ....
.... to have a credit card.

2 The department store opened a year ago.
FOR   The department store ....
.... a year.

3 Mary plans on returning her new MP3 player.
GOING Mary ....
.... her new MP3 player.

4 The shop allows payment by cash or credit card.
EITHER You ....
.... by cash or credit card.

5 I can't wait to get my new computer.
FORWARD I'm really ....
.... my new computer.

6 I don't feel like shopping today.
PREFER I'd ....
.... today.

7 Your new lap top is faster than mine.
AS   My lap top ....
.... yours.

8 It's not a problem for me to go to the chemist.
MIND   I ....
.... to the chemist.

9 There are no other refrigerators on the market better than this one.
FAR   This ....
.... refrigerator on the market.

10 She is not allowed by her parents to shop online.
LET   Her parents ....
.... online.

11 Amber hasn't been shopping for over two months.
MORE   It ....
.... two months since Amber has been shopping.

12 My parents thought that it wasn't worth spending so much money on a new laptop.
POINT My parents thought there ....
.... spending so much money on a new laptop.

Vocabulary

1 a) ★ **Match the words to make phrases.**

1	go	A	money to charity
2	wear	B	stray animals
3	feel	C	embarrassed
4	make	D	old materials
5	donate	E	scruffy clothes
6	recycle	F	at a soup kitchen
7	look after	G	small talk
8	cross	H	the road
9	have	I	undercover
10	volunteer	J	no official identity

b) ★★ **Use some of the phrases from Ex. 1a in the correct form to complete the sentences.**

1 The community is encouraging residents to .... in order to reduce waste.

2 Molly .... as an elderly lady for a day; no one knew she was really only 25!

3 Tim often .... like worn out jeans and old T-shirts.

4 Joan .... in her community; she serves hot meals to homeless people every week.

5 Henry finds it easy to .... at parties; he chats about everyday topics like sport and movies.

6 We should .... and not let them roam on the streets.

2 ★ **Fill in: for, across, into, out, of, up and off.**

1 John dozed .... watching the late news.

2 This chair isn't very comfortable; it digs .... my back.

3 The dog curled .... next to the fireplace and fell asleep.

4 We tried to get rid .... the annoying salesman by telling him we didn't have any money.

5 Tracy set .... to investigate what happened to the missing money.

6 I headed .... the quietest place in the library to study.

7 They were walking in the park when they came .... a lost puppy.

3 ★ **Fill in** criticises, eye-opening, chatty, embarrassed, invisible, treat, debts, accused **in the correct form.**

1 Tom couldn't believe the poverty he saw in India; it was a really .... experience.

2 We should all .... the elderly with respect.

3 Polly felt really .... when Tom was rude to the waitress.

4 Now that Jill is unemployed she is having difficulty paying her ....

5 Maggie often .... her sister for the way she dresses.

6 Barbara is a(n) .... person who enjoys speaking to people when she's out and about.

7 The shop assistant .... the young man of stealing the jacket.

8 People walk by Patty, who's homeless, every day as if they don't see her; she feels ....

Grammar

4 ★ **Rewrite the sentences. Use:** could, should, can/can't, mustn't **or** didn't have to.

1 It's forbidden to park your car here. ....

2 It wasn't necessary for Jo to make a donation. ....

3 It's impossible for Alan to get unemployment benefits. ....

4 Is it OK if I borrow your car? ....

5 John had the ability to write when he was three years old. ....

6 It's a good idea to hold a fundraiser. ....

Vocabulary

1 ★ **Fill in:** *appalling, nerve-racking, reputation, hygiene, affection.*

1 Children must be taught personal .... habits from an early age.
2 Street children in Brazil live in .... shacks.
3 Their mother never showed them much love and ....
4 He had the .... of being a good lecturer.
5 Speaking in front of the classroom can be a(n) .... experience for many students.

2 ★ **Choose the correct words.**

1 Max had a **privileged/worthwhile** childhood; his family was wealthy and they took trips around the world.
2 If Sally hadn't volunteered, she would have **missed out/given up** on a great experience!
3 After the earthquake, workers built a **makeshift/poverty** school out of cheap materials.
4 A **fallen/broken** home is one in which the parents have separated or divorced.
5 People in favelas live in very bad **conditions/situations**, with no running water or electricity.
6 The roof of our house is **leaking/dripping** and letting water in.
7 Some homeless people **turn to/look after** crime to support themselves.

3 ★ **Fill in the sentences with the correct word derived from the word in brackets.**

1 The teachers in this school are all very .... and helpful. **(FRIEND)**
2 Children see too much .... on TV these days. **(VIOLENT)**
3 The .... of the town are worried about toxic waste in the river. **(RESIDE)**
4 Brazil has a .... of approximately 190 million people. **(POPULATE)**

Grammar

4 ★ **Put the verbs in brackets in the correct tense.**

1 If I were you, I .... **(spend)** my summer holiday volunteering.
2 If you .... **(listen)** in class, you would have understood how to do the assignment.
3 Samantha wishes she .... **(have)** a job.
4 If I had the time and money, I .... **(go)** backpacking around the world.
5 When you give money to shelters, you .... **(help)** many homeless people.
6 It's chilly; I wish I .... **(bring)** a sweater.
7 If he .... **(study)** hard, he will pass his exam.
8 If people .... **(drink)**, contaminated water, they get sick.

Listening

5 ★ 🎧 **You'll hear an interview with a young woman called Samantha who worked on a charity project in India. Listen and write *T* (true) or *F* (false).**

1 Samantha found out about the charity project from a TV program. ....
2 She tells us that climate change has caused people to move to slums. ....
3 Her job was to build water facilities. ....
4 The locals are now helping with the project. ....
5 Samantha feels the experience changed her character. ....

Vocabulary

1 ★ **Fill in:** *legends, loyal, solstice, traditions, stands, performances, mystical.*

Glastonbury Festival

Have the time of your life!

Every year thousands of **1)** .... fans come to the Glastonbury Festival to see live **2)** .... of their favourite bands. The festival is usually on the first weekend after the summer **3)** .... It occurs in a **4)** .... place, in the Vale of Avalon, an area that has a number of **5)** .... and spiritual **6)** .... But music is not the only attraction at the festival; there is also a great selection of food **7)** .... to visit! It's sure to be a great weekend so don't miss it!

2 ★ **Choose the correct word.**

1 After they had **pitched/raised** their tent in a field, they went to walk around the festival.

2 Kim **explored/wandered** around the festival, stopping to enjoy the different performers and entertainers.

3 Festival organisers **attract/promote** green issues by encouraging festival-goers to recycle and leave the site tidy.

4 Please **encourage/support** Greenpeace by coming to our demonstration tomorrow.

3 ★ **Fill in:** *for (x2), of, over, in.*

1 They held a concert to raise money .... charity.
2 People should have the right to freedom .... expression.
3 He wandered .... to the stage to see his favourite band up close.
4 The city is famous .... its diverse cultural events all year round.
5 If .... doubt, call the charity organisers.

Speaking

4 ★ **Use the sentences to complete the dialogue.**

A And what's the expiration date?
B Can I get your full name and address, please?
C I'd like to make a single donation of £50, please.
D I'd like to make a donation, please.
E Could you give me your credit or debit card number, please?

> A: Hello, Oxfam. How can I help you?
> B: 1 ☐
> A: Would you like to make a single donation or a regular monthly donation?
> B: 2 ☐
> A: That's great. 3 ☐
> B: Sure, it's Sally Harding and my address is 118 Colechester Street, London.
> A: 4 ☐
> B: Yes, it's 8765 9687 9465 8364.
> A: 5 ☐
> B: It's October of this year.
> A: OK, that's all. Thank you so much.
> B: You're welcome.

5 ★★ **Use the leaflet below and your own ideas to write a dialogue similar to the dialogue in Ex. 4.**

We are working to **protect** endangered species such as pandas, tigers and whales!

Provide help to an animal in danger for as little as £3 a month!

Donate by post, online or call
0-800-125-8598

Cheerleader for Nature

Meet Mireya Mayor, a former cheerleader who is now known as "the female Indiana Jones," and with good reason! This brave biologist has travelled to many of the Earth's most remote places in order to find and protect rare animals.

1 [ ] Mireya has certainly lived a wild life, from swimming with sharks in Mexico, to being chased by giraffes in Namibia, to drinking cow's blood in Tanzania. She's even survived a plane crash in the Congo. But just how did this fashion loving, cheerleading, Cuban-American city girl who had never been camping in her life become a mountain climbing explorer who sleeps in a hammock? A college anthropology class is the answer.

2 [ ] Mireya originally studied English Literature and Philosophy and planned to become a lawyer when an anthropology class opened her eyes to the natural world. Mireya was amazed that some of these incredible animals that faced extinction had never been studied and decided to earn a PhD in Anthropology.

3 [ ] Following that, Mireya became National Geographic's first female wildlife correspondent. Her quest: to put the spotlight on rare animals in danger. Since then, Mireya has explored some of the most remote and dangerous corners of the globe, looking for some of the most difficult to find animals in the world.

4 [ ] It was during a trip to the rainforests of Madagascar that Mireya discovered an unknown species of Lemur. "There we were, tromping through remote areas of jungle," remembers Mireya, "rain pouring, tents blowing into the air, looking for a nocturnal animal that happens to be the smallest primate in the world." Her dedicated search paid off; Madagascar's president declared the little lemurs'

habitat a national park, tripled the number of protected areas in the nation, and established a $50 million conservation trust fund. Not a bad result!

5 [ ] Travelling to such remote places, explorers often face danger and Mireya is no exception. Once, Mireya had to eat leaves to calm down an angry 400-pound gorilla in the Congo and another time, she had a very close encounter with a tarantula the size of a dinner plate in South America. Luckily, the tarantula didn't bite her. In fact, Mireya seemed to bring out the spider's playful side! "It had been sitting on my hand," explains Mireya, "and then it started climbing up my arm, and then it went to the top of my head and the locals thought it was hilarious."

6 [ ] When Mireya isn't facing such hair-raising moments as those, she tours schools and universities as an inspirational speaker. She's also written a book about her experiences, called Pink Boots and a Machete, a reference to the fact that the female Indiana Jones still remembers her cheerleading days!

A LOOKING TO THE FUTURE
B A CHANGE OF DIRECTION
C AN INCREDIBLE ACHIEVEMENT
D FROM GIRL-NEXT-DOOR TO ADVENTURER
E ENCOURAGING WORDS
F A RISKY BUSINESS
G IN SEARCH OF SPECIAL CREATURES

Reading

1 ★ Read the text and match the headings (A-G) to the paragraphs (1-6). There is one extra heading.

Vocabulary

2 ★ Match the words to make phrases.

1	brave	A	tribes
2	hostile	B	pit viper
3	go on a jungle	C	expedition
4	hair-raising	D	of wasps
5	deadly	E	moment(s)
6	swarm	F	explorer
7	natural	G	with exhaustion
8	inject	H	a bow
9	collapse	I	with antibiotics
10	draw	J	wonder

Grammar

3 ★ Fill in who, which, where, whose, adding commas where necessary.

1 Wateraid and Oxfam are two charities .... the Glastonbury Festival supports.
2 Simon .... is an expedition leader agreed to take us on a tour of the jungle.
3 Jenny is the girl .... worked with poor children in India last year.
4 The favela .... the children live is one of the largest slums in South America.
5 John .... brother is my best friend is teaching street children in Brazil.
6 The snake .... we saw was one of the most dangerous in the world.

35

3f

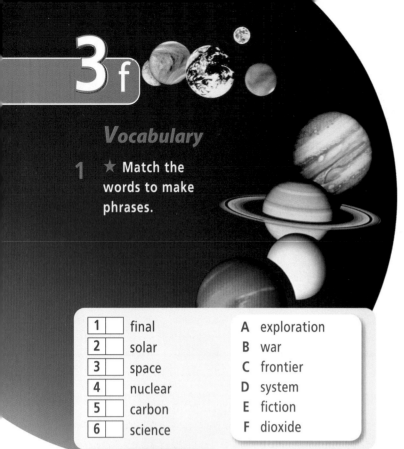

Vocabulary

1 ★ **Match the words to make phrases.**

1	final	A	exploration
2	solar	B	war
3	space	C	frontier
4	nuclear	D	system
5	carbon	E	fiction
6	science	F	dioxide

2 ★ **Complete the sentences with the phrases from Ex. 1.**

1 The Earth's atmosphere contains .... gas.
2 Space is often referred to as the ....; the unexplored territory.
3 The .... is made up of all the planets that orbit the sun.
4 Every new step we make in .... advances our knowledge of the universe.
5 The .... film is set on Mars.
6 The threat of .... is frightening.

3 ★ **Choose the correct word.**

1 With new technologies the possibilities for space travel are **continuous/endless**.
2 The Earth has rich **supplies/resources** like natural gas and oil.
3 Solar panels **construct/generate** electricity from sunlight.
4 Mankind still has many challenges to **pass/ overcome** before space colonisation becomes a reality.
5 The Russian satellite will **leap/orbit** the earth for the next six years.
6 Astronomers revealed that a comet could **extract/ wipe** out life on Earth.

4 ★ **Fill in:** *harsh, catastrophe, race, colonies, warms up, release, afford, self-sufficient.*

1 In the future, scientists hope to build .... in space.
2 The weather always .... in summer.
3 Not all governments can .... to invest money in space travel.
4 One day, new technologies will make humans .... in space as they will be able to produce what they need.
5 Cars .... toxic emissions that damage our environment.
6 Global warming could lead to an environmental ....
7 Astronauts wear space suits to protect them from the .... environment of outer space.
8 Will the human .... survive in the future?

Grammar

5 ★ **Rewrite the following as *mixed conditional* sentences.**

1 Mark didn't study, so he won't pass his science test.
   ....
2 Jane arrived on time, so she will have enough time to visit the planetarium.
   ....
3 He isn't well-qualified, so he didn't get the job at the space centre.
   ....
4 They didn't buy cinema tickets, so they can't see the new science fiction film tonight.
   ....
5 Emily wasn't told about it, so she isn't at the science fair now.
   ....
6 The researcher was working late last night, so he is exhausted now.
   ....
7 Sally doesn't take her studies seriously, so she didn't get into university.
   ....

Meet the Rubbish Warrior

Reading

1 ★ **Read the article. For questions 1-6, choose the correct answer** *A, B, C or D.*

1 How did Michael Reynolds get the name the 'Rubbish Warrior'?

   A from his use of recycling

   B due to the large amount of recycling he does every day

   C from being the first to recycle

   D because he recycles almost every type of rubbish

2 'Earthships'

   A do not cost anything to run.

   B recycle their own water.

   C don't consume energy.

   D can generate their own electricity.

3 What problem did Michael encounter when he started building earthships?

   A He couldn't find materials.

   B Other architects interfered with his work.

   C His designs did not comply with building regulations.

   D Nobody wanted his work.

4 What finally helped Michael's work become accepted?

   A changes in building regulations

   B the architectural community

   C rebuilding after disasters

   D building homes in New Mexico

5 Michaels believes 'biotecture'

   A is the answer to all environmental problems.

   B will solve some important environmental issues.

   C will spread around the world.

   D will solve our energy shortages.

6 Michael feels 'biotects'

   A create new ecosystems.

   B shouldn't use natural resources.

   C should fight consumerism.

   D create a new lifestyle.

He has been called the 'The King of Rubbish', 'The Rubbish Architect' and most recently the 'The Rubbish Warrior'. Michael Reynolds doesn't just collect rubbish and recycle it; he turns it into sustainable green homes known as 'earthships'. These eco-friendly houses are made from natural and recycled materials. Anything from old tyres, glass, plastic bottles and tins to old electrical appliances and cars are used as building materials. The homes are self-sufficient with solar panels and wind turbines to generate electricity. They also have rainwater collection systems and a constant inside temperature that allows residents to grow a small vegetable and fruit garden indoors. All these design factors contribute to the total independence of the home by using natural resources. By providing their own power and water, operation costs of these earthships are low with little to no utility bills. Building materials are also inexpensive, making these homes affordable for everyone.

Trained as an architect, Michael responded to concerns back in the 1970s about the ever increasing rubbish problem and environmental crisis by building sustainable homes out of the rubbish. 'Thirty five years ago I saw dark clouds on the horizon ... Lots of people also saw the environmental crisis coming but weren't inspired to do anything. They thought I was a fool going to the dump and recycling rubbish before recycling even existed.' Michael says, looking back. Well, no one is laughing at him anymore. After years of being snubbed by the architectural community and battling outdated building laws, Michael's work is now being taken very seriously. He started with building homes for himself and like-minded people in New Mexico. The owners appreciated the homes and understood their importance but publicly they were still seen as radicals. The value of Michael's work came into the spotlight when he and his team were invited to the tsunami hit area of the Bay of Bengal in 2004. Michael and his team passed on their knowledge to the desperate people there while at the same time building several critical shelters with the tons of rubbish left behind from the disaster. This provided Michael with the opportunity to experiment and create some of his most inspired designs while not being restricted by building regulations. The homes are earthquake and hurricane proof and built to collect rainwater. Micheal and his crew have visited other disaster areas to help rebuild communities including areas hit by hurricane Katrina and more recently the earthquake in Haiti in 2010. As word catches on, his designs have spread to every corner of the globe. Michael has even created a name for his type of work, 'biotecture' to describe the designing of buildings with the goal of sustainability. According to Michael it's a sort of 'combination of biology and architecture' that addresses a number of serious problems now facing mankind. When rubbish becomes the building material, less waste goes to over-burdened landfill sites.

Shortages of water and energy are eased when households create their own supply. Michael calls himself and others working like him ' biotects' and sees their creations not just as homes but as an alternative way of living. "Earthships are a model of the future that goes beyond house and architecture," he explains. Residents become an active part of their local ecosystem, living hand in hand with nature and not just consuming it. It's a sustainable way of living that this warrior will continue to fight for.

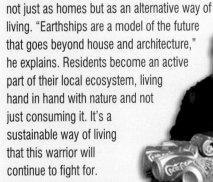

Vocabulary

1 ★ Fill in: *grazed, diseases, threat, harmful, released*.

1 .... pesticides sprayed on vegetables can have a really bad effect on our health.
2 Improved cleanliness helps to prevent the spread of ....
3 The fire at the factory .... poisonous gases into the atmosphere.
4 Sea pollution is a terrible .... to sea creatures such as whales and dolphins.
5 Several sheep .... on the long grass in the field.

2 ★ Fill in: *for, to, under, out, down*.

1 The Arctic glaciers are .... threat from global warming.
2 If deforestation continues, thousands of animal species will die ....
3 Forests are home .... many animal and plant species.
4 We are all responsible .... protecting the environment.
5 Loggers cut .... trees and destroy animal habitats.

3 ★ Fill in: *on, out, in (x2), over*.

1 Hang ...., Peter. I'll be ready in a few minutes.
2 The thief demanded that the man hand .... his wallet.
3 I have to hand .... my science project by 3 pm today.
4 Bill is handing .... festival flyers to passers-by.
5 They have just started an environmental club at school. Why don't we join ....?

Listening

4 ★ 🎧 **You'll hear people talking in eight different situations. For questions 1-8, choose the correct answer** *A, B* **or** *C.*

1 You hear a woman talking about volunteering at a community centre. What does she do at the centre now?
A spends time with the elderly
B helps with art classes for children
C teaches computer skills to the disabled

2 You hear a man talking on the radio about a festival. What can festival-goers do in the afternoon?
A listen to bands
B play in the annual football matches
C see exhibits on environmental issues

3 You hear a woman talking about a charity ski race. How did she feel at the end of the race?
A thrilled   B disappointed   C proud

4 You hear a filmmaker being interviewed on the radio. Why did he make the film?
A to raise money for a charity
B to inform people about a problem
C to make money for his film school

5 You hear a man talking. What is he?
A disabled   B homeless   C elderly

6 You hear a woman talking to her friend. Why is she talking to him?
A to offer him help
B to give him a warning
C to convince him about something

7 You hear a lecture about illiteracy. What is the lecturer describing?
A a solution to the problem
B the causes of the problem
C the impact of the problem

8 You hear a teenager talking about an animal shelter. How does she feel about the shelter?
A It needs more money.
B It needs more volunteers.
C It doesn't help many animals.

Writing (an opinion essay)

1 ★ **Read the rubric and answer the questions.**

> Your college English magazine is asking for essays on the following statement: *It's better for elderly relatives to be looked after in nursing homes.* Write your essay for the magazine, stating your opinion and giving reasons/examples to support it.

1 What do you have to write? ....
2 Which two reasons can you think of to support the statement? ....
3 What can the opposite viewpoint be? ....
....

2 ★ **Read the essay. Which of your ideas in Ex. 1 are mentioned?**

▶ In many countries these days, elderly people often choose to live in nursing homes and not with their families. **In my opinion**, this can be a really good idea as their needs can often be best met there.

▶ **First of all**, a carefully-chosen nursing home can offer excellent care and facilities for an elderly person. **For example**, they often have great facilities – such as TV rooms – and special events where the residents can socialise. **In addition**, they have professional care staff such as trained nurses.

▶ **Secondly**, many elderly people do not wish to be too dependent on their families. They do not want to put a burden on their family members' busy lives, by taking care of them 24 hours every day.

▶ **On the other hand**, some people believe that it should always be the family's responsibility to look after elderly relatives. They argue that they looked after you when you were a child and so now you should give them the love and care they need.

▶ **All in all, I believe that**, while it is the choice of each family, it is often better for an elderly person to live in a carefully-chosen nursing home. **This way**, they can live more independent lives in an environment that caters to all their needs.

3 ★ **Which paragraph contains:**

1 the writer's first viewpoint & example/reason? ....
2 the writer's opinion? ....
3 the writer's second viewpoint & example/reason? ....
4 the writer's opinion restated? ....
5 an opposing viewpoint & example/reason? ....

4 a) ★ **Underline the writer's opinion in the model essay.**

b) ★ **Complete the table with information from the model essay.**

paragraph	viewpoint	reasons/examples
2	*A nursing home can offer …*	*They often have great facilities …*
3		
4		

5 a) ★ **Complete the table with the linkers in bold in the model.**

listing points	
adding more points	
introduce an opinion	
introduce an opposite viewpoint	
introduce examples/ reasons	
show results	
conclude	

b) ★ **Add these linkers to the table.**

- Moreover • In the first place
- Although • Such as • To sum up
- As a result • It seems to me
- Lastly/Finally • However • Also

6 ★ Choose the correct linker.

1 If recycling were mandatory, it would reduce waste. **However/Moreover**, it would help the environment.

2 Volunteer work is rewarding. **For example/Such as** it helps young people to develop their confidence.

3 Space exploration is very costly. **On the other hand/So**, it would help mankind discover new things.

4 **All things considered/Although**, I feel that making recycling mandatory would be an more excellent way to help the environment.

5 We should reduce the price of public transport. **Secondly/As a consequence**, people would be likely to use buses instead of cars.

6 The agency helps unemployed people to find work. **For instance/To sum up**, they provide education and skills training.

7 ★ Rewrite the sentences using the linking words in brackets.

1 The government is going to reduce the speed limit. There will be fewer traffic accidents. **(Consequently)** ....

2 The homeless shelter is going to be demolished. The charity will have to relocate. **(As a result)** ....

3 Recycling bins will be installed in the city. People will be able to dispose of their waste. **(So)** ....

8 a) ★ Replace the topic sentences in the main body paragraphs in the essay in Ex. 2 with other appropriate ones.

b) ★ Read the topic sentences and write suitable supporting sentences using the prompts. Use appropriate linkers.

1 Cycling lanes should be created in the city.
• encourages people to exercise
• reduces traffic and pollution

2 Firstly, many people feel that stray animals should be put in a shelter.
• keeps the streets clean
• helps animals find a new home

9 ★ Read the rubric, then match the viewpoints (1-3) to the examples/reasons (A-C). Try to think of an opposing viewpoint and examples/reasons.

Your teacher has asked you to write an essay, giving your opinion on the topic:
"Unemployed people should do volunteer work in their community in order to get unemployment benefits."
Write your essay (200-250 words).

1		a chance to learn new skills
2		prevent a feeling of being useless
3		will stop lazy people from taking advantage of the benefits

A unemployed people can become depressed without a purpose in life

B they will no longer be able to claim benefits without any effort

C teamwork and organisational skills will be useful for future jobs

10 ★★ Use ideas from Ex. 9 and sentences from the *Useful language* box to write your opinion essay on the topic (200-250 words).

Useful language

State topic & opinion: Unemployed people ... In my opinion ...
Present viewpoints: Firstly ... For example ... Moreover ...
Present opposite viewpoints: On the other hand, it could be argued ...
Restate opinion: All in all, I believe ... This way ...

English in Use
Word Formation

1 ★ Read the text and complete the gaps with the words derived from the words in bold.

Most people would think that shark charming is a **1)** .... pastime, but not Italian diver Cristina Zenato! She can hold a ten-foot shark **2)** .... in her hand. How does she manage that? She can induce the fish into a state of **3)** .... simply by rubbing the jelly-filled pores around its nose and mouth. She uses her **4)** .... to immobilise sharks in order to educate other divers or tend to the animals' wounds in case of an **5)** .... Cristina has been working with sharks for 15 years and wants to spread the news about this endangered species and increase public **6)** ....!

DANGER

VERTICAL

PARALYSE

ABLE

INJURE

AWARE

Key Word Transformations

2 ★ Complete the gapped sentences so that they have a similar meaning to the original ones, using the words given.

1 It isn't necessary for you to attend the event.
HAVE You .... the event.

2 Tom worked at a wildlife park.
WHERE The place ....
.... a wildlife park.

3 If you don't follow the hiking trail, you will get lost.
UNLESS You will get lost ....
.... the hiking trail.

4 It's a shame that we didn't go to the festival.
WISH We ....
.... to the festival.

5 Using public transport regularly is a good idea.
SHOULD We .... regularly.

Speaking

Choose the correct response.

1 A: How can I help you?
   B: a I've been reading your leaflets.
      b I'd like to make a donation, please.

2 A: I think we must stop cutting down trees.
   B: a I totally agree.
      b In my opinion.

3 A: Could you give me your credit card number?
   B: a Yes, it expires in May.
      b Yes, it's 7895 5541 5474 2552.

4 A: How much would you like to donate?
   B: a £15 a month.
      b On the 15th of the month.

5 A: May I speak to Mr Davis, please?
   B: a That's great.
      b Certainly.

6 A: Could I get your address, please?
   B: a It's Jeff Taylor.
      b It's 589 Maple Street.

7 A: When does the card expire?
   B: a In May next year.
      b It's a debit card.

8 A: Thank you for your donation.
   B: a Goodbye and thank you again.
      b You're very welcome.

9 A: Would you like to leave a message?
   B: a Could you ask Mrs Jones to call me back?
      b And a contact number?

10 A: We should protect endangered animals.
   B: a I think that too.
      b The way I see it.

11 A: What kind of donation would you like to make?
   B: a It's a credit card.
      b A single donation of £15.

12 A: We should recycle more waste.
   B: a You're completely right.
      b Don't you think so?

41

3

Language & Grammar Review

Choose the correct answer.

1 A lot of people look ..... stray cats.
   A after   **B** up   **C** to   **D** out

2 Ann's first English class was a ..... experience.
   A puffy-eyed   **C** hard-working
   B sharp-toothed   **D** nerve-wracking

3 Ed Stafford ..... many challenges while walking through the Amazon.
   A made   **B** met   **C** faced   **D** approached

4 The hot, humid air made Beth's hair ..... .
   A pale   **B** frizzy   **C** scruffy   **D** puffy

5 The mayor wants to ..... public awareness about the town's rubbish problem.
   A gather   **B** organise   **C** reach   **D** raise

6 Gold, oil and wood are all ..... resources.
   A natural   **C** common
   B physical   **D** familiar

7 I was once chased by a swarm of .....!
   A snakes   **B** wasps   **C** fish   **D** eels

8 Tim is staying with a(n) ..... family while studying in Brazil.
   A unofficial   **C** host
   B private   **D** adopted

9 Jim hates making ..... talk with people.
   A quick   **B** simple   **C** basic   **D** small

10 The brightly-coloured poster was designed to ..... people's attention.
   A reach   **B** gather   **C** grab   **D** spread

11 The charity held a demonstration to help ..... their cause.
   A donate   **C** conserve
   B promote   **D** generate

12 A: What's the expiration date?
   B: .....
   A It's 553-9465.   **C** 45 Springhill Drive.
   B March next year.   **D** £30, please.

13 The protesters succeeded ..... stopping a plan to build a new factory in town.
   A in   **B** on   **C** for   **D** over

14 The old hotel has been ..... into a homeless shelter.
   A generated   **C** constructed
   B turned   **D** conserved

15 If I ..... rich, I would donate lots of money to charity.
   A am   **B** were   **C** be   **D** was being

16 Visitors ..... take pictures in the museum. It's forbidden.
   A shouldn't   **C** don't have to
   B mustn't   **D** couldn't

17 I wish I ..... more free time.
   A would have   **C** had
   B have   **D** was having

18 If you don't study, then you ..... pass the test.
   A didn't   **C** wouldn't
   B couldn't   **D** won't

19 If Tom had invited Jane to the lecture, she ..... here now.
   A will be   **C** would have been
   B would be   **D** will have been

20 If only I ..... to my parents' advice.
   A will listen   **C** had listened
   B listen   **D** was listening

21 What ..... do if you found some money?
   A would you   **C** will you
   B do you   **D** have you

22 Tom, ... was a sales clerk, is now homeless.
   A whose   **B** that   **C** which   **D** who

23 Stella ..... volunteer at the shelter this weekend; she has to study.
   A mustn't   **C** can't
   B doesn't have to   **D** couldn't

24 When people don't find jobs, the crime rate ..... .
   A will rise   **C** would rise
   B rises   **D** will be rising

25 If the charity had the money, it ..... a larger shelter by now.
   A would build   **C** had built
   B would be building   **D** would have built

Reading Task

Read the text. For each question choose the correct answer *A*, *B*, *C* or *D*.

Into the Great White North

As the group of five adventurers watched their small plane fly away, a sudden wave of panic spread through them. They realised they were all alone and the only way out of the massive valley where they stood was to launch their canoes and paddle down the Kongakut River 209 km to the Arctic Ocean. A plane was scheduled to pick them up there two weeks later. Despite being very experienced trekkers, the team was unsure of what to expect as such a journey had never been completed before.

This adventure-hungry team are volunteers for an organisation known as Across the Atlas which organises extreme adventure expeditions that raise money through sponsorships and donations. The money raised is then given to non-profit organisations and causes. The challenge this time was to trek, ski and canoe across one of the most remote places on Earth: the upper Kongakut Valley in northern Alaska. The team's goal was to support efforts to protect wildlife and conservation of this unique area of the world. Proceeds raised by the team would go to the Colorado Cancer Foundation.

The first task of the trip was to climb the Alaskan Continental Divide which runs from the base of the Kongakut River to the Arctic Ocean. Unfortunately, due to global warming, there was little snow, so the team was unable to ski the surrounding mountains as planned and had to settle only on hiking the divide. The hike turned out to be a strenuous task, involving crossing raging rivers and climbing steep mountainous terrain. After a gruelling day covering 4,500 feet, the team reached the top to enjoy stunning views of the surrounding valleys. They encountered hundreds of fearless caribou that appeared to have never seen humans before.

With the continental divide conquered, the team assembled their inflatable canoes for the journey downriver. To their amazement, the river was extremely shallow in many sections so the team had to push and drag their fully-loaded boats downstream. The first couple of days the team managed to travel only 3-5 kilometres per day instead of the estimated 24 km per day. This was very discouraging and tiring for the team. Fortunately, the river finally deepened and narrowed allowing the canoes to pick up speed. The canoes eventually encountered some challenging rapids which were the most difficult the adventurers had ever experienced. The team was thrilled to see ancient glaciers on the river and at one point paddled through one to find themselves surrounded by blue ice.

Finally, the river met the Arctic Ocean and the team built shelters on the beach and watched in the distance as waves crashed against drifting icebergs. The next day they set off in their canoes to meet their plane at the landing strip. Along the way, they saw a polar bear. The bear began to follow them for some distance, but eventually gave up. At the landing strip they set up camp to enjoy one final evening in the Arctic wilderness before meeting the plane the next day. As they sat around the campsite for the last time, the five adventurers knew how the first explorers must have felt after discovering a new land!

1 Upon arrival at the Valley the team
   A didn't know which direction to go.
   B felt concerned about the task ahead.
   C realised the plane had left without them.
   D lacked experience for such a trip.

2 The Across the Atlas organisation
   A hired the adventure team.
   B is an tourist travel agency.
   C is a wildlife conservation group.
   D donates money to various charities.

3 The team didn't ski on the trip
   A because the climb took the entire day.
   B due to hundreds of caribou.
   C due to the lack of snow.
   D due to very steep mountains.

4 While canoeing, the team was surprised
   A by the depth of the river.
   B at the difficulty of the river rapids.
   C by the glaciers floating on the river.
   D at how far the ocean was.

5 When the team arrived at the Ocean,
   A they encountered a polar bear.
   B they camped on the beach.
   C they paddled to the landing strip.
   D they waited for the plane.

3

Building Up Vocabulary

1 **Complete the sentences using one of the words in the box.**

> • waste • leftover • scrap

1 Peter had a great idea, so he wrote it down on a .... of paper.

2 We can reduce .... by recycling cans and bottles.

3 Try not to be wasteful by throwing out any .... food.

> • donation • allowance • grant

4 Debbie receives a travel .... every month in her new job.

5 Fred makes a monthly .... to a charity that cares for children in need.

6 James was lucky enough to receive a(n) .... to pay for his university fees.

> • endangered • threatened • extinct

7 The museum contains replicas of .... species like the dinosaur.

8 The world's rainforests are being .... by deforestation.

9 Pandas are a(n) .... species that are protected by the World Wildlife Fund.

> • urban • rural • commercial

10 Maria enjoys .... life as there are always things to do in a big city.

11 Danny works in an office in the .... district of town.

12 Mike wanted to experience .... living so he moved to the countryside.

> • settlement • colony • community

13 Scientists hope to establish a .... in outer space.

14 Next year, the mayor plans to build a new .... hall.

15 The tribe lives in a small .... deep in the rainforest.

> • renew • restore • repair

16 When your car breaks down, you can take it to a mechanic for ....

17 You must .... your passport every ten years.

18 Experts are working hard to .... the ancient building to its former glory.

> • subscription • contribution • payment

19 I pay a monthly .... for my favourite fashion magazine.

20 The shop allows .... by either cash or credit card.

21 She made a small .... to the charity.

2 **Complete the sentences with a word derived from the words in bold.**

Can you imagine having hundreds of cats roaming around inside your house? Well, for Lynea Lattanzio, that's **1)** .... (**EXACT**) how she likes it! Lynea is the proud **2)** .... (**FOUND**) of the largest no-cage cat sanctuary in California. Inside Lynea's 12-acre home, there are over 700 feline **3)** .... (**INHABIT**); and she is the only person living among them! Her **4)** .... (**OBSESS**) with cats started during her childhood years. She had longed for a kitten, but her mother would not allow it. As a result, she decided to rescue them in later life. She even enrolled in a veterinary **5)** .... (**TRAIN**) course in order to administer healthcare to the animals. Indeed, Lynea is so **6)** .... (**PASSION**) about cats that she has rescued around 19,000 of them! It's very **7)** .... (**DEMAND**) work, but fortunately Lynea isn't alone! She has the support and **8)** .... (**DEDICATE**) of 25 members of staff to help keep the shelter running **9)** .... (**SMOOTH**). However, caring for so many animals is very **10)** .... (**EXPENSE**) work, and Lynea receives no government **11)** .... (**FUND**). Instead, the charity relies on public donations to cover their costs, and Lynea has been deeply touched by the continued **12)** .... (**GENEROUS**) of all of their donors.

Language Knowledge – Module 3

1 Choose the correct Item.

1 If we hadn't raised the money, the shelter ..... now.
A would be closed   C had been closed
B will close   D was closed

2 By this time next month, we ..... enough food to send to the orphanage.
A will collect   C will have collected
B have collected   D are collecting

3 You ..... bring lunch to the charity run; they will have food stands there.
A mustn't   C can't
B don't have to   D shouldn't

4 The factory ..... waste in the river for years before the government stopped them.
A had dumped   C were dumping
B had been dumping   D have dumped

5 The conservation group, ... works to protect the rainforest, needs volunteers.
A whose   B where   C which   D who

6 ..... people in the town recycle their rubbish.
A Plenty   B Much   C Every   D Most

7 Mike wishes he ..... clean up the beach but he was sick.
A helped   C would help
B had helped   D was helping

2 Fill in the gaps. Use the appropriate forms of the word in brackets when given.

1 If Bill .... (know) about the fun run, he would have joined .... the race.

2 It is Candice .... raised the most money for charity .... holding a fundraiser.

3 I .... like to help, but I have a headache and I think it's getting .... (bad).

4 I wish there .... (be) more cycle lanes in town because I enjoy ....
(ride) my bicycle.

5 The animals .... live in the rainforest will suffer .... we do not stop cutting down trees.

Key Word Transformations

3 Complete the sentences using the word in bold. Use two to five words.

1 It's a shame I can't go to the charity dance.
ABLE   I wish ....
.... to the charity dance.

2 We volunteered for the environmental day because our teacher asked us to.
HAVE   If our teacher hadn't asked us, ...
....
for the environmental day.

3 I really want to find a job.
ONLY   If ....
.... a job.

4 Sarah donated £1,000 to the shelter.
ONE   Sarah ....
.... donated £1,000 to the shelter.

5 It's forbidden to throw rubbish in the park.
NOT   You...
.... rubbish in the park.

6 Max didn't volunteer at the homeless shelter.
WHO   It ....
.... at the homeless shelter.

7 She has sold as many raffle tickets as I have.
NUMBER   She has sold ....
.... raffle tickets as I have.

8 She needn't have cleaned up all the house.
HAVE   She ....
.... up all the house.

9 It's a shame that they closed the homeless shelter.
ONLY   If ....
.... the homeless shelter.

10 My mother used to volunteer at that school.
IS   That ....
.... my mother used to volunteer.

11 Jill regrets spending so much money at the festival.
WISHES   Jill ....
.... so much money at the festival.

12 It wasn't a good idea to quit your job.
HAVE   You ....
.... your job.

45

4a

Vocabulary

1 ★ **Fill in:** *saucer, autopsy, eye-witness, sightings, footprints, sceptic, wreckage.*

1 Some teenagers found strange .... in the sand that didn't look human.
2 Ben thought he saw a flying .... hovering over the city.
3 Scientists performed a(n) .... to look inside the strange creature.
4 Danny is a .... who does not believe UFOs exist.
5 Army officials are investigating the .... of a plane crash.
6 There have been many UFO .... around Roswell.
7 One .... claimed that she saw strange lights in the sky.

2 ★ **Choose the correct word.**

1 Lisa went on a **trip/tour** to Roswell hoping to see a UFO.
2 Investigators **examined/experienced** the debris but found no evidence of any spacecraft.
3 He had a great **sight/view** of the area from his balcony.
4 The **events/facts** that happened in Roswell remain a mystery to this day.
5 The aircraft **soared/burst** high above the clouds.
6 The man gave journalists a **report/witness** on the UFO sighting.
7 Helicopters that **hovered/floated** over Roswell were thought to be UFOs.

3 ★ **Fill in the correct adjective:** *oval-shaped, impressive, intelligent, eerie.*

1 Some people believe that there is .... life in the universe.
2 Sally looked up and saw a(n) .... object with large windows in the sky.
3 Dean felt uneasy when he walked down the dark .... road.
4 An eye-witness said the massive spacecraft was a(n) .... sight.

Grammar

4 ★ **Rewrite the newspaper headlines in the passive.**

A PHOTOGRAPHER FILMED STRANGE OBJECT IN THE SKY
B EXPLORERS DISCOVER UNUSUAL CRAFT IN HIMALAYAS
C BELGIAN UFO HOAX HAS FOOLED THOUSANDS
D MAYOR WILL OPEN NEW PLANETARIUM TOMORROW

A ....
B ....
C ....
D ....

5 ★ **Fill in** *by* **or** *with.*

1 Alan claimed that he was abducted .... aliens.
2 The UFO was seen .... a local resident.
3 Some pieces of the destroyed spaceship were found .... metal detectors.
4 The autopsy was performed .... a doctor.
5 Locals were fooled by a fake alien body built .... rubber and cardboard.

6 ★ **Complete the text with the** *passive* **form of the verbs.**

Unusual Lights reported

A series of mysterious lights **1)** .... (spot) above Cambridge late Sunday night. Video footage of the unusual sighting **2)** .... (capture) by eye-witness Steven Morgan, an amateur astronomer. The strange phenomenon **3)** .... (observe) by Morgan while he was studying a passing meteor shower. In an interview with local journalists, he claimed the lights were a bright blue colour. At the moment, the video footage **4)** .... (examine) by experts at London University to determine whether it is a hoax. An official report **5)** .... (not/release) yet. However, it **6)** .... (believe) by some who have viewed the video that the lights were fireworks from a nearby festival. Expert opinion on the matter **7)** .... (reveal) in the upcoming days.

Vocabulary

1 ★ **Fill in:** *hair samples, specimen, life-size, countless, mobility, native.*

1 Using a needle, scientists took a blood .... from the creature to study.
2 There have been .... sightings of Bigfoot over the years.
3 Some .... tribes of Central America believe in a monster called 'El Chupacabra'.
4 Researchers found .... of an unknown creature in a cave.
5 The museum has got a .... model of a dinosaur.
6 Scientists believe that Bigfoot moves like an ape with limited ....

2 ★ **Choose the correct word.**

1 Dinosaurs have been **extinct/unknown** for a long time.
2 The monster let out a terrible **scratch/screech**.
3 Before starting the experiment, the scientist **glanced/gazed** at her watch.
4 The forest felt eerie as the hunter **peered/glared** into the darkness.
5 She **peeped/stared** through the keyhole and thought she saw a ghost!
6 Ben **gazed/stared** through his telescope at the stars in the sky.
7 As the hunter approached the animal, the angry beast **glared/glanced** at him.
8 He caught a **glimpse/glance** of something strange in the woods.

3 ★ **Fill in:** *to (x2), on, with.*

1 .... date, nobody has captured a Bigfoot.
2 The scientist is an expert .... prehistoric animals.
3 When I feel scared, I turn .... my mother for comfort.
4 Sceptics take eye-witness accounts of UFOs .... a pinch of salt.

4 ★ **Complete the text with these words.**

- prehistoric
- secretive
- legendary
- sightings
- sceptics
- hoax
- evidence

In Scotland there is a **1)** .... tale of a beast called the Loch Ness Monster that lives in the waters of Loch Ness. To the locals it is simply known as 'Nessie'. The word 'loch' is Scottish for 'lake'. The loch is very deep and long, which makes it an ideal place for such a shy and **2)** .... creature to hide. There have been many recorded **3)** .... of the monster going back as far as the 6th century. The first photographic **4)** .... was captured in 1934 by Dr Kenneth Wilson, a physician from London. The picture apparently shows a **5)** .... dinosaur-like beast with a long neck emerging out of the murky waters. The photo created quite a fuss and is still the centre of controversy to this day. Some **6)** .... argue that the photograph is either a **7)** .... or an honest mistake. They believe that what people have seen are seals or otters that are sometimes found in the loch, or even objects such as tree trunks. Whatever lives in the loch, it brings many tourists each year hoping to see it!

Grammar

5 ★ **Complete the sentences in the** *passive.*

1 People think the creature walks like a gorilla.
The creature ....
2 They think the government found a UFO.
The government ....
3 Experts believe that he didn't see a ghost.
He ....
4 They report that natives have spotted Bigfoot.
It ....
5 People say the Loch Ness Monster exists.
The Loch Ness monster ....

Vocabulary

1 ★ **Fill in:** *cruel, trials, torture, graveyard, beheaded, usher, haunted.*

1 In medieval times, ... were held in the Tower of London courthouse.
2 The tombstones in the .... looked eerie at night.
3 At the funfair, we took a ride in the .... house.
4 The London Dungeons have a .... history.
5 When we entered the theatre, the .... led us to our seats.
6 In medieval times to make criminals confess, they would sometimes .... them.
7 King Henry VIII had his wife .... in the Tower of London.

2 ★ **Fill in the correct word derived from the word in the brackets.**

1 Ann gasped when she saw a .... face in the window. **(GHOST)**
2 The criminal was sentenced to life .... **(IMPRISON)**
3 There were many public .... in medieval times. **(EXECUTE)**
4 Ghost sightings in London were a common .... **(OCCUR)**
5 There have been many .... performances at the Theatre Royal. **(SUCCESS)**

Grammar

3 ★ **Choose the correct** *question tag.*

1 Sally will come on the tour, **will she/won't she?**
2 Let's visit the Castle, **will we/shall we?**
3 Don't forget to bring the tickets, **do you/will you?**
4 He isn't scared of the dark, **isn't he/is he?**
5 Chris can't come to the haunted house, **could he/can he?**
6 They went to the theatre, **didn't they/weren't they?**
7 John likes going sightseeing, **does he/doesn't he?**

Speaking

4 ★ **Use the sentences to complete the dialogue.**

A Could you tell me what the ticket price includes, please?
B That will be £25, please.
C When would you like to go?
D How many tickets would you like?
E That sounds great!
F It starts at Mercat Cross at 7 pm.
G Is this where I can buy tickets for the Ghosts and Ghouls tour?

A: Good afternoon. **1** ⬚
B: Yes, it is.
A: Great. **2** ⬚
B: Sure. It includes a tour of Edinburgh's dark past and entry to the underground vaults. You also get a free drink at Meggat's Cellar at the end.
A: **3** ⬚ I'd like to buy some tickets, please.
B: Sure. **4** ⬚
A: Tonight if possible.
B: That's fine. **5** ⬚
A: Could I have 1 adult and 2 children, please?
B: OK. **6** ⬚
A: Great. Here you are. Could you tell me where the tour starts from?
B: Of course. **7** ⬚
A: Thank you.
B: My pleasure. Enjoy your visit.

5 ★★ **Write a similar dialogue. Use the advert below and the dialogue in Ex. 4 as a model.**

THE YORK GHOST WALK
THE MOST HAUNTED CITY IN THE WORLD

The tour experience:
▸ Walking tour of York's haunted locations.
▸ Spine-tingling stories, told by our professional tour guides.
▸ Historical re-enactments.

Tours start at the Roman Column by York Minster every night at 7pm. Cost: Adults £5, Children £3.

Book early to avoid disappointment!

Reading

1 ★ Read the text. For questions 1-15, choose from the texts (A-D).

Which person ...

was enjoying their hobby when it happened?	1	remains puzzled by their experience?	10
tried to find out more about the event?	2	was performing a chore when it occurred?	11
was an adolescent when it happened?	3	inherited special abilities?	12
says they will never forget their experience?	4	had their experience due to a change they made	13
has a history of detecting certain phenomena?	5		
was panic-stricken when it happened?	6 / 7	noticed a change in their surroundings before it happened?	14
lost money because of their experience?	8		
continues to observe the phenomenon?	9	was at ease during their experience?	15

Mysterious Experiences

Have you ever had something strange happen to you? Weird things happen to ordinary people more often than you think. Enter the world of the unexplainable ...

A The Shadow People – Dwayne Rogers

For years my family and I would go to our lake house. I used to enjoy spending time with my brothers there – and being close to nature. But when I was thirteen years old, the scariest thing happened to me there – something that will stay with me throughout my lifetime. Late one afternoon, my brothers and I went fishing at our favourite spot. As we sat there, I got the strangest feeling that we were being watched. I looked around and there on the distant shore I saw many dark shapes gathering together. They appeared to be staring at us. It was quite unnerving as more and more of these dark shapes kept arriving until there were at least fifty of them. My brothers who had been chatting away all afternoon suddenly stopped talking and looked over at these shapes. They looked like people; they had dark human-shaped silhouettes but they had no faces. It was quite an alarming sight and I was terrified. It didn't take long for my youngest brother to start packing up his fishing gear and the rest of us followed suit. As we got up to leave, I glanced back at the shore. All the shadow people had disappeared!

B The Scarecrow Mystery – Ryan Miller

My wife and I bought an old farmhouse in an auction after the old owner passed away. We planned to sell it for a profit to local developers. One day, I gathered up the rubbish, pulled out the old scarecrow from the cornfield and threw everything on a bonfire. Outside the house, I put up a 'For Sale' sign. The next morning my wife and I returned to the house and gasped at what we saw; the sign was missing and in its place now stood the scarecrow that I was sure I had burned. In fear, I was driven to sell the property at a fraction of the cost. But, occasionally, I drive by the farm and I can still see the scarecrow staring out at me!

C A Bizarre Encounter – Shelly White

I myself am very clairvoyant, as my grandmother had been before me which means that I can sense things that can't be explained. But I had never actually had a close encounter with a spirit until the time I went on a camping trip with my friend Annabelle. In the middle of the night, I suddenly woke up feeling very cold. Our tent was freezing and a pale mist descended upon us. I sensed the presence of a spirit but felt oddly calm. I looked over to my friend Annabelle, but she was fast asleep. That's when I saw it: the shape of a woman hovering above my sleeping friend. I put on my glasses to get a closer look. The apparition had reddish hair and was wearing a black cloak with a hood. It tried to make eye contact, but it seemed to be staring past me into the distance. Suddenly, Annabelle turned in her sleep and then, just like that, the apparition vanished into thin air!

D A Strange Light – Jeremy Mathews

I am an astronomer and have been observing the stars for many years. I'm always on the look out for passing meteor showers or other strange phenomenon. But one night I witnessed an incident that has baffled me to this day. I was out walking my dog and as I looked up at the starry sky, a bright flashing light caught my gaze. I didn't pay much attention at first since I knew the airport was only few miles off. However, it soon became apparent that the light wasn't moving and it seemed to be too low for an airplane in flight. In any case, I couldn't hear anything; there was no sound! The more I looked, the less it appeared to be an aircraft. The light remained stationary for several minutes and then it moved abruptly until it was no longer visible in the sky. It travelled at a speed that was faster than any aircraft I have ever witnessed. This aroused my curiosity and I made an inquiry at the local newspaper. Apparently, no one else had reported anything similar.

Vocabulary

1 a) ★ **Match the words to make phrases.**

1	conduct	A	the Earth
2	make	B	of an egg
3	bring	C	in two
4	become	D	experiments
5	run	E	extinct
6	hatch out	F	back to life
7	rule	G	a breakthrough
8	break	H	tests

b) ★★ **Use some of the sentences above to complete the sentences.**

1 In order to learn new things, scientists must .... in a laboratory.
2 There are no more dinosaurs alive on Earth as they have ....
3 Scientists would like to .... in genetic testing.
4 Dinosaurs used to .... because they were stronger than other animals.
5 Like a bird, a baby dinosaur would ....

2 ★ **Fill in:** *vessels, relatives, prehistoric, techniques, organic, map.*

1 Scientists found .... material in dinosaur bones.
2 Scientists hope to clone dinosaurs using advanced ....
3 Snakes and lizards are distant .... of dinosaurs.
4 Scientists are trying to complete the genetic .... of a dinosaur.
5 The Triceratops was a giant land mammal that lived in .... times.
6 Blood .... were found in a dinosaur bone.

3 ★ **Fill in:** *revive, excavate, preserve, roam, clone* **in the correct form.**

1 DNA samples can be .... in a freezer.
2 Scientists believe they will be able to .... extinct animals in the future.
3 Archaeologists are very careful when they .... artefacts from a site.
4 Dinosaurs .... the Earth over 65 million years ago.
5 Scientists have already .... one sheep from another.

Grammar

4 ★ **Fill in the gaps with the correct reflexive/ emphatic pronouns.**

1 Brian introduced .... to the rest of the tour group.
2 We really enjoyed .... on the field trip to the archeological site.
3 The scientists .... are unsure about the results of the experiment.
4 She .... discovered the dinosaur bone.
5 Did you conduct the experiment ....?

Listening

5 ★ 🎧 **You will hear an interview with a young man who is a paleontologist. Listen and check (✓) T (true) or F (false).**

	T	F
1 The Sprinter was a good hunter.		
2 There are many dinosaur remains in the Valley of the Moon.		
3 The researchers are only interested in dinosaurs.		
4 It took the dinosaur species a long time to develop.		
5 Jeff does not enjoy his work because it is too difficult.		

Vocabulary

1 ★ Match the type of book to its title.

A A Rose for Maggie

B Voyage to Venus

C The Escape

D Haunted

E Murder on the Orient Express

F The Legend of James Dean

G The Last Crusaders

H Dragonflight

1		horror story
2		science fiction
3		biography
4		fantasy

5		romance
6		thriller
7		crime
8		historical fiction

2 ★ Complete the sentences with the correct adjective.

• boring • thrilling • silly • relaxing
• unrealistic • frightening • fascinating

1 Reading is .... and helps me to unwind after school.
2 Historical fiction is so .... that it puts me to sleep.
3 Emma thought the characters were .... because they never did anything wrong.
4 Gracie refuses to read ghost stories because she finds them ....
5 The main characters embarked upon a(n) .... adventure.
6 The book gave a(n) .... insight into the life of the famous artist.
7 The main character was quite .... and made me laugh!

3 ★ Choose the correct word.

1 There were several **clever/mysterious** events in the book that made me wonder what would happen next.
2 The main character was very **shallow/dull** because he only seemed to care about money.
3 Jane found the end of the novel **confusing/unexpected** and felt the author did not explain what had happened.
4 James found the book so **fast-paced/gripping** that he could not stop reading!
5 The series was **unrealistic/unimaginative** because the plot was the same in every book!
6 The story was **surprising/interesting** because it taught me about dinosaurs.
7 Katrina thought the book was very **predictable/original** and had guessed the ending half-way through.

Speaking

4 ★ Choose the correct response.

1 A: What is your favourite type of book?
B: **a** It's Harry Potter.
b It's science fiction.

2 A: What's the main character like?
B: **a** It's quite predictable.
b He's evil but interesting!

3 A: Why don't you like fantasy novels?
B: **a** I find them unrealistic.
b I don't think I'd buy one.

4 A: What did you think of the plot?
B: **a** It's likeable.
b It's slow-paced.

5 A: What do you think of horror novels?
B: **a** I'm afraid not.
b I don't like those types of books.

Vocabulary

1 ★ **Fill in:** *irritably, viciously, sting, complete, enclosure, carving.*

1 She used a .... knife to cut up the roast.
2 The dog lunged .... at the intruder.
3 The animals were kept in a small .... so they could not escape.
4 The bee .... caused her arm to swell up.
5 "Aren't you ready yet?" he asked ....
6 Once they entered the cave they were in .... darkness.

2 ★ **Complete the sentences with the correct form of the verbs from the list.**

• whip • cross • settle • hack • break
• wriggle • smack • mist

1 They returned to the house to find someone had .... in.
2 The runner .... the finish line and set a new world record.
3 We should wait until the wind has .... down before going outside.
4 John .... his way through the dense jungle with a large knife.
5 The jellyfish's stings .... and slapped across my arm causing horrible pain.
6 The boys .... the ball against the side of the house.
7 The rain .... up her glasses and she was unable to see.
8 The worm .... into the soil to hide.

3 ★ **Choose the correct participle.**

1 Can you help me pick **up/out** a nice dress to wear tonight?
2 She kept **up/on** working even though she was tired.
3 Jane was let **down/out** of the hospital yesterday.
4 Some of the children were teasing and picking **on/out** Bill.
5 If you don't come, you'll be letting me **down/out**.
6 Most films stars have bodyguards to keep **from/away** fans.

Listening

4 ★ 🎧 **You will hear an interview with an author about her book. For questions 1-10 complete the sentences.**

The interviewer describes Kelly's book as a
[_____ **1**] and a combination of styles.

Kelly says in her book a
[_____ **2**] meet an alien.

The alien in the book is based on an
[_____ **3**] description.

People who usually read
[_____ **4**] will also enjoy the book.

Kelly spent a year studying well-known
[_____ **5**] .

Kelly gives the example of the
[_____ **6**] as strong proof of supernatural phenomena.

Kelly has written numerous
[_____ **7**] on the supernatural.

Kelly consulted with UFO [_____ **8**] while writing her book.

The book will be in bookshops in
[_____ **9**] .

Kelly's next project is to work on a
[_____ **10**] about a haunted town.

Writing
(a book review)

1 a) ★ Read the book review and put the paragraphs in the correct order.

A The story is set in the future after Peeta has been captured by the government. The main character, Katniss, is now part of the rebellion against those responsible for the Hunger Games. Together with the rebels, she attacks the district to free Peeta. They manage to save him and together they plan to overthrow the government. Will Katniss be able to put an end to the Hunger Games once and for all?

B *Mockingjay*, by Suzanne Collins, is the third book in the popular *Hunger Games* series. It is a thrilling science-fiction novel which continues the story of Katniss Everdeen and her friend, Peeta Mellark, as they try to stop the 'Hunger Games' that force poor children to fight for food.

C I would definitely recommend this book to anyone who enjoys reading science fiction and has read the first two books. It's an entertaining sequel and you will not be able to put it down!

D The fast-paced plot is extremely clever. It is full of many unpredictable twists and turns. It also contains some touching moments and an original romance unlike any other love story. What adds to the novel's appeal is that the main character is not always likeable. She is moody and angry at the world. However, she is appealing because she is brave and caring. This makes her character realistic.

b) ★ Which paragraph contains:

1 a summary of the plot? ....
2 the writer's opinion/recommendation with reasons? ....
3 background information about the book? ....
4 general comments about the book? ....

2 ★ Which adjectives does the writer use to describe these nouns?

1 .... moments
2 .... plot
3 .... science-fiction novel
4 .... sequel
5 .... romance
6 .... twists and turns

3 ★ Complete the spidergram. Put the words below in the correct boxes.

- shallow • horror • gripping • original
- biography • likeable • evil • fantasy
- unimaginative

Book Type
....
....
....

Characters
....
....
....

book review

Plot
....
....
....

4 ★ Fill in: *funny, exciting, predictable, heartwarming, confusing, surprising, informative, mysterious.*

1 I was moved by the .... romance between the main characters.
2 The story was full of .... twists; I never knew what was going to happen next.
3 It was a(n) .... adventure story that had me hooked from the very beginning!
4 Non-fiction tends to be very .... and teaches you new things.
5 It was a .... story about a strange occurrence.
6 The story was so .... that I had guessed the ending right from the start.
7 The plot was quite ....; I was completely lost!
8 The author was so .... that I couldn't stop laughing.

5 ★ Choose the correct words/phrases.

1 The **chief/main** character is Katniss Everdeen.
2 The science-fiction novel *Voyage to Venus* is **set/based** in space.
3 The book is **set in/based on** the inspirational life story of Ghandi.
4 The novel was so entertaining that I couldn't **put it down/throw it away**.
5 *A Christmas Carol* **plays the part/tells the story** of Ebenezer Scrooge.
6 I was totally **absorbed/involved** in the exciting book I was reading.
7 Although it was educational, I found the book quite **thick/dull**.
8 The end of the book had a really unexpected **plot/twist**!

6 a) ★ Complete the reviews with:

- won't regret it • I've ever read
- don't bother • is definitely for you
- to be a bestseller • highly recommend it
- well worth reading • make sure it's this one

A This is the most fascinating novel **1)** ....
.... If you're a fan of historical fiction, then this book **2)** ....

B If you read only one book this summer,
3) .... I guarantee you
4) ....

C This is a very well-written book. I would
5) .... to anyone who enjoys exciting crime thrillers.

D This series is **6)** ....
Judging by the popularity of the first book, this sequel is bound **7)** ....!

E The plot was weak and the characters were really boring. **8)** .... reading this book; choose a different one instead!

b) ★ Which sentence does the writer use to recommend the book in the review in Ex. 1?

....
....

7 a) ★ Read the rubric and think of a book you've recently read and complete the table.

A magazine is asking for a book review. Write your review for the magazine describing the plot, making general comments and giving your recommendation (200-250 words).

Background information (title, type, author)	....
Main points of the plot	....
General comments (plot, characters, beginning, ending)	....
Recommendation and reasons	....

b) ★ Answer the questions.

1 What are you writing? ....
2 What tense(s) will you use? ....
3 What must you include? ....
....

8 ★★ Use your answers from Ex. 7 and the *Useful language* box to write your review.

Useful language

Background: This a fascinating book written by ...; The story is set in ...
Main points of the plot: The story is about... The plot/beginning/ending is rather boring/predictable/gripping ...
General Comments: It is interesting/slow etc ...; The main character is shallow/ likeable ...; The ending is rather disappointing/surprising ...; The book is full of funny/dull moments ...
Recommendations: I thoroughly recommend this book ...; This is a highly entertaining read ...; Don't bother reading this. It's...

54

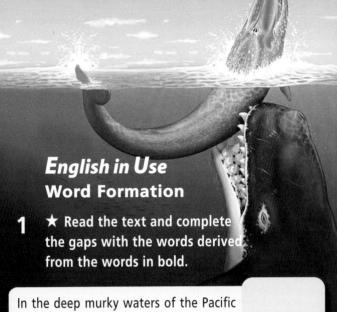

English in Use
Word Formation

1 ★ Read the text and complete the gaps with the words derived from the words in bold.

In the deep murky waters of the Pacific Ocean, **1)** .... have discovered the fossils of an ancient predator. The creature is a giant whale with **2)** .... teeth twice as long as those of a dinosaur! This huge beast from **3)** .... times is thought to have eaten other whales for dinner! Researchers are unsure of how the **4)** .... creature became extinct. However, its **5)** .... is similar to today's sperm whale. **6)** ...., the sperm whales of today are much friendlier creatures!

SCIENCE

SPIKE

HISTORIC

TERRIFY

APPEAR

FORTUNATE

Key Word Transformations

2 ★ Complete the gapped sentences so that they have a similar meaning to the original ones, using the word given.

1 Did the student discover the dinosaur skeleton?
BY   Do you know if the ....
.... the student?

2 Many people say that a monster lives in the lake.
SAID   A monster ....
.... live in the lake.

3 The archeologists thought that the dinosaur fossils were amazing.
BY   The archeologists ....
.... the dinosaur fossils.

4 Witnesses said they saw strange bright lights in the sky.
REPORTED   Strange bright lights in the sky .... witnesses.

5 John went alone into the haunted house.
HIMSELF   John was ....
he went into the haunted house.

Speaking

Choose the correct response.

1 A: I'd like to buy some tickets, please.
B: **a** How many would you like?
   b Could you tell me the price?

2 A: That's £17, please.
B: **a** Here you are.
   b That sounds great.

3 A: Could you tell me what the ticket price includes, please?
B: **a** The tour starts on the high Street.
   b It's a guided tour of London.

4 A: Where does the tour start from?
B: **a** Every half hour.
   b At the main entrance.

5 A: What did you think of the main character in *Twilight*?
B: **a** Very interesting and likeable.
   b It was really imaginative!

6 A: When would you like to go on the tour?
B: **a** Tonight if possible.
   b It starts at 6 o'clock.

7 A: What did you think of the plot?
B: **a** It was funny and original!
   b Very shallow!

8 A: What's your favourite type of book?
B: **a** I enjoy biographies.
   b *Eclipse* was brilliant.

9 A: Is this where I can buy tickets for the tour?
B: **a** When would you like to go?
   b Yes, it certainly is.

10 A: What did you think about the ending of the book?
B: **a** It was disappointing.
   b It was a thriller.

11 A: What is the book about?
B: **a** A detective who investigates a murder.
   b It's a mystery novel.

12 A: How many tickets would you like?
B: **a** They're valid for 3 days.
   b 1 adult and 2 children.

4

Language & Grammar Review

Choose the correct answer.

1 Scientists hope to ..... a breakthrough in cloning.
A have **B** reach **C** make **D** get

2 Ann picked ..... the fossil to look at it.
A on **B** out **C** up **D** off

3 Her heart ..... when she realised there was no ghost.
A broke **B** sank **C** fell **D** dripped

4 Roswell is becoming a famous tourist ..... .
A base **B** mark **C** point **D** spot

5 She is one of the world's ..... experts on UFOs.
A leading **C** original
B legendary **D** apparent

6 He heard ..... from an unknown creature.
A scratches **C** images
B screeches **D** occurrences

7 The hunter ..... into the dark cave.
A peered **B** glanced **C** stared **D** glimpsed

8 What a ..... read! I can't put it down.
A gripping **C** predictable
B likeable **D** satisfying

9 The leaves ..... in the wind.
A scratched **C** whistled
B rustled **D** crunched

10 The Naga fireballs are a(n) ..... phenomenon!
A doubtful **C** baffling
B confusing **D** ambitious

11 Scientists continue to ..... experiments on dinosaur DNA.
A gather **B** conduct **C** run **D** preserve

12 A: When would you like to go?
B: ..... .
A Every hour.
B It's 3 o'clock.
C They're valid for 7 days.
D This afternoon.

13 Scientists need to create a genetic ..... of a dinosaur before they can clone it.
A base **B** map **C** maze **D** plan

14 The man was ..... after he fainted.
A revived **C** reactivated
B reserved **D** reluctant

15 A strange creature ..... by a hunter in the woods.
A captured **C** was captured
B is captured **D** is capturing

16 The unusual bones ..... by paleontologists at the museum.
A are examining **C** examined
B are examined **D** are being examined

17 You won't go to the haunted house, ... you?
A won't **B** are **C** will **D** shall

18 Witnesses ..... by the police when I arrived.
A were interviewed
B have been interviewed
C were being interviewed
D are being interviewed

19 Sam likes scary stories, ... he?
A isn't **B** does **C** didn't **D** doesn't

20 Paul enjoyed .....on the ghost tour.
A itself **B** himself **C** myself **D** yourself

21 150 years ago, it ..... believed that mountain gorillas didn't exist.
A was **B** is being **C** is **D** has been

22 There have been many UFO sightings in ..... Nevada Desert.
A – **B** the **C** a **D** an

23 Jill and Kay enjoyed ..... on the UFO tour.
A yourselves **C** ourselves
B themselves **D** herself

24 The new museum ..... opened next week.
A will be **B** is **C** are **D** has been

25 A large ape-like creature ..... near the lake yesterday.
A is spotted **C** is being spotted
B was spotted **D** has been spotted

Reading Task

Read the text. Seven sentences have been removed from the article. Choose from the sentences (A-H) the one that fits each gap (1-7). There is one extra sentence.

The Zone of Silence

Deserts are often considered eerie, isolated places. However, there is one desert spot which takes this isolation one step further.

Six hundred kilometres from the US border in the Chihuahua Desert of Mexico lies an area that has perplexed scientists for decades. **1** This is why it has become known as the Zone of Silence.

The mysterious Zone of Silence was first discovered in the 1930s when a Mexican pilot reported problems while flying over the region. **2** However, the phenomenon was not confirmed until 1970 when an American rocket flew hundreds of kilometres off course and crashed into the area! It was suspected that an invisible force within the desert had caused this strange occurrence. But nobody could explain what this curious force could be.

In order to uncover the mystery of the peculiar desert, government investigators were sent out to the crash site. **3** Since then, a research centre has been constructed at the heart of the zone and scientists from around the world have come to study the area. Despite all this attention, the reason behind the sound wave silence remains a mystery to this day.

The mystery becomes even more intriguing with the high number of UFO sightings that have been witnessed over the years in the zone. **4** Most of the eye-witness accounts of alien encounters describe strange human-like creatures with long blonde hair, wearing raincoats and hats.

Many of the mysterious lights in the night sky can be attributed to the high concentration of meteor strikes in the zone. The area seems to be a magnet for space debris, and has even attracted the largest meteorite ever recorded on Earth. **5**

So does anyone actually live in this creepy area? Well actually, they do! **6** It seems that almost all of the people living there have a story to tell about a strange light in the sky or other mysterious occurrences. They have also learned to live without television and with weak radio signals.

Curiously enough, the Zone of Silence with all its UFO and meteor attraction is located on the same latitude as another mysterious planetary spot: the Bermuda Triangle in the Atlantic Ocean. **7** Could this just be a coincidence, or could this invisible line point towards an even greater mystery that has yet to unfold?

A Reports of strange lights, flying saucers, burning bushes and alien encounters have made the zone a UFO hotspot.

B This car-sized fireball struck the zone in 1969, producing a shockwave that could be heard many kilometres away!

C He claimed that he could not transmit radio signals and that his plane instruments seemed to fail.

D This infamous stretch of water has long been known as an area where countless ships and planes have disappeared.

E For unexplained reasons, no radio, television or satellite signals can be transmitted in the area.

F Some scientists believe that region was once submerged beneath the sea.

G Just 40 kilometres from the zone lies the town of Ceballos, where residents have got used to the unique attributes of the area.

H Upon arrival they became immediately aware of the 'silence' when they couldn't communicate with each other via radio transmissions.

4

Building Up Vocabulary

1 **Complete the sentences using one of the words in the box.**

• eerie • ghostly • creepy

1 Upon hearing the news, James turned .... pale.
2 Beth is scared of spiders and finds them very ....!
3 There was a(n) .... atmosphere in the haunted house.

• fierce • savage • untamed

4 The creature turned towards me and gave me a .... look.
5 That horse is ....; it can't be ridden.
6 They encountered a .... tribe living in the Amazon

• speculation • observation • surveillance

7 The criminals have been under police .... for many weeks.
8 Paul gazed through the viewfinder at the top of the .... tower.
9 There is a lot of .... about the cause of the phenomenon.

• invisible • cloudy • murky

10 There is no visibility in the .... depths of the muddy river.
11 The ghost slowly faded and eventually became ....
12 That water looks a little ....; you shouldn't drink it.

• convincing • realistic • true-to-life

13 His explanation was so .... that we believed it.
14 We need to be more .... about the possible existence of UFOs.
15 The characters in the book are so .... that I feel I know them.

• startled • distressed • alarmed

16 The bear was .... because it had been caught in a trap.
17 Rory was .... by an unexpected knock on his door.
18 Authorities are .... by reports of a strange creature in the forest.

• speculate • forecast • predict

19 The fortune-teller claims to be able to .... the future.
20 Some scientists .... that the fireballs are meteorites falling from the sky.
21 It is .... to snow next week.

2 **Complete the sentences with a word derived from the words in bold.**

For decades, **1)** .... **(MYSTERY)** flashes of light have been seen above the **2)** .... **(PEACE)** valley of Hessdalen in Norway. This **3)** .... **(USUAL)** phenomenon began in 1981, when hundreds of sightings were reported by **4)** .... **(VARY)** eye-witnesses. Scientists were so intrigued by the phenomenon that they installed advanced computerised **5)** .... **(EQUIP)** to monitor the area. But despite 25 years of research, the mystery continues to baffle the **6)** .... **(SCIENCE)** community. One theory is that the lights are caused by water seeping into rocks in the valley. When this water freezes, it is thought to generate **7)** .... **(ELECTRIC)**. This spark could then ignite gases in the air, creating a flash of light. However, there is little **8)** .... **(EVIDENT)** to support this theory and it has been heavily criticised as being physically **9)** .... **(POSSIBLE)**. Sceptics have suggested that the lights could be caused by planes approaching a nearby airport, but as the lights have been seen in the sky for hours, this theory seems quite **10)** .... **(LIKE)**. Whatever the cause of the mystery, it is a **11)** .... **(REMARK)** sight to see and attracts countless **12)** .... **(TOUR)** to the area each year.

Language Knowledge – Module 4

1 Choose the correct item.

1 You believe in ghosts, ... you?
A aren't   B do   C don't   D can't

2 Sightings of the Loch Ness Monster date back to ..... 6th century.
A a   B the   C –   D an

3 Joe made the discovery ..... .
A itself   C themselves
B himself   D ourselves

4 If Tim wasn't so scared, he ..... a video of the ghost.
A will take   C took
B had taken   D would have taken

5 Strange lights ..... in the sky last night.
A were spotted   C have been spotted
B are being spotted   D had been spotted

6 In the future, scientists ..... living dinosaurs.
A are recreating
B will have been recreating
C are going to recreate
D will recreate

7 The Bigfoot pictures ..... at tomorrow's press conference.
A are showing   C have been shown
B were shown   D will be shown

2 Fill in the gaps. Use the appropriate forms of the word in brackets when given.

1 The UFO sighting that was witnessed .... some tourists last night is .... **(investigate)**

2 Thanks to .... photographer's help, scientists were able to gather .... **(far)** evidence about the phenomenon.

3 The hunter uses traps .... **(catch)** animals .... live in the forest.

4 It .... **(believe)** that the Yeti has a lack .... mobility and walks like an ape.

5 Ted can't wait .... **(see)** the Dinosaur exhibition at .... Natural History Museum.

Key Word Transformations

3 Complete the sentences using the words in bold. Use two to five words.

1 People say the creature is very dangerous.
BE   The creature ....
.... very dangerous.

2 The photographer took a lot of pictures for the news story.
TAKEN   A lot of pictures ....
.... photographer
for the news story.

3 Experts have looked into the UFO video footage.
INVESTIGATED   The UFO video footage ....
.... experts.

4 Kristy went alone on the ghost walk.
HERSELF   Kristy was ....
.... she went on the ghost walk.

5 The strange creature was last seen a month ago.
FOR   The strange creature ....
.... a month.

6 They don't think he saw a Yeti.
THOUGHT   He is .... a Yeti.

7 I myself wrote the ghost story.
ME   The ghost story ....
.... alone.

8 It was too dark to see the creature clearly.
ENOUGH   There ....
.... to see the creature clearly.

9 It's a shame they didn't get a picture of the spaceship.
HAD   If ....
.... a picture of the spaceship.

10 I don't want to go into the haunted house.
PREFER   I ....
.... into the haunted house.

11 Eyewitnesses claim that they have spotted a UFO.
CLAIMED   A UFO ....
.... spotted.

12 Paul saw the strange lights because his car broke down.
SEEN   If Paul's car hadn't broken down, he
.... the strange lights.

Vocabulary

1 a) ★ Match the words to form phrases.

1	balance	A	the splits
2	break	B	barefoot
3	lie	C	full of energy
4	walk	D	your body
5	fight	E	on a bed of nails
6	do	F	bricks
7	feel	G	blindfolded

b) ★★ Use some of the phrases from Ex. 1a in the correct form to complete the sentences.

1 He .... after he does his exercise routine at the gym.

2 How could he .... on hot coals without getting burnt?

3 The monks .... but know where their opponent is at all times.

4 He can .... with just his hands.

2 ★ Fill in: *courage, pride, discipline, humility, strength, relief.*

1 A Shaolin monk must have .... to control both body and mind.

2 Training at the academy gave him new inner ....

3 To Carl's .... , he didn't have to run up the mountain.

4 The monks take a lot of .... in their training.

5 He needs to have the .... to overcome his fear of Kung Fu.

6 The monks are not arrogant; instead, they believe in ....

3 ★ Choose the correct word.

1 Hard work **makes/builds** character.

2 The mountains will **take/bring** your breath away.

3 Mary works hard to **determine/achieve** her goals.

4 The monk **sent/threw** himself into the air.

5 He **crouched/crawled** down like a tiger.

6 You must **hold/stand** still with your legs bent to do the position.

7 The monk **spun/knelt** across the stage.

4 ★ Complete the text with the correct words derived from the words in bold.

THE ART OF KUNG FU

Most people gasp in **1)** .... when they watch what the masters of Kung Fu can do. The masters make it look easy, but it takes years of practise and **2)** .... to learn to do these incredible moves. Most students feel like a **3)** .... at the beginning and it can be a humbling experience. Once a student has learned the more advanced moves, there is no room for **4)** .... though. The masters focus on teaching their students the importance of discipline and mental strength. Students attend **5)** .... classes to improve their mental control. Only when students have achieved both mental and physical control can they call themselves Masters of Kung Fu!

AMAZE

PATIENT

FAIL

ARROGANT

MEDITATE

Grammar

5 ★ Rewrite the sentences in reported speech.

1 "Tomorrow we will run up the mountain," our coach said.
   ....

2 "I really enjoy martial arts," Peter said.
   ....

3 "Paul has taken Kung Fu before," said Joe.
   ....

4 "Kay is training at a Shaolin School," Tina said.
   ....

5 "We studied Tai Chi last year in school," they said.
   ....

6 "I was exercising at the gym," she said.
   ....

7 "The students will practise after lunch," the teacher said.
   ....

Vocabulary

1 ★ Fill in: *crash, analyst, negotiation, sensation, occasional.*

1 The music videos posted online have become a web ....
2 It is the job of a financial .... to give investment advice to companies.
3 Steve is good at his job; however, he still makes the .... error.
4 A good lawyer must have strong .... skills.
5 He did a four-week .... course.

2 ★ Choose the correct word.

1 This summer, I'll **enrol/study** in a nursing course.
2 John **admitted/claimed** that he had made a mistake.
3 Having little money as a child has **complicated/motivated** him to succeed in life.
4 The lecturer has a very **talkative/chatty** style.
5 Danny **researched/investigated** martial arts for his assignment.
6 The lecturer had lost the interest of his **audience/crowd** after ten minutes.

3 ★ Fill in: *attracted, prefers, stumble, converted, scribbled, complicated.*

1 After quitting his job, Salman Khan now spends most of his day in a .... cupboard at home.
2 From here, Salman has recorded thousands of lectures which have .... millions of viewers on the internet!
3 Students feel that Salman makes .... subjects seem easier.
4 However, all you will ever see of Salman is his .... handwriting since he never films himself in the videos.
5 Not to worry though, because even Salman's cousin .... the digital Salman to the real one!
6 If you ever use *YouTube*, chances are you might across one of Salman's lessons yourself!

Grammar

4 ★ Fill in: *said, told* or *asked* then report the sentences.

1 'Where is the lecture theatre?' Steve .... me.
....
2 'Have you studied for the exam?' Paul .... John.
....
3 'Call me later!' Daisy .... to Ruth.
....
4 'When will we get our test results back?' I .... my teacher.
....
5 'Be quiet!' the librarian .... them.
....
6 'Don't write on the blackboard!' She .... to me.
....
7 'Is he the new headteacher?' Tim .... me.
....
8 'Don't eat in the class!' he .... us.
....
9 'Can you help me move this desk?' Tina .... Jill.
....

Listening

5 ★ 🎧 You will hear five different people talking about going to university. For questions (1-5) choose from the list (A-F) their plans after they finish school. Use the letters only once. There is one extra letter which you do not need to use.

A will study history
B is going to take a gap year before university
C isn't going to university
D hasn't decided what to study yet
E is going to study abroad
F wants to work in the travel industry

Speaker 1	
Speaker 2	
Speaker 3	
Speaker 4	
Speaker 5	

5 c, d

Vocabulary

1 ★ **Fill in:** *participants*, *challenge*, *opportunity*, *tough*, *extra-curricular*, *expedition*, *progress*, *faint-hearted*, *potential*, *focused*, *skills*, *disciplined*.

1 If you work hard, you should be able to reach your full ....

2 The explorer wants to climb Mount Everest because he enjoys a difficult ....

3 After school, Mandy takes part in many .... activities, such as dancing.

4 Even though his .... was slow, Gavin became an excellent swimmer.

5 The maths problem was ...., but in the end she managed to solve it.

6 Many jobs today require computer ....

7 In order to study well, students must be .... with no distractions.

8 Military training has helped to make Stewart a highly .... person.

9 When given the ...., you should always try new things.

10 Brave explorers are planning a(n) .... to the South Pole.

11 Skydiving is not for the ....!

12 Before the race began, the .... did some warm-up exercises.

Speaking

2 ★ **Replace the phrases with synonymous ones from the list.**

- Someone has borrowed that book.
- Would you like me to keep it for you?
- Here you are.
- Let me have a look on my computer.
- The books are due back one week from today.

1 Would you like me to reserve it?

....

2 I'll check my computer for you.

....

3 You have to return the books in one week.

....

4 There you go.

....

5 That book is out right now.

....

3 ★ **Choose the correct response.**

1 A: Hi, I wonder if you could help me.
   B: **a** Sure. What's the problem?
   b I need a book for my IT class.

2 A: What's the title of the book?
   B: **a** Alright. Just one moment.
   b It's *Easy PC* by Mark Foster.

3 A: When will it be back in?
   B: **a** It's out right now.
   b In two days.

4 A: I can call you when I have the book.
   B: **a** It's due next week.
   b That would be great.

5 A: Can I take out these books, please?
   B: **a** Can I see your library card?
   b Can you leave a phone number?

4 ★★ **Use the sentences in Exs 3 & 4 to act out your own dialogue at the library. Follow the plan.**

A	**B**
Ask librarian for help. →	Reply.
Say what book you ⤢	Ask for title/author.
are looking for.	
Reply. ←	Say it's unavailable &
Ask when it will be ↙	ask if they'd like to
back in.	reserve it.
Give phone number & ↙	Reply & ask for A's
then ask if you can	phone number.
take out some books. ↘	Ask to see library card.
Offer card. ←	Tell A when books
Thank librarian. ←	must be returned.
	End conversation.

Reading

1 ★ **Read the article. For questions 1-6, choose the correct answer** *A, B, C* **or** *D*.

A ticket to a better life

As I departed from my hotel in central Mumbai, the glowing sun lit up the beautiful architecture of India's richest city. I marvelled at the majestic Gateway of India and world-renowned Taj Mahal Palace Hotel. Here and there, people bustled around, ready to start their day.
5 But my time in Mumbai would not be spent in this vibrant and affluent city. Instead, I was headed for one of the largest slums on Earth. Entering the slum was like stepping into a war zone. Endless rows of crumbling shacks were crammed together amidst piles of rubbish and debris. Here, the sweltering sun only served to intensify
10 the stench of raw sewage and to add hardship to already difficult lives. I sighed in dismay as I watched children working on the streets. But fortunately, there was a ray of hope.
A bright yellow school bus rumbled through the busy streets and parked itself beside a row of grubby, splintered shelters.
15 Immediately, a group of barefoot children rushed and pushed aboard, chatting excitedly. However, the children on this bus were not going anywhere. While other buses were busy transporting people, this one took its passengers on a different kind of journey. It brought education to disadvantaged children.
20 So this is where I come in. I'd signed up for a programme called School on Wheels, which aims to improve literacy in impoverished areas. Although I had volunteered in many disadvantaged schools around India, teaching on a bus was a first for me! My new classroom was no larger than a hallway, but adequately equipped
25 with a blackboard and educational materials. I warmly greeted my new students who had perched themselves on wooden benches on either side of the bus.
"My name is Mina Kapoor," I informed the wide-eyed faces before me, "I'm going to teach you how to read and write." I referred to an alphabet poster which another volunteer had tacked to the wall and 30 slowly began to introduce the symbols to the children. As I did so, they each attempted to copy down the letters onto slates on their laps. However, as the lesson progressed, they became increasingly distracted. Without any previous schooling, these children simply didn't know how to sit still. But rather than enforcing discipline, I just 35 took a deep breath and began to sing.
The first time I did this, the children listened and watched in awe. But by the end of my six month stint, the class would join in! To my pride, they had also learnt the basics of Hindu and English, and were now ready to enter a public school. 40
On my last day, I felt incredibly emotional. Although our time together was limited, I felt I had truly got to know my students, and sincerely hoped that I had made a difference in their lives. Would they go on to enrol in school? And more importantly, would they stay there and graduate? A quarter of the children who participate in 45 the School on Wheels programme progress into the public school system. I looked at my class. Of my 24 students, I realised that only eight might receive a life-changing education. I knew I should have been glad, but I couldn't help but feel that I could do so much more. As I pondered this, one of my students approached me with a shiny 50 black pebble. She placed it in my hands with a warm smile. "Thank you teacher," she whispered.

1 What was the writer's first impression of Mumbai?
   A An evidently wealthy area.
   B A place with stunning architecture.
   C An overwhelmingly crowded city.
   D A poor and dirty slum.

2 What is the cause of the writer's distress as she enters the slum?
   A The poor housing conditions.
   B The blazing heat of the sun.
   C The smell of waste.
   D The children watching her.

3 How does the writer describe the attitude of the children?
   A enthusiastic   C impulsive
   B apprehensive   D impatient

4 The writer uses the phrase "this is where I come in" (line 20) to describe
   A the moment she entered the bus.
   B the location at which she embarked.
   C her purpose for being in the slum.
   D her relationship with the children.

5 What did the writer find unusual about her new teaching environment?
   A It was an unconventional classroom.
   B It lacked space for the students.
   C It had substandard teaching equipment.
   D It offered no seating for the children.

6 How does the writer reflect upon her experience?
   A She was filled with sadness.
   B She thought it was a life-changing experience.
   C She wished that she could achieve more.
   D She didn't feel appreciated.

Vocabulary

1 ⭐ **Fill in:** *groom, grubby, needy, rehearsal, sample, cup, run-down, poisonous.*

1 The singer will have one last .... before tonight's live performance.
2 While working in the dusty ranch, Jack's clothes became rather ....
3 Volunteers rebuilt a .... hospital to provide healthcare for the poor community.
4 The explorer was shocked to see a .... rattlesnake in the bush!
5 To keep a horse's coat healthy, the farmer must .... it regularly.
6 Although Joanne likes animals, working as a beekeeper isn't really her .... of tea.
7 The volunteer travelled to Africa to help poor and .... children.
8 Gavin enjoys travelling because he loves to .... the local food!

2 ⭐ **Choose the correct word.**

1 You must wear safety gloves if you **work/ practise** as a beekeeper.
2 Juliet moved to Italy to **study/read** opera with a professional Italian singer.
3 Every Friday, Jason goes to the local school to **coach/aim** young football players.
4 In the Brazilian rainforest, charity workers help to **rehabilitate/shear** injured animals.
5 It's exhilarating to **drive/saddle** sled dogs through the snow!
6 Eva cares for the environment, so she wants to go to Fiji to **conserve/mend** coral reefs.

3 ⭐ **Fill in:** *out (x2), for, away, up, back.*

1 Lisa was burnt .... from working long hours.
2 He rolled .... his jeans before wading across the river.
3 A football pitch had been marked .... on the grass.
4 When life becomes hectic, it's good to take a step .... to clear your head.
5 Delicious Swiss chocolate is to die ....!
6 The farmer had to chase .... birds to protect his crops.

Grammar

4 ⭐ **Underline the appropriate time word and put the verbs in brackets into the correct form.**

1 Send me a text **as soon as/until** you .... (arrive) in Italy.
2 Make sure you saddle the horse **before/until** you .... (ride) it.
3 She had learnt to ride a horse **since/by the time** she .... (leave) the ranch.
4 **When/Since** I .... (finish) university, I will get a job.
5 The children went home **by the time/after** they .... (play) football.
6 She didn't go on holiday **until/after** she .... (save) some money.

5 ⭐ **Fill in:** *as soon as, by the time, while, after, before, since.*

Last Summer, I went to Sunset Ranch for an experience of a lifetime, I got to be a cowboy for a day!
1) .... I arrived at the ranch, I was greeted by Jude, my very own wrangler! He led me to the stables, and **2)** .... some basic training, we headed out for a trail ride across the rugged outback! It was incredible! Back at the ranch, Jude showed me how to herd cattle. He made it look easy, but it was really hard work! **3)** .... we were finished, I was exhausted so I decided to take a nap.
I woke up as the afternoon air began to cool. Jude told me we had to build a fire **4)** .... we could cook our evening meal. We gathered some wood and Jude lit the fire using only stones! Then, we cooked and ate our food **5)** .... the evening sun disappeared behind the mountains. It was truly beautiful. **6)** .... going to Sunset Ranch, I've started horse riding. It's not as fun as being a cowboy in the outback, but it's the next best thing!

Reading

1 ★ Read the text and mark the sentences *T* (True) or *F* (False).

Going Global

These days, it seems like almost everything is going global, so why not higher education? Traditionally, universities have been limited by their location, but in the future, universities will reach beyond their campuses. The growing Internet has made education more accessible and allows students to study when they want. Already more than 33% of students study part-time with most of these being mature students (over 25 years of age). Many more students are leaving secondary school to study at online universities.

To keep up with the changing times, universities aim to have multiple campuses across a range of different countries, all linked via information technology. To achieve this, universities are working together to create a network of locations around the world. This has even more advantages for students, as they will be able to custom-make their degrees at different universities, across different countries. For example, one semester you may choose to study Shakespeare in Japan; then the next semester you could be jetting off to study creative writing in Dubai. No matter which institute or course you choose, all of your modules will contribute towards one ultimate goal: your degree.

So you see, the doors have truly been flung open! With a global university, all courses in all countries suddenly become available. In the future, we could see mega-universities consisting of over 100,000 students with most of them studying online! Not only that, but all of these students and their professors will be able to communicate using interactive software. Education will indeed be limitless, and that is globalisation at its very best. Higher education of the future will cross borders with a movement of people and ideas: on campus and beyond.

	T	F
1 Most part-time students are young people just out of secondary school.		
2 In the future, universities will form partnerships together.		
3 Learning in the future will be more flexible.		
4 At a global university, only certain courses will count towards your degree.		
5 Universities of the future will have fewer students.		

Vocabulary

2 ★ **Choose the correct word.**

1 Diana is studying **modern/up-to-date** languages so that she can travel around the world.

2 James is training to be a mechanic at a vocational **university/college**.

3 Many people choose to enrol in **further/farther** education courses.

4 I hired a private **tutor/lecturer** to help me with my French.

5 There are several learning **buildings/institutions** in the city.

6 Could you tell me where the lecture **theatre/classroom** is?

3 ★ **Fill in:** *convenient, tuition, access, comfortable, shy, residence, promotes, exchange.*

1 Universities charge their students .... fees.

2 It is .... for Colin that his college is so close to his house.

3 Sally was very .... on her first day at school as she didn't know anyone.

4 Jason was not .... with the idea of giving a class presentation.

5 The university halls of .... are located on campus grounds.

6 The advantage of working in groups is that it .... interaction.

7 The teacher asked her class to brainstorm the topic then .... their ideas.

8 All classrooms have computers with Internet ....

Vocabulary

1 ★ **Fill in:** *remember, recalled, erupted, barking, reminded, snarled, memorise.*

1 Sharon .... happy times from her childhood.
2 When the volcano ...., it sent a large cloud of ash into the sky.
3 Always .... to turn off the lights before you leave the house.
4 Lewis was woken by the sound of a .... dog outside his house.
5 Janet's dog showed its teeth and .... angrily at the intruder.
6 The actor had to .... his lines for the performance.
7 The secretary .... him of his appointment at 2 o'clock.

2 ★ **Fill in:** *down (x2), in, of, out, for, up.*

1 Dean let me .... when he forgot about my birthday.
2 You should exercise regularly to keep yourself .... top form.
3 Helen can't remember long strings .... information so she must write things down.
4 Sarah was less stressed when she spaced .... her study schedule.
5 The problem was difficult but Barney came .... with the solution.
6 If you break .... a Maths problem, it's easier to solve.
7 Cramming .... exams is not an effective way to study.

3 ★ **Choose the correct participle.**

1 Before the exam, the teacher passed **out/up** test papers to the students.
2 Joanna was saddened to hear that her old professor had passed **up/away**.
3 After dinner, my friends asked me to stick **around/at** for a chat.
4 Gary's father asked him to think **over/up** his decision to drop out of college.
5 Each group had an hour to think **through/up** a good idea for their class presentation.

Listening

4 ★ 🎧 **You will hear people talking in eight different situations. For questions 1-8, choose the correct answer (*A, B* or *C*).**

1 You hear a young girl talking on the radio. Why did she teach art?
   A She wanted a break from university.
   B She needed teaching experience.
   C It was one of her ambitions.

2 You hear a young man talking. What does he work as?
   A a chef   **B** a doctor   **C** a waiter

3 You hear a lecturer talking to his students about a writer. How does the lecturer feel about the writer?
   A He finds his novels too long.
   B He likes that his work is very detailed.
   C He thinks his work is too hard to read.

4 You hear a man talking to a librarian. Why has he phoned the library?
   A to order a book
   B to make an enquiry
   C to complain

5 You hear part of a news broadcast about education online. What is the reporter describing?
   A the pros and cons of online lectures
   B the reasons why students don't go to lectures anymore
   C the different ways that students can learn

6 You hear a photographer being interviewed on the radio. Why did she decide to become a photographer?
   A to fulfil a lifelong ambition
   B to make money
   C to help a friend

7 You hear a girl talking about her extra-curricular activity. How does she feel before she competes?
   A awkward   **B** nervous   **C** excited

8 You hear a backpacker talking about visiting a mountain village. How did she travel to the top of the mountain?
   A by taxi   **B** on foot   **C** by bus

Writing (a for-and-against essay)

1 ★ Read the essay and complete the table.

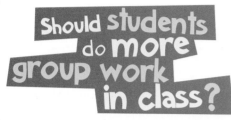
Should students do more group work in class?

A Many students enjoy working with their friends in class, but teachers often tell students to work quietly and alone. Is this the best way to learn, or should students do more group work in class?

B **Without a doubt**, there are many advantages to group work. **Some people argue that** it creates a more comfortable classroom environment **because** students can ask each other questions that they may be embarrassed to ask a teacher. **In addition**, group work encourages students to listen to the opinions of others. This improves teamwork, which is an important skill in the workplace.

C **On the other hand**, there are also arguments against group work in classrooms. **Firstly**, students may become distracted and chat about subjects that are not related to school. **As a result**, no work is achieved. **Another disadvantage** is that during group work, only certain opinions are heard. **For example**, one student may try to control the group, or another could be too shy to speak, making group work quite unfair.

D **All in all**, there are both advantages and disadvantages to doing group work. **It seems to me** that some tasks are performed better when people work together as a team. However, others, like writing, are probably best tackled alone.

Advantages	Examples/Justifications
....	....
....	....
Disadvantages	**Examples/Justifications**
....	....
....	....

2 ★ Which paragraph:

1		contains the writer's opinion?
2		presents the topic?
3		gives the arguments against?
4		gives the arguments for?

3 ★ Complete the table with the linkers in bold in the model.

List/add points	
List advantages	
List disadvantages	
Introduce examples/ justifications	
Show contrast	
Introduce a conclusion	
Give your opinion	

4 ★ Replace the words in bold in the essay with the ones below.

- I believe • to begin with • to sum up
- another argument against it • for instance
- one point in favour is • furthermore
- therefore • first of all • in contrast • since

5 ★ Choose the correct linking words.

1 **Therefore/To start with**, playing learning games in the classroom has many advantages. **For instance/Moreover**, it gets students more interested and involved in the lesson.

2 **Some people argue that/Many people are against** students should learn a second language **since/like** it helps them to get a job in later life.

3 **In conclusion/However**, some people feel that it isn't necessary for all people to attend university. **Such as/For example**, some people would be better off going to a vocational college instead.

4 **Another disadvantage is that/In my opinion**, online learning is an excellent way to learn **as/therefore** it allows many students to participate from all over the world.

67

6 ★ Replace the topic sentences in the main body paragraphs in the text with your own ones.

....
....
....

7 ★ Expand the prompts into complete sentences. Then write an appropriate topic sentence for each paragraph.

....

A debate/class/be/good way/develop/social skills/ students learn/listen/other people's opinions

....

....

B debate/class/be/bad idea/waste/time/better spent/study/other subjects

....

8 a) ★ Match the arguments to the supporting ideas.

2	saves parents money
3	reduces bullying
1	uncomfortable
4	limits creativity

school uniform

A they can be ill-fitting and awkward to wear

B students can't express themselves through their clothing

C school uniforms are cheaper than popular designer clothes

D students won't get picked on for looking different

b) ★ Use the ideas to write a paragraph presenting the advantages of wearing school uniforms.

9 a) ★ Read the rubric and match the viewpoints to the reasons/examples.

A website is asking for student opinions on the following issue: *Should students study Art in schools?* Write a for-and-against essay discussing the advantages and disadvantages of this proposal (200-250 words).

Viewpoints

1	It makes students more creative.
2	It's a waste of time.
3	It's expensive.
4	It's relaxing and fun.

Reasons/Examples

A The money spent on materials could be used to buy textbooks or to improve the school.

B It gives students a break from studying textbooks and problem-solving.

C It's not useful and students might be better off studying other subjects instead.

D Students learn to express themselves through drawings, which they cannot do in subjects like maths.

b) ★ Answer the questions.

1 What are you writing? ....
....
2 What will each paragraph include? ....
....
3 How will you begin/end your essay? ....
....

10 ★★ Use the ideas in Ex. 9 or your own ideas to write your essay.

Useful language

Presenting the topic: Many students enjoy ... Some people believe ...
Advantages: There are many advantages ... Some people argue that...
Disadvantages: On the other hand... Another disadvantage is...
Conclude & give your opinion: All in all... It seems to me...

English in Use
Word Formation

1 ★ **Read the text and complete the gaps with the words derived from the word in bold.**

If you step into the studio of painter John Bramblitt, you will find a vast array of 1) .... artwork. However, John is no ordinary artist. In fact, the talented painter is blind! How does John paint without being able to see? Well, he has developed his own special 2) .... Firstly, he outlines his objects with thick paint and then he uses his hands to feel the outlines and fill in the gaps with colour. The result is a striking 3) .... canvas. John had never painted before in his life. It was only after he lost his vision that he felt he needed to be 4) .... Indeed, John's paintings are so breathtaking, they have been compared with the work of 5) .... artists like Van Gogh! It is no surprise then that his paintings are very popular and have been sold at many art 6) .... around America!

IMPRESS

PROCEED

COLOUR

CREATE

FAME

EXHIBIT

Key Word Transformations

2 ★ **Complete the gapped sentences so that they have a similar meaning to the original ones, using the words given.**

1 He finished school and immediately went home.
   AS   He went home ....
   .... school.

2 "I'm sorry I missed the meeting," she said.
   FOR   She ....
   .... the meeting.

3 The last time Lisa saw Peter was last year.
   SINCE   Lisa .... last year.

4 "Have you written your essay?" Ann asked him.
   WHETHER Ann asked him ....
   .... his essay.

5 The school has a new computer lab because of donations.
   THANKS It .... that the school has a new computer lab.

Speaking

Choose the correct response.

1 A: What's the problem?
   B: **a** I'm looking for a book.
      b I wonder if you could help me.

2 A: Someone has borrowed that book.
   B: **a** When will it be back in?
      b It should be brought back in three days.

3 A: Can I take out these books, please?
   B: **a** Sure, your library card, please.
      b They are due back next week.

4 A: I need a book for my history class.
   B: **a** I'll check on the computer for you.
      b What's the title?

5 A: Can I see your library card, please?
   B: **a** Yes, that would be great.
      b OK, here it is.

6 A: When is it due back in?
   B: **a** Would you like to reserve it?
      b One week from today.

7 A: I can call you when I have it.
   B: **a** There you go.   **b** Yes, please.

8 A: You have to return the books in seven days.
   B: **a** No problem, thank you.
      b OK. Just a moment.

9 A: Hi, I wonder if you could help me.
   B: **a** Of course.
      b That would be great.

10 A: Online learning is easy to access.
   B: **a** It seems to be a computer class.
      b On the other hand, it could isolate students.

11 A: Would you like to reserve it?
   B: **a** Sure. Here it is.   **b** Yes, please.

12 A: What's the title of the book you need?
   B: **a** I'll check on my computer for you.
      b It's *French Made Easy* by Lily White.

Language & Grammar Review

Choose the correct answer.

1 Tom is taking a ..... course in web design that is only 3 weeks long.
   A fast   B heavy   C smash   D crash

2 The tuition ..... at this university are very high.
   A costs   B expenses   C fees   D charges

3 The performers will have one last ..... before the show.
   A lesson   C rehearsal
   B lecture   D class

4 The beautiful lake just ..... my breathe away!
   A gasped   B got   C took   D grabbed

5 A: Would you like to reserve the book?
   B: .....
   A Yes, here it is.
   B OK, I'll check the computer.
   C No, thank you.
   D I'll call you when I have it.

6 Jan is ..... out from studying and wants to take a gap year.
   A burnt   B drained   C gone   D dropped

7 Marc is a ..... example for young people everywhere.
   A shining   C starry
   B glowing   D sparkling

8 Tracy will go travelling ..... she finishes university.
   A by the time   C when
   B since   D until

9 The School on Wheels ..... education to disadvantaged children.
   A provides   C produces
   B supplies   D creates

10 What extra-curricular ..... do you like?
   A courses   C activities
   B events   D occasions

11 She couldn't pass ..... the opportunity to travel to Africa.
   A away   B around   C out   D up

12 Ben ..... that I watch the film online.
   A explained   C suggested
   B told   D said

13 ..... I complete my degree, I will go abroad.
   A By the time   C As soon as
   B Until   D Since

14 Mona asked ..... time it was.
   A where   B if   C what   D whether

15 Mike said he had ordered the book ..... .
   A last night   C tonight
   B the night before   D yesterday

16 Joy ..... me of cheating on the test.
   A reminded   C warned
   B denied   D accused

17 They asked me ..... I had a university degree.
   A what   B when   C where   D whether

18 Tracey said she ..... for a gap year next week.
   A had left   C left
   B has left   D was leaving

19 He has an informal ..... style in his lectures.
   A chatty   B talkative   C childish   D wordy

20 The professor didn't begin his lecture ..... all the students were seated.
   A by the time   C since
   B after   D until

21 The travel pictures really ..... Holly's imagination.
   A caught   B grabbed   C got   D captured

22 Kelly explained ...... to get to her house.
   A that   B how   C why   D where

23 Cory told Shelly ...... in his book.
   A don't write   C not to write
   B wrote   D didn't write

24 Bill ...... for being late.
   A accused   C explained
   B apologised   D denied

25 "Don't be late with your assignments," she ..... us.
   A said   B told   C asked   D suggested

Reading Task

Read the text. For each question choose the correct answer A, B, C or D.

Like Nothing on Earth!

I couldn't believe my eyes as people in blue space suits floated around on the screen in front of me. They were laughing and trying to catch objects drifting past them. A voice spoke "Imagine floating like an astronaut. Experience true weightlessness, just as NASA's astronauts do, aboard our specially modified Boeing 727 airplane, the Zero G aircraft!" The video came to an end and our instructor switched on the lights before speaking to us. "So are we ready then?" I could never have imagined what I was about to do! It all started a few months ago when a friend of mine encouraged me to enter a competition on a local radio station. The winner would get to experience an 'anti-gravity' flight operated by a company called Zero G. An opportunity like this is rare as the starting price for a ticket is over £3,000. The only other way to access such a flight is to qualify as a student for one of the educational programmes offered. So you can imagine my surprise when I got a call saying I had won.

The day of the flight finally arrived and it was a bright, cool morning as our small group made their way to a large airplane hanger. Our instructor was there to greet us and we were each given our own blue space suits. Next, we sat down to watch an informational video. It explained that we would experience 'micro gravity' or zero gravity as our plane did a series of steep climbs and descents. It was during the descents that we would experience zero gravity that would last about 30 seconds and then gravity would suddenly return. Finally, the video demonstrated some safety techniques such as keeping our feet

down or risk landing on our heads. Just before boarding the plane our instructor recommended not getting caught up with doing flips and turns but instead trying to enjoy the unique sensation of weightlessness. I would later realise how important his suggestion really was.

The plane took off and soon we were high above the clouds. Suddenly it was time. "Feet down!" called out our instructor. Whoosh! My body rose abruptly from the floor and I was floating light as a feather! I tried to turn but there was nothing to hold on to. An arm caught my foot and sent me slowly spinning towards the ceiling. I was hovering effortlessly near the ceiling when all of a sudden the pilot pulled up and I fell to the floor! This happened another 12 more times during the flight. I felt like a pinball bouncing around in all directions before crashing to the ground again. On the last time, I remembered what our instructor had said; I just laid back and took in the amazing sensation of weightlessness.

Before I knew it, we were back on the ground and taking pictures in front of our spacecraft. The feeling of zero gravity is almost impossible to explain. Unlike skydiving and free falling, a person does not feel the pull of gravity. Nothing I've experienced before can come close to what it's like to float in anti-gravity. It's something everyone should experience for themselves. I know I'm glad I did as it was a once in a lifetime experience that I'll never forget!

1 The Zero G aircraft
 A belongs to NASA.
 B was specially made for space travel.
 C is an astronaut training plane.
 D was adapted for zero gravity flights.

2 The writer was able to go on the anti-gravity flight because
 A his friend won it on a local radio station.
 B it was prize he won.
 C he won the money for it in a competition.
 D he qualified for an educational programme.

3 Before the flight, the instructor
 A demonstrated flips and turns for the flight.
 B explained safety techniques for the flight.
 C gave some important advice about the flight.
 D explained how zero gravity is achieved.

4 When zero gravity begins, the writer describes his body as
 A rising slowly off the ground.
 B spinning out of control to the ceiling.
 C a pinball being bounced about.
 D going quickly up in the air.

5 The writer feels the zero gravity experience is
 A difficult to describe.
 B similar to free falling.
 C not something everyone should try.
 D something he definitely wants to do again.

5

Building Up Vocabulary

1 Complete the sentences using one of the words in the box.

> • instructions • manual
> • handbook

1 The doctor often refers to his medical .... when he has a problem.

2 The examiner asked John to follow his .... during the driving test.

3 When there is a problem with the device, always consult the ....

> • faculty • campus
> • department

4 Many students don't have to travel to university as they live on ....

5 The university is recruiting some new professors to join the ....

6 The science .... is holding a competition for young inventors.

> • colleague • associate
> • assistant

7 The director is meeting with a business .... to discuss future plans.

8 Debra is a teaching .... who helps the teacher during class.

9 Adam has become good friends with his .... at work.

> • professional • trainee
> • apprentice

10 Martin is a(n) .... golfer who has won the world championship twice.

11 The new .... in the office has just graduated from university.

12 Larry works as a(n) .... to a carpenter.

> • degree • certificate • license

13 You must have a .... to drive a car.

14 When Annie finished her training course, she received a .... of completion.

15 After studying for five years, Christine has earned a .... in law.

> • reward • trophy • compensation

16 The police are offering a .... for any information on the criminals.

17 Joe was paid .... from his insurance company for the loss of his car.

18 After winning the tennis tournament, Andy received a ....

> • break • gap • term

19 Lisa plans to take a .... year before starting university.

20 Students must submit their thesis by the end of ....

21 The school will have a month-long .... during the summer.

2 Complete the sentences with the word derived from the words in bold.

Wouldn't learning be a lot easier if we could just implant knowledge into our brains? While this may seem **1)** .... **(POSSIBLE)**, new research suggests that it could soon be a **2)** .... **(REAL)**! Scientists have found that when we learn, pictures **3)** .... **(GRADUAL)** form in our brains. This requires hours of practice, but over time, a memory or skill is acquired. Using new technology, scientists have managed to monitor brain **4)** .... **(ACTIVE)** to locate the areas of the brain which respond to learning. Using this **5)** .... **(INFORM)**, they have been able to artificially stimulate the brain, and as a result, improved a person's **6)** .... **(PERFORM)** in certain tasks. Not only that, but the test subjects were totally **7)** .... **(AWARE)** that they were being taught anything, making learning completely **8)** .... **(EFFORT)**! Although the experiment has only worked on one area of the brain, scientists are **9)** .... **(HOPE)** that this method could enhance various skills, such as **10)** .... **(ATHLETE)** ability. However, critics warn that the power to plant thoughts into the brain is an extremely **11)** .... **(HAZARD)** tool, and if it were to be used **12)** .... **(RESPONSIBLY)**, it could have very serious consequences.

5

Language Knowledge – Module 5

1 Choose the correct Item.

1 I had been waiting an hour ..... the bus arrived.
   A after   B before   C until   D since

2 He ..... me that the essay was due on Monday.
   A reminded   C explained
   B remembered   D ordered

3 She asked ..... I liked going to university.
   A when   B what   C where   D if

4 The lecture ..... and posted online yesterday.
   A is recorded   C was recorded
   B had recorded   D has been recorded

5 She explained that Sam ..... on a gap year and would be back in a month.
   A had been B has been C was   D is

6 By this Friday, Molly ..... writing all her exams.
   A had finished   C will finish
   B will have finished D is finishing

7 Celia plans to do her masters degree ..... she returns from Africa.
   A as soon as B while C since D until

8 The more you exercise, the ..... you become.
   A fit   C fittest
   B fitter   D more fit

2 Fill in the gaps. Use the appropriate forms of the word in brackets when given.

1 I .... the student where the lecture hall was, but she told me she .... (not/know).

2 Patty's mother promised her that she .... (buy) her a new laptop if she did well in her exams.

3 When the professor accused the student .... cheating, she left the room without .... (say) a word.

4 Tim .... a huge mistake when he refused .... (submit) his homework.

5 If you want to avoid .... (fail) your exams, you .... better study hard.

Key Word Transformations

3 Complete the sentences using the word in bold. Use two to five words.

1 "I'm sorry I didn't go to the party," Gary said.
   APOLOGISED Gary .... to the party.

2 Sarah began learning French one month ago.
   HAS Sarah .... one month.

3 "My computer doesn't work," Theresa said.
   COMPLAINED Theresa .... work.

4 She went to university immediately after finishing secondary school.
   SOON She went to university .... secondary school.

5 "Are you going on holiday to Italy this summer?" James asked.
   IF James asked me .... on holiday to Italy that summer.

6 The exam wasn't as easy as I had expected.
   MORE The exam .... I had expected.

7 "Sure I'll help you with your essay," she told me.
   AGREED She .... with my essay.

8 You should study more
   WERE If .... study more.

9 Once everyone arrived she began the seminar.
   BEFORE She waited .... she began the seminar.

10 Newspapers report that some students cheated on their entrance exams.
   ARE Some students .... on their entrance exams.

11 "Don't write in the workbook," our teacher said.
   TOLD Our teacher .... in the workbook.

12 Only experienced teachers can apply for the position.
   HAVE Only teachers .... can apply for the position.

73

Vocabulary

1 ★ **Fill in:** *muscular, unflattering, glossy, flawless, manicured, enhanced, rippling, inadequate, frizzy.*

1 Janet always has beautifully .... nails.
2 Paul has been lifting weights for years and now he's quite ....
3 Photos of supermodels are digitally .... to remove imperfections.
4 Kate went to the salon to get her .... hair straightened.
5 Debbie chose not to buy the dress as it was .... when she tried it on.
6 Images of celebrities make teenagers feel .... in comparison.
7 The bodybuilder showed off his .... muscles on stage.
8 Even without makeup, Lisa has a(n) .... complexion.
9 Top models in .... magazines promote a body image that is impossible to achieve.

2 ★ **Circle the odd word out.**

1 straight – pointy – curly – wavy **hair**
2 pale – dark-skinned – wrinkled – tanned **complexion**
3 square – oval – long – shaven **face**
4 bushy – rosy – plucked – thin **eyebrows**

3 ★ **Fill in the appropriate synonym/ adjective from the list.**

• eager • shy • impolite • reliable • caring
• outgoing • ill-tempered • organised

1 kind-hearted   ....
2 ambitious   ....
3 moody   ....
4 rude   ....
5 fun-loving   ....
6 trustworthy   ....
7 introverted   ....
8 efficient   ....

4 ★ **Choose the correct word.**

1 Kate's **inside/inner** voice tells her that she doesn't look good enough.
2 Many people shed their puppy **fat/weight** in later life.
3 As you grow older, your body **adjusts/alters** in shape.
4 Exercising regularly can help to **flex/boost** your self-confidence.
5 If he wasn't famous, I wouldn't **look/think** twice at him!
6 In order to lose weight, you must **reject/resist** the temptation to eat fattening foods.
7 You should embrace the features that make you a(n) **unique/alone** individual.

Grammar

5 ★ **Rewrite the sentences using the causative.**

1 The hairdresser has cut Tom's hair.
....
2 Mary will knit Jane's jumper.
....
3 The beautician is plucking Anna's eyebrows.
....
4 Someone should hem your trousers.
....
5 The plastic surgeon removed John's stitches.
....

6 ★ **Choose the correct words.**

1 Pam **can't/mustn't** have gone to the hairdresser's. Her car is parked outside her house.
2 Anna's hair is bright red. She **must/can** have dyed it.
3 Jack says he **can/may** shave off his beard because his wife doesn't like it.
4 Sue says she **might/must** have cosmetic surgery, but she isn't sure.
5 That **can't/mustn't** be Timothy. He's got a moustache.
6 It's possible that Jennifer **could/must** get a perm.
7 Richard **must/can** be exhausted. He's gone to take a nap.

Vocabulary

1 ★ **Read the definitions and complete the types of people.**

1 Someone who is aggressive and knows how to get what they want.
st _ _ _ _ r _ _ _ _ _ r

2 Someone who thinks they know everything.
k _ _ _ _ - _ _ _ - _ _ l

3 Someone who likes to cause difficulties.
t _ _ _ _ _ _ _ m _ _ _ _ r

4 Someone who is not very organised.
s _ _ _ _ _ _ _ b _ _ _ _ n

5 Someone who never stops complaining.
w _ _ _ _ _ _ r

6 Someone who looks down on others.
s _ _ b

7 Someone who overreacts to everything.
d _ _ _ _ _ q _ _ _ n

8 Someone who talks all the time.
c _ _ _ _ _ _ _ b _ x

9 Someone who likes to order others around.
b _ _ _ _ y b _ _ _ _ s

2 ★ **Fill in:** *exaggerate, contribute, intimidate, admit, dominate, encourage, dismiss, moan, interrupt,* **in the correct form.**

1 Jason always .... me when I'm talking.

2 Mary .... to always gossiping about her friends.

3 Kelly .... the conversation all the time and never lets me speak.

4 She .... my idea without even giving me a chance to explain it.

5 Jane .... everything that happens and makes such a big deal all the time.

6 You shouldn't let bullies .... you!

7 Stella complains and .... about every little thing; she's never happy.

8 You .... to gossip by saying negative things about people.

9 Don't .... him to act silly!

3 ★ **Fill in:** *in (x2), with (x2), up, down, on, out (x2), back.*

10 Tips
for Dealing with
Difficult People

1 Avoid getting involved .... gossip.

2 Just agree .... complainers and they will stop.

3 Always stand .... for yourself and your friends.

4 Never back .... to intimidating people.

5 Don't put up .... aggressive behaviour.

6 Don't take an interest .... emotional outbursts.

7 Ignore people who are trying to find .... negative things about others.

8 Don't pass .... negative comments about others.

9 Never shout .... at aggressive people; it only encourages them.

10 Ignore people when they blow things .... of proportion.

Grammar

4 ★★ **Choose the correct words.**

1 Mike talks **as if/so that** he knows everything.

2 **As a result/The reason why** I left was to discourage her silly behaviour.

3 I interrupted Peter **in order to/so that** tell him what happened.

4 She is **so/such** emotional that no one wants to be around her.

5 Mark doesn't talk to Maria **due to/because** her gossiping all the time.

6 He acts **as though/so** he is in charge all the time.

7 Tracy complains all the time **so as to/as a result** get attention.

8 She is **such/so** a negative person that I can't stand her.

9 Joe argues all the time. **The reason why/As a result** everyone avoids him.

75

6 c, d

Vocabulary

1 ★ **Fill in:** *chant, routine, tribe, pit, welcome, stick, traditional, weapon.*

1 The leader of the .... wore a headdress made of colourful feathers.

2 The villagers wore a .... outfit made of grass and feathers.

3 In order to go hunting, the villager made a .... from a sturdy stick.

4 When they dance, the natives beat drums and .... loudly.

5 The villager stumbled and fell into a deep ....

6 When they arrived at the village, all the natives bowed to .... their guests.

7 The girls jumped and spun as part of their dance ....

8 It is considered quite rude to .... out your tongue!

2 ★ **Fill in the sentences with the correct words derived from the words in brackets.**

1 The dancers wore .... outfits during their performance. **(TRADITION)**

2 The football .... were dressed in their team colours. **(SUPPORT)**

3 As part of the festival, the .... had a huge feast in the village. **(INHABIT)**

4 The .... involved singing and dancing to the beat of a drum! **(CELEBRATE)**

3 ★ **Choose the correct word.**

1 Before the match, the player greeted his **enemy/ opponent** by shaking his hand.

2 When the dancers **stamp/slap** their feet at the same time, it sounds like thunder!

3 When the volcano erupted, the natives had to **flee/fly** the village!

4 The Sun Dance **originates/begins** from the tribes of North America.

5 As they went into **battle/war** with another tribe, the villagers banged their drums.

6 After the fight, the tribe had a feast to celebrate their **triumph/achievement**.

7 The tribesmen carved unique **engravings/tattoos** into wooden statues.

Speaking

4 ★ **Use the sentences to complete the dialogue. One sentence isn't necessary.**

A Monday afternoon, if possible?

B I'm calling to see if I can rearrange my eye exam.

C I had to work late at short notice.

D Oh no, that's awful.

E It was supposed to be at 3:30pm today.

F Could you make Tuesday the 10th at 2pm?

A: Hello, Clearvision Opticians.

B: Hello there. This is Gina Robertson. **1** ☐ There's been a family emergency.

A: **2** ☐ What time was your appointment?

B: **3** ☐ It's with Dr. Howard.

A: OK. When would you like to rearrange it?

B: **4** ☐

A: I'm afraid Dr. Howard isn't available that day. **5** ☐

B: Erm, yes, that should be OK.

A: Great. We'll see you on Tuesday, then.

B: OK. Thank you very much.

A: My pleasure. Goodbye.

5 ★★ **Imagine you want to call and rearrange a hairdresser's appointment. Use the sentences from Ex. 4 and the plan below to write a similar dialogue.**

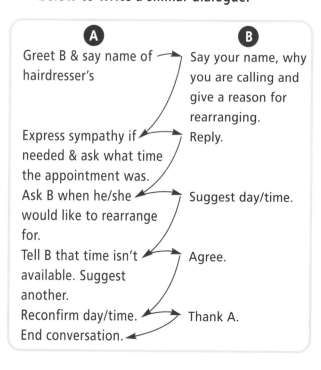

A	**B**
Greet B & say name of hairdresser's	Say your name, why you are calling and give a reason for rearranging.
Express sympathy if needed & ask what time the appointment was.	Reply.
Ask B when he/she would like to rearrange for.	Suggest day/time.
Tell B that time isn't available. Suggest another.	Agree.
Reconfirm day/time. End conversation.	Thank A.

76

Vocabulary

1 ★ **Fill in:** *confidently, intensely, drooping, rubbing, convince, distinguish, subconscious.*

1 People don't realise that they create a(n) .... barrier when they hold an object in front of them.

2 She tried to .... me she was telling the truth, but I still didn't believe her.

3 Sue smiled .... when she realised that she knew the correct answer.

4 He believes that .... your ears is a sign of lying.

5 Mr. Stanton can .... between someone telling the truth and someone telling a lie.

6 She stared at me .... and I knew she was lying.

7 He tried to smile but the corners of his mouth were .... and I knew he was sad.

2 ★ **Choose the correct item.**

1 People can't control muscle **spasms/flashes**.

2 Her cheek had a nervous **response/twitch** when she was talking.

3 He's as good as a lie **finder/detector** and can tell who is not telling the truth in an interview.

4 His face suddenly turned bright red; it was a tell-tale **signal/sign** he was lying.

5 She was so nervous that she tried to **hide/conceal** behind the books in her hands.

6 The most important thing is to trust your **nature/instincts** when dealing with people.

3 ★ **Fill in:** *keep an eye on, pull the wool over my eyes, get cold feet, give her a hand, pull your leg, get it off your chest,* **in the correct form.**

1 Many actors .... before a performance.

2 Don't take him so seriously; he's just ....

3 Can you .... the children while I'm gone?

4 Jane has a lot of cleaning up to do. Can you ....?

5 I was sure that Carl was telling the truth, but he really ....!

6 Why don't you tell me what's bothering you and just ....?

Reading

4 ★ **Read the text and mark the sentences** *T* (true), *F* (false) or *DS* (doesn't say).

 # What is your body saying about you?

You accidentally meet your boss at a party. You're smiling and speaking in a friendly tone, but your body is saying 'I feel uncomfortable and I can't wait to get away from you.' Obviously this is not a message you want to send. Body language (everything you communicate without actually speaking) says a lot about a person. All the physical gestures we make are subconsciously interpreted by others. Some gestures project a positive message and some a negative one. The key is to be aware which is which and try to control the messages we send.

Positive Messages

Mothers are always after their children to sit or stand straight. And they are right to do so. An upright not too tense posture sends a powerful message that you are confident. Of course maintaining eye contact shows that you are trustworthy and forthright. But be careful not to stare and appear too aggressive. Make sure to nod and lean slightly towards a person when engaged in a conversation. This shows you're listening and interested. Finally, always smile and be pleasant. Smiling too much or in an unnatural way, however, makes you look insincere and silly.

Negative Messages

Most people are totally oblivious to the negative signals they are sending with their gestures. Crossing your hands or legs sends a message of defensiveness or distance. Don't touch your face and hair or fidget with your clothes. These are sure signs that you are nervous or being dishonest. On the other hand, putting your hand on your hips or behind your head sends a message of arrogance. Looking down or around often screams out you're bored. Foot tapping or shifting your body weight around can also indicate boredom or even stress. Either way it doesn't look good. So the next time you move your body or hands focus on what you might be signalling. It can really make a difference in how people see you.

1 People intentionally look for meaning in body language. ....

2 It's possible to fully control our body language. ....

3 The way you stand tells a lot about how you feel about yourself. ....

4 Smiling is always a positive body gesture. ....

5 Placing your hands anywhere on your body sends a message of anxiety. ....

Vocabulary

1 ★ **Fill in:** *aquatic, mimic, adapt, vocal, whistles, flippers, gestures, wound.*

1 Dolphins use their .... to steer underwater.

2 Wild dolphins can easily .... to a life in an aquarium.

3 It took several weeks for the dolphin's .... to heal.

4 A dolphin's .... chords can produce sounds that humans can't hear.

5 Hand .... are helpful when communicating with animals.

6 The dolphin is a(n) .... mammal.

7 When dolphins talk to each other, they use clicks and ....

8 If you shake your leg, a dolphin can .... your behaviour by shaking its tail!

2 ★ **Match the words to make phrases.**

1	a pack	A	of birds
2	a pod	B	of kittens
3	a colony	C	of bees
4	a school	D	of ants
5	a swarm	E	of lions
6	a pride	F	of fish
7	a herd	G	of dolphins
8	a flock	H	of elephants
9	a litter	I	of dogs

3 ★ **Choose the correct word.**

1 The tour guide is **common/familiar** with all the animals in the nature reserve.

2 When your pet is sick, don't allow it to make **touch/contact** with other animals.

3 A pod of whales was spotted off the **coast/shore** of Alaska.

4 Pollution has a negative **impression/impact** on marine wildlife.

5 After months of talking, the politicians finally **resolved/concluded** their problem.

6 Dolphins use clicking **signals/signs** to find food and to detect other aquatic animals.

7 Officials are **investigating/experimenting** the cause of the oil spill.

Grammar

4 ★ **Use the words/phrases to rewrite the sentences, using inversion.**

1 The fisherman has hardly ever seen a dolphin out at sea.
Seldom ....

2 Lara didn't realise how clever dolphins were until she went to the aquarium.
Only after ....

3 I seldom swim in the sea.
Rarely ....

4 They had no idea the dolphin show had already started!
Little ....

5 If you see a dolphin, be sure to take a photo!
Should ....

6 Emma had a hectic day so she took a well-earned rest.
Such ....

7 If I'd known about the sea-life centre, I would have gone to visit it.
Had ....

8 If I were you, I'd go to see the aquarium.
Were ....

Listening

5 ★ 🎧 **You will hear an interview with a wildlife photographer and conservationist. For questions 1-6, complete the sentences.**

The pink river dolphin has a(n)
.... **1** on its back.

It was difficult to take photographs because the water was .... **2** .

The dolphins relaxed after the crew gave them some .... **3** .

The pink river dolphin has now become a(n)
.... **4** .

Pink dolphins are being poisoned by
.... **5** from gold mines.

Dolphins can't reach food due to the building of many .... **6** .

Reading

1 ★ **Read the text. For questions 1-15, choose from the types of communication (A-D).**

Which type of communication ...

can be heard?	1 ☐ 2 ☐
was used on a memorable occasion?	3 ☐
mimics oral communication?	4 ☐
has symbols that can be used in two ways?	5 ☐
sends a signal from an elevated place?	6 ☐ 7 ☐
is inherited through a family tradition?	8 ☐
is still considered a fast and reliable form of communication?	9 ☐

requires a talented sender?	10 ☐
has different ways of transmission?	11 ☐
sends a message created on the ground?	12 ☐
cannot be read by some people?	13 ☐
is not only used to send messages?	14 ☐
changes meaning depending on the time and place it is sent?	15 ☐

Did you get my message?

People are always sending messages. Take a look at a few unusual ways to get a message across ...

A In the dark of the night on the 14th April, 1912 the RMS Titanic struck an iceberg. As the ship sank, it sent out a distress signal using Morse code. The code, sent by radio, consisted of long and short sound pulses that appear on paper as dots and dashes. The Titanic's message was immediately received, but unfortunately it took hours for a rescue boat to reach the sinking ship. Still, the efficiency of Morse code undoubtedly saved many lives on that fateful day. In Morse code, each letter of the alphabet and numbers are represented by the pattern of short and long pulses. Whether sent by sound, light or symbols on paper, Morse code even today is a quick and effective way to send a message.

B High above the Rocky Mountains, puffs of smoke from a fire rise up in the air forming spirals, circles, lines and patterns. The fire belongs to an Native American tribe. However, it is not intended for warmth or cooking, but rather to communicate a message to other tribe members. Indians used smoke signals created in a 'fire bowl' to send a variety of messages. These were large saucer-shaped vessels that were dug into the soil at high altitudes, making the smoke signal clearly visible over long distances. The signals created were commonly used to alert allies of approaching danger, or to call fellow tribesmen to a meeting. Each tribe had their own signalling system to keep their messages private from their enemies.

C A lone boat is spotted in a harbour by a large ship. Two coloured flags with shapes on them are flying high above the boat. Upon seeing the flags, the captain of the ship immediately knows a man has fallen overboard and sends help. Flags like these are called maritime flags and are used for communication at sea. There is a flag representing each letter of the alphabet and the numbers. Ships can use the flags to spell out words or combine the two to create a specific message. The meaning of the message is determined by where and when the message is sent.

D The sound of tribal drumming booms across the African plains. Many miles away, a villager is listening intently to the beat. He drums enthusiastically in response. This drumming is the most elaborate form of primitive communication. Due to the fact that the language used by some Nigerian tribes is tonal (each syllable of a word contains either a high, middle or low pitch), drumming can be used to imitate the spoken word. Using this method, complex messages can be sent and understood by villages up to 30km away! Since drums are considered to be a symbol of power in West Africa, only the most skilled drummers are employed for this role. This esteemed ability is often passed down from father to son, and earns the musician great respect among the tribal community. Of course, drumming is also an integral part of African culture, and besides communication, plays an important role in ceremonies and celebrations.

Vocabulary

1 ★ **Fill in:** *rub, release, signal, pass on, invade, stick out.*

1 When snakes hiss, they .... their long tongues to catch food.

2 Some plants .... chemicals to protect themselves from insects.

3 Rabbits thump their hind legs on the ground as a warning .... when they are in danger.

4 Some insects use touch and sound to .... information to other insects.

5 Horses .... noses when they like each other!

6 If you .... a dog's territory, it might bite you.

2 ★ **Fill in:** *predators, prey, antennae, pile, camouflage, texture, display, source.*

1 Some animals can disguise themselves using their powers of ....

2 Lions are large .... that hunt deer.

3 Ants use their .... to communicate and identify scents.

4 A frog's skin has a smooth ....

5 A cat uses its claws to catch its ....

6 Bamboo is the main .... of food for pandas.

7 When male peacocks spread out their blue and green feathers, they reveal an elaborate .... of colour.

8 The ants were attracted to a .... of breadcrumbs.

3 ★ **Choose the correct participle.**

1 Dean had to fill **out/up** forms to apply for university.

2 I was late because I was held **up/on** in traffic.

3 James will try **on/out** for the school football team.

4 Before going hiking, Gina filled **up/out** her water bottle.

5 It's always a good idea to try **out/on** shoes before you buy them.

6 Luckily, the rain held **off/on** until after the rugby match had finished.

7 Hold **out/on** a minute, I'm not ready yet!

Listening

4 ★ 🎧 **You will hear an interview with a wildlife expert. For questions 1-7, choose the best answer (*A, B or C*).**

1 Why was the Wolong National Nature Sanctuary established?
  A to protect all the plants and animals in Wolong
  B to shelter rare and endangered animals
  C to save the giant panda

2 What is the main threat to pandas?
  A human settlements
  B over-hunting
  C lack of bamboo

3 What is the purpose of bamboo corridors?
  A to provide more food for pandas
  B to connect the bamboo forests
  C to allow humans to live alongside pandas

4 How does Jason feel about keeping animals in captivity?
  A he thinks captivity is good for wild animals
  B he feels it is necessary for pandas
  C he thinks pandas would be better off in the wild

5 What is the panda sanctuary's ultimate goal?
  A to become a tourist attraction
  B to teach people about the panda
  C to release pandas into the wild

6 What must captive pandas learn to do?
  A defend their territory
  B avoid other animals
  C find bamboo

7 In Jason's opinion, what area is best to release a panda back into the wild?
  A an area with many wild pandas
  B an area where pandas don't live anymore
  C an area where pandas have never lived

Writing (an article describing a person)

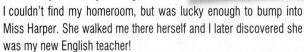

1   a)   ★ Read the model.

1▶ I met Miss Harper three years ago. It was my first day of high school. I couldn't find my homeroom, but was lucky enough to bump into Miss Harper. She walked me there herself and I later discovered she was my new English teacher!

2▶ Miss Harper is in her mid-thirties and is quite pretty. She is pale-skinned with curly red hair, beautiful almond-shaped eyes and a long face. As well as being attractive, Miss Harper is a very fashionable woman. She's always smartly-dressed and never looks shabby.

3▶ I've never met anyone as considerate as Miss Harper. She's always supportive, encouraging me to speak up in class. Moreover, she has a great sense of humour, with the ability to make everyone laugh. Her easy-going personality makes me feel comfortable around her. She's a great listener and is extremely easy to talk to. Although she can be quite strict at times, I know it's only because she wants us to learn.

4▶ Miss Harper is an amazing person. She became a teacher so that she could help other people. She's highly respected among her colleagues and students, and even received the National Teacher of the Year award! As well as being a great teacher, Miss Harper is also a very creative person. In her spare time, she loves to paint and draw. She is exceptionally talented and has even sold her work in an art gallery!

5▶ All in all, Miss Harper is both sensitive and kind. Most importantly, she has taught me how to be a positive person. Her selfless and hard-working nature is very inspiring. She is truly an incredible teacher.

b)   ★ Which paragraph (1-5) describes:

clothes? ☐ personality? ☐ hobbies/ interests? ☐ achievements? ☐ name/ relationship to writer? ☐ feelings about the person? ☐ facial features? ☐ when/where/ how the writer met them? ☐

2   ★ Replace the topic sentences in the article with the topic sentences below.

1 Miss Harper is attractive and looks younger than her age.
2 I really admire Miss Harper.
3 To sum up, Miss Harper is a wonderful person.
4 I'll never forget the moment when I met Miss Harper.
5 Miss Harper is a very kind-hearted woman.

3   ★ Choose the correct word.

1 Georgia tends to be quite **disorganised/ pessimistic**, and often expects things to go wrong.
2 Ewan is always smiling and happy. He's such a(n) **cheerful/easy-going** person.
3 Dan is always thinking of others. He's such a **confident/considerate** guy.
4 Since Gayle is so **supportive/reserved**, I sometimes can't tell how she feels.
5 Jennifer always tries to help and care for others. She's the most **kind-hearted/outgoing** person I know.

4   ★ Fill in: *trustworthy, stubborn, intelligent, lazy, selfless, absent-minded, shy, sociable.*

1 Jill doesn't like being active and can be rather .... at times.
2 Liam tends to be a little awkward around other people because he's quite a .... person.
3 Denise is the life and soul of the party! She's such a .... girl.
4 Phillip often puts other people's needs before his own. He's such a .... boy.
5 I know I can rely on Emma to keep a secret. She's completely ....
6 Fred always gets the best marks in class. He's the most .... person I know.
7 Nicola may be smart, but she tends to be a little .... and is always forgetting where she put things!
8 Although he is a great friend, Graham can be quite .... and never admits when he is wrong!

5   ★ Link the sentences using the words/ phrases in brackets:

1 Ann has long brown hair. She often wears it in a pony-tail. **(which)** ....
....
2 Darren has wrinkles around his eyes. He looks older than his age. **(that make him look)** ....
....
3 Janice is a beautiful girl. She has an oval face and a small nose. **(with)** ....
....
4 John is a very fashionable person. He likes to wear designer clothes. **(who)** ....
....

6 ★ Fill in the gaps with the correct linking word.

• despite • and • both • however

A Serena is **1)** .... tall **2)** .... slim. **3)** ...., she is often badly-dressed. **4)** .... being unfashionable, she is still an amazing friend!

• moreover • as well as • although

B **1)** .... being sociable, Nathan is also very trustworthy. **2)** ...., he is always helpful, **3)** .... he tends to be quite absent-minded.

• but • also • in spite of

C Gerald enjoys running. He is **1)** .... keen on playing football, **2)** .... he is not very good at it! **3)** .... his lack of talent, he always tries to do his best.

• nevertheless • and • on the other hand

D My sister Fran is kind **1)** .... thoughtful. **2)** ...., she can be a little lazy at times. **3)** ...., I still think she's the best sister in the world!

• in addition • and • even though • both

E **1)** .... Frank is **2)** .... smart **3)** .... funny, he tends to be very disorganised. **4)** ...., he is sometimes rather unreliable.

7 ★ Read the rubric and complete the table. Then answer the questions.

You have seen the following advertisement in your local newspaper:

Enter our Writing Competition
Write an article about a classmate you admire and you could win £200! Write about the person, describing their appearance, personality, interests and achievements, stating why you admire them, and how you feel about them.

Name:	....
Age:	....
Appearance:	....
Character:	....
Hobbies/Interests:	....
Achievements:	....
Your comments & feelings:	....

1 What do you have to write? ....
....

2 What tense(s) will you use? ....
....

3 How many paragraphs will you write?.............
....

4 What information could you include in each paragraph? ....
....
....

8 ★★ Use your answers from Ex. 7 and the sentences from the *Useful Language* box to write your article (200-250 words).

Useful language

Para 1:	The classmate I most admire is... I met them ...
Para 2:	He/She is tall/short/of medium height ..., thin/plump, looks smartly/badly dressed ...
Para 3:	I've never met anyone as ..., He/She is very cheerful/lazy ...
Para 4:	He's/She's a very active person ..., He/She can sometimes be rather ...
Para 5:	All in all ..., He/She is ...

English in Use
Word Formation

1 ★ Read the text and complete the gaps with the words derived from the word in bold.

Did you know that in one bat cave, you could find as many as 20 million bats? In spite of their **1)** .... numbers, bats miraculously never fly into each other! How is this possible? Bats emit ultrasonic sounds which bounce back to themselves, allowing them to judge the size and distance of objects. In short, they use their ears to 'see'! Bats can achieve this with such incredible **2)** .... that they can even detect a tiny ant upon the ground! Not only that, but they also use their voices to sing like birds! In fact, bats have some of the most intricate **3)** .... systems in the animal kingdom. They actually use their songs to talk to each other and have been found to have **4)** .... vocal patterns, just like humans. Indeed, scientists are so amazed by bats, they believe that by studying bat language, they could provide better treatment for human **5)** .... disorders!

ORDINARY

ACCURATE

COMMUNICATE

DISTINCT

SPEAK

Key Word Transformations

2 ★ Complete the gapped sentences so that they have a similar meaning to the original ones, using the words given.

1 The painter will paint Susan's house tomorrow.
   HAVE Susan ....
   .... tomorrow.

2 Anna hardly ever complains about her work.
   DOES Seldom ....
   .... about her work.

3 John had just left when Jill started gossiping about him.
   SOONER No ....
   ...... Jill started gossiping about him.

4 He is an interesting lecturer and as a result everyone attends his classes.
   SUCH He's ....
   .... everyone attends his classes.

5 Anna arranged for a famous hairdresser to style her hair.
   HAD Anna ....
   .... a famous hairdresser.

Speaking

Choose the correct response.

1 A: What time was your lesson?
   B: **a** How about next Thursday?
      b It was supposed to be at 2pm.

2 A: I had to work late at short notice.
   B: **a** Oh, dear!
      b How about tomorrow?

3 A: When would you like to rearrange it for?
   B: **a** OK, see you on the 16th.
      b Is Monday available?

4 A: I'm calling to see if I can rearrange my appointment?
   B: **a** Did you come on Thursday?
      b What time was it supposed to be?

5 A: Could you make Tuesday at 3pm?
   B: **a** That should be fine.
      b That time isn't available.

6 A: How about Wednesday at 1pm?
   B: **a** I'm sorry that time is booked.
      b I should be fine by then.

7 A: It's annoying when you crack your knuckles.
   B: **a** I find it really irritating.
      b I'm really sorry.

8 A: Do you mind not talking down to people?
   B: **a** I don't mean to.
      b You're always doing that.

9 A: Could you please allow me to speak?
   B: **a** Stop interrupting me.
      b I didn't realise I was doing that.

10 A: You always insist on your own way!
   B: **a** Please don't get tongue-tied.
      b I'll try not to do it again.

11 A: I twisted my ankle.
   B: **a** That should be fine!
      b That's awful!

12 A: See you on the 21st!
   B: **a** Great. Thank you.
      b That's such a shame!

6

Language & Grammar Review

Choose the correct answer.

1 She has ..... eyebrows.
A plucked   C raised
B curly   D stamped

2 You don't annoy me; I'm just pulling your .....!
A feet   B hand   C leg   D nose

3 The start of the meeting was held ..... until the boss arrived.
A on   B up   C off   D out

4 A: Could you make Saturday at 10am?
B: .....
A That time isn't available.
B It was supposed to be at 1pm.
C That should be fine.
D That's a shame.

5 Ronald has brown hair and ..... cheeks.
A full   C long
B tanned   D chubby

6 No one knows how Sue feels because she is ..... .
A ill-tempered   C introverted
B impolite   D intimidated

7 The oil spill had a huge ..... on all marine life.
A impact   C instinct
B implant   D impression

8 Joy is too shy; she should be more ..... .
A aggressive   C argumentative
B assertive   D active

9 Those two can't ..... on anything.
A accept   B admit   C agree   D adapt

10 Stop ..... and sit still. You look nervous.
A rubbing   C fidgeting
B stamping   D drooping

11 Jack shouts at people to ..... them.
A intimidate   C dominate
B interrupt   D dismiss

12 Those twins look so alike, it's hard to ..... between them.
A detect   C direct
B depict   D distinguish

13 Don't try to ..... the wool over my eyes!
A pull   B pass   C rub   D spin

14 The deer was spotted by a ..... of lions.
A herd   B pack   C pride   D pod

15 Seldom ..... about others.
A Tony gossips   C gossips Tony
B does Tony gossip   D is gossiping Tony

16 The team is celebrating. They ..... have won.
A could   B should   C must   D might

17 Denise always exaggerates! She's ..... a drama queen!
A so   B such   C too   D much

18 Some plants release chemicals ..... protect themselves from animals.
A so that   C due to
B so as to   D because

19 Rarely ..... to the zoo.
A we went   C we go
B do we go   D go we

20 Mary ..... her nails done yesterday.
A had   C have had
B have   D are having

21 He doesn't make eye-contact when he's talking to me. I think he ..... be lying.
A should   C might
B would   D couldn't

22 He's so rude and talks to me ..... I know nothing.
A so that   C as a result
B as though   D because

23 Darren is ..... bossy! He's always telling people what to do.
A so that   B so   C such   D much

24 Gary loves dolphins and ..... does Julie.
A also   B nor   C so   D neither

25 Jo ..... her hair dyed at the moment.
A will have   C is having
B has been having   D has

Reading Task

Read the text. In each question choose the correct answer *A, B, C* **or** *D*.

Cultural Show Offs!

Men painted as skeletons terrorise the crowd with sharp primitive bows. Mudmen covered in dried mud and wearing huge mud masks shake 10 centimetre long fingernails menacingly at their audience. This is obviously no ordinary show; in fact there is no show quite like traditional 'sing sing' dances from one of the hundreds of tribes of Papua New Guinea.

Fifty years ago, a visitor would have a lot to fear from one of these tribal groups who often attacked and killed other rival groups. Nowadays, however, these groups have left their hostilities in the past and now celebrate their cultural differences through music, song and dance at a variety of shows held throughout Papua New Guinea.

It used to be that these gatherings were an opportunity to celebrate marriages, trade useful items or reduce tensions between enemy tribes. Today, 'sing sing' celebrations such as the one held in Mount Hagen deep in the mountains of Papua New Guinea attract hundreds of tribal groups. Tribal groups from all over the country, many of them on foot, journey through the dense jungle of the mountains to the town of Mount Hagan to take part in the 'sing sing' show. The Mount Hagan show is the equivalent to a large dance competition with groups performing 'sing sing' dances for prize money, a chance to show off their ancestral heritage, but most of all for the glory that first prize at this show brings to the tribe. Although the show brings in local crowds of more than 50,000, very few tourists attend the event due to its remote location.

Recently, these 'sing sing' shows are being promoted outside the country and many tourists are becoming aware of these unique cultural gatherings. In the past locals preferred that tourists did not attend, but slowly they are becoming more open to foreign audiences.

Those who are privileged enough to be part of the audience at the Mount Hagen show are in for an incredible cultural journey. Over the course of two days more than 50 cultural groups take to a muddy field to perform their unique 'sing sing' dances. Tribesmen like the Huli Wigmen with colourful painted bodies and faces and wearing elaborate headdresses (wigs) made of exotic feathers parade out onto the field. To the sound of beating drums, the Huli Wigmen begin to sway in their long grass skirts as they perform their traditional bird dance in honour of the famous birds of paradise found in the highlands of their territory. Other tribes such as the Asaro Mudmen, wearing huge mud masks and shaking fierce weapons, perform silent dances once used to terrify their enemies. Other dances act out tribal stories with the popular Simbu skeleton dancers performing an attack on a magical beast.

As group after group perform, the field becomes alive with music, colour and tantalising dances. Even after the formal competition has ended, the dancing and singing continues for hours as the groups continue to celebrate with the sounds of chanting and drums. And although the field is an obvious mixture of different cultures with different beliefs, there is a sense of community amid this colourful gathering.

1 The purpose of the shows is
- **A** to avoid conflict between rival tribes.
- **B** to celebrate marriages between tribes.
- **C** to honour each tribes' cultural identity.
- **D** to share and trade valuable goods.

2 The main reason many tribes attend the Mount Hagen show is
- **A** for the prize money.
- **B** for the prestige of winning.
- **C** to show off their cultural history.
- **D** to perform in front of large crowds.

3 The Mount Hagan Show is not a tourist attraction because
- **A** it is difficult to get to.
- **B** it is not promoted abroad.
- **C** it is unknown to tourists.
- **D** locals don't want tourists there.

4 The Huli Wigmen performance
- **A** doesn't include music.
- **B** is based on a mythical story.
- **C** celebrates a local animal.
- **D** demonstrates a wartime dance.

5 According to the text, the Mount Hagan show ends
- **A** with an understanding of the different cultural beliefs.
- **B** with individual cultural groups performing a song or a chant.
- **C** with the creation of a new tribal community.
- **D** with a feeling of unity amongst the tribes.

6

Building Up Vocabulary

1 **Complete the sentences using one of the words in the box.**

> • trend • craze • fashion

1 The designers will show off their creations at a .... show.

2 There is a growing .... for teen plastic surgery.

3 That latest dance .... has become popular across the world.

> • personality • character • identity

4 The main .... in the film is a teenage boy called Luke.

5 James has a great .... and is always smiling even when things go wrong.

6 You must carry your .... card with you at all times.

> • operation • procedure • process

7 The normal .... for cosmetic surgery is to meet with the plastic surgeon and discuss the treatment first.

8 Ann is going to hospital to have a(n) .... on her leg.

9 After having surgery, the recovery .... can be long and painful.

> • independent • liberate • free

10 The caged animal was set .... into the wild.

11 When you live alone, you must learn to become ....

12 The military plans to .... all the prisoners of war.

> • secretive • reserved • confidential

13 Josie is very .... about whether or not she had cosmetic surgery.

14 Consultations between a doctor and their patients are strictly ....

15 Liam is a .... person who rarely socialises with others.

> • appeals • interests • attracts

16 The brightly coloured mural .... a great deal of attention from passers-by.

17 My friend Mike and I have similar ....

18 The idea of losing weight without dieting .... to me.

> • drawbacks • obstacles • barriers

19 One of the .... of getting a tattoo is that it is permanent.

20 The council have installed .... along the riverbank to prevent flooding when it rains heavily.

21 The .... on the course were challenging, but Ben's team finished the race first.

2 **Complete the sentences with the word derived from the words in bold.**

Do you need to shed a few pounds? Or are you looking to improve your **1)** .... **(FIT)** level? Well, if you are, come to Alpine Boot Camp! Our camp is tailored to meet your individual **2)** .... **(REQUIRE)** by focusing on your unique physical strengths. Our week-long **3)** .... **(INTENSE)** programme is guaranteed to improve your overall health as we push your **4)** .... **(ENDURE)** to the limit! All **5)** .... **(PARTICIPATE)** should be prepared for the toughest, but most **6)** .... **(REWARD)** week of their lives! Throughout your stay with us, our fully qualified **7)** .... **(INSTRUCT)** will take you on a breathtaking journey across the **8)** .... **(SPECTACLE)** French Alps. At the end of each day, you can put up your feet at our **9)** .... **(LUXURY)** hotel and spa. Then after dinner, feel free to attend our **10)** .... **(OPTION)** seminars which focus on health **11)** .... **(MANAGE)** and ways to avoid unhealthy habits. By the end of the week, your body and mind will feel completely revitalised. So what are you waiting for? Join us today for an **12)** .... **(FORGETTABLE)** experience of a lifetime!

Language Knowledge – Module 6

1 Choose the correct item.

1 Ellie is at the salon; she ..... her eyebrows plucked.
A has   C had
B will have had   D is having

2 Steve acts ..... he knows everything.
A so that   C as if
B as a result   D so as to

3 ..... a long time has Terry worked at the zoo that she knows all the animals.
A Rarely   B Such   C Seldom   D So

4 She ..... that she was the best hairdresser in the salon.
A advised   C complained
B boasted   D offered

5 I'm not sure where Cindy is. She ..... be at the library.
A must   B should   C will   D might

6 You will come to my party, ... you?
A will   B aren't   C won't   D shall

7 Carl went to the garage ..... have his car repaired.
A so that   C so as
B as a result   D in order to

2 Fill in the gaps. Use the appropriate forms of the words in brackets when given.

1 Are you saying you .... **(never/be)** to a salon in your life? You .... be joking!

2 She is .... a gossip that I find myself .... **(avoid)** her at all times.

3 I think you should .... **(your hair/dye)** by a professional; .... **(do)** it yourself is a bad idea.

4 You .... speak to Doctor Hope now; she .... **(wait)** for you in her office.

5 The documentary about river dolphins .... risk of extinction .... **(start)** at 7:30. Can you record it for me?

Key Word Transformations

3 Complete the sentences using the words in bold. Use two to five words.

1 It's possible that Sue didn't get the message.
MIGHT   Sue ....
.... the message.

2 Bill's constant complaining caused many people to leave his party early.
RESULT   Many people left Bill's party early ...
.... his constant complaining.

3 Someone stole Ann's wallet while she was on the train.
HAD   Ann ....
.... while she was on the train.

4 Tara went to Jim's house so that she could talk to him.
ORDER   Tara went to Jim's house ....
.... to him.

5 You won't get the job unless you meet the manager.
BY   Only ....
.... you get the job.

6 David said that Vicki had lied to her friends.
ACCUSED David ....
.... to her friends.

7 Many doctors say that plastic surgery is dangerous.
IS   Plastic surgery ....
.... dangerous.

8 I would like to go on holiday but I can't afford to.
COULD   I wish ....
.... but I can't afford to.

9 Professional decorators are painting Susan's house.
HAVING   Susan ....
.... by professional decorators.

10 She seemed to be anxious about something.
IF   She looked ....
.... anxious about something.

11 I've never spoken to such a rude person.
THE   He is ....
.... have ever spoken to.

Present Simple

Form

AFFIRMATIVE	I/You/We/They **run**. He/She/It **runs**.
NEGATIVE	I/You/We/They **do not/don't run**. He/She/It **does not/doesn't run**.
INTERROGATIVE	**Do** I/you/we/they **run**? **Does** he/she/it **run**?
SHORT ANSWERS	**Yes**, I/you/we/they **do**. **Yes**, he/she/it **does**. **No**, I/you/we/they **don't**. **No**, he/she/it **doesn't**.

Spelling (3rd-person singular affirmative)
- Most verbs take **-s** in the 3rd-person singular.
  I sit – she sits
- Verbs ending in **-ss**, **-sh**, **-ch**, **-x** or **-o** take **-es**.
  I pass – he passes, I wash – he washes, I teach – he teaches, I fix – he fixes, I do – he does
- Verbs ending in **consonant + y** drop the **-y** and take **-ies**.
  I fly – he flies
- Verbs ending in **vowel + y** take **-s**. *I say – he says*

Use
We use the **present simple** for:
- **daily routines/repeated actions** (especially with adverbs of frequency: **often**, **usually**, **always**, etc).
  She starts work at 9 am.
- **habits.** *They always do their shopping on Friday.*
- **permanent states.** *He works as a teacher.*
- **timetables/schedules** (present/future meaning).
  The museum opens at 10 am.
- **general truths** and **laws of nature.** *Water boils at 100°C.*
- **reviews/sports commentaries/narrations**
  The young actor gives an excellent performance in Cats.

Time expressions used with the *present simple*: every day/month/hour/summer/morning/evening, etc, usually, often, sometimes, always etc, on Sundays/Tuesdays, etc.

Adverbs of frequency

- **Adverbs of frequency** tell us how often sth happens. These are: always (100%), usually (75%), often (50%), sometimes (25%), never (0%).
- **Adverbs of frequency** go **before** the **main verb** but **after** the auxiliary verbs **be**, **have**, **do** and modals such as **will**, **may**, etc. *He usually sleeps early on Sundays. They are usually at work at this time of day.*

Present Continuous

Form: verb **to be** (am/is/are) + main verb **-ing**

AFFIRMATIVE	NEGATIVE
I'm eating. You're eating. He/She/It's eating. We/You/They're eating.	I'm not eating. You aren't eating. He/She/It isn't eating. We/You/They aren't eating.

INTERROGATIVE	
Am I eating? Are you eating?	Is he/she/it eating? Are we/you/they eating?

SHORT ANSWERS	
Yes, I am. Yes, you are. Yes, he/she/it is. Yes, we/you/they are.	No, I'm not. No, you aren't. No, he/she/it isn't. No, we/you/they aren't.

Spelling of the present participle
- Most verbs take **-ing** after the base form of the main verb.
  ask – asking, spend – spending
- Verbs ending in **-e** drop the **-e** and take **-ing**.
  wake – waking, dance – dancing
- Verbs ending in **vowel + consonant** and which are stressed on the last syllable, **double the consonant** and take **-ing**. *stop – stopping, regret – regretting* **BUT** *happen – happening* (stress on 1st syllable)

Use
We use the **present continuous** for:
- actions happening **now**, at the moment of speaking
  Tim is swimming right now.
- actions happening **around the time of speaking**.
  They are painting their house these days.
- **fixed arrangements** in the **near future**, especially when we know the time and the place.
  Ben is having a party on Saturday.
- **temporary situations.**
  Patty is working at her uncle's shop this summer.
- **changing or developing situations.**
  He is getting better at tennis.
- frequently **repeated actions** with **always**, **constantly**, **continually** to express annoyance or criticism.
  He's always forgetting to bring his wallet.

Note: The following verbs do not usually have a continuous form: have (= possess), like, love, hate, want, know, remember, forget, understand, think, believe, cost, etc. *I want to ask you something.*

Time expressions used with the *present continuous*: now, at the moment, at present, nowadays, these days, today, tomorrow, next month, etc.

Present Simple vs Present Continuous

PRESENT SIMPLE	PRESENT CONTINUOUS
timetables *The film starts at 6.*	future arrangements *I'm going out on Sunday.*
permanent states & facts *They live in the country.*	temporary situations *He's working from home this week.*
habits/routines *He goes jogging every morning.*	actions happening now/ around the time of speaking *She's sleeping at the moment.*

Stative Verbs

Stative verbs are verbs which describe a state rather than an action, and do not usually have a continuous form.
These are:

*   verbs of the **senses** (*appear, feel, hear, look, see, smell, sound, taste, etc*).
    *This jumper **feels** soft.*
*   verbs of **perception** (believe, forget, know, understand, etc).
    *I don't **understand** what the problem is.*
*   verbs which express **feelings** and **emotions** (*desire, enjoy, hate, like, love, prefer, want, etc*).
    *I **like** swimming.*
*   other verbs: **belong**, **contain**, **cost**, **fit**, **have**, **keep**, **need**, **owe**, **own**, etc.
    *She **owes** me £25.*

Some of these verbs can be used in continuous tenses, but with a difference in meaning.

PRESENT SIMPLE	PRESENT CONTINUOUS
*I **think** he's lying.* (= believe)	*I **am thinking** of moving.* (= am considering)
*He **has** a sports car.* (= owns, possesses)	*I **am having** dinner.* (= eating) *She **is having** a break.* (= taking)
*I can **see** the river from my room.* (= it is visible) *I **see** what your point is.* (= understand)	*He's **seeing** a new client tomorrow.* (= meeting)
*This tea **tastes** very sweet.* (= it is/has the flavour of)	*Tom **is tasting** the sauce to see if it has enough pepper.* (= is trying)
*These flowers **smell** nice.* (= have the aroma)	*The cat **is smelling** its food.* (= is sniffing)
*You **appear** to be angry.* (= seem)	*Liz **is appearing** in New York this week.* (= is performing)

Note: The verb **enjoy** can be used in continuous tenses to express a **specific preference**.
*I really **enjoy** eating out.* (general preference)
BUT
*I'm **enjoying** a nice dinner at home.* (specific preference)
The verbs **look** (when we refer to somebody's appearance), **feel** (when we experience a particular emotion), **hurt** and **ache** can be used in simple or continuous tenses with no difference in meaning.
*Beth **looks** very elegant tonight. = Beth **is looking** very elegant tonight.*

Present Simple – Present Continuous

1 **Put the verbs in brackets into the *present simple* or the *present continuous*, then match the sentences to the correct description.**

1	F	Gabriel *watches* (watch) the 8 o'clock news every evening.
2		The brave man .... (jump) into the fire and .... (save) the child.
3		The storm .... (grow) more violent by the minute.
4		When a volcano .... (erupt), lava .... (flow) out of its crater.
5		That gash in your leg .... (bleed) too much; it needs stitches.
6		What time .... (Sportsline/start)?
7		Chris .... (eat) chocolate when he's nervous.
8		Why .... (you/always/call) us so late at night?
9		Experts .... (fly) in later today to assess the extent of the damage.
10		Paul .... (not/work) this week; he's on holiday leave.
11		People who .... (live) in coastal areas are most at risk when a tsunami hits.
12		Jamieson .... (pass) the ball to Harris, who .... (shoot) the winning 3-point basket for his team.

A expressing annoyance for a frequently repeated action

B a general truth or law of nature

C timetable or schedule

D action happening at or around the moment of speaking

E temporary situation

F daily routine

G fixed arrangement in the near future

H permanent state

I changing or developing situation

J sports commentary

K habit

L narration

2 Tick (✓) the appropriate gap to show the correct position of the *adverb of frequency*.

1 ..... Patrick ✓ checks the weather forecast before he goes sailing. **(always)**

2 The people of New Orleans ..... will ..... forget the tragedy that the 2005 hurricane brought to their homes. **(never)**

3 Sitcoms ..... are ..... very entertaining ..... . **(often)**

4 Linda ..... thinks ..... back to the time she got lost in the mountains. **(sometimes)**

5 Our science teacher ..... says that tornadoes don't ..... last for more than an hour. **(usually)**

6 Does ..... Mary ..... record her favourite sitcom .....? **(always)**

3 Put the verbs in brackets into the correct form of the *present simple* or the *present continuous*.

1 A: *Is it raining* again? **(it/rain)**
   B: Yes, and whenever it .... **(rain)** for so long, the streets .... **(flood)**.

2 A: .... **(you/ever/watch)** game shows?
   B: Yes, in fact I ....
      (take part) in one next week!

3 A: Where .... **(Liam/live)**?
   B: In London, but he .... **(spend)** this week with his parents in Liverpool.

4 A: .... **(the authorities/still/look)** for the missing climber?
   B: I .... **(not/know)**. I
      .... **(watch)** the news to find out.

5 A: Why .... **(Sally/constantly/complain)** about her maths teacher? I'm tired of listening to her!
   B: Because she .... **(think)** he's too strict and unfair.

6 A: .... **(you/always/go)** windsurfing in summer?
   B: Yes, and I .... **(think)** of taking up paragliding too.

7 A: What .... **(you/do)** ?
   B: I .... **(pack)** my suitcase.

4 Put the verbs in brackets into the correct form of the *present simple* or the *present continuous*.

Dear Diary,
It's my second day in Departamento de Yoro in the Honduras, and something really bizarre **1)** is happening **(happen)** right now. Hundreds of fish **2)** .... **(fall)** from the sky! I **3)** .... **(not/believe)** what I **4)** .... **(look)** at! I know this event **5)** .... **(occur)** in the area every summer, but witnessing the actual thing is something else. What I can **6)** .... **(see)** from my window is totally awesome! Some people **7)** .... **(run)** to take cover, while others **8)** .... **(collect)** fish for the evening's meal. The children **9)** .... **(seem)** to be having the most fun, though. They **10)** .... **(grab)** the silvery creatures and they **11)** .... **(throw)** them at their friends, in some kind of fun game. Tomorrow, I **12)** .... **(go)** to the local library to see if I can find some information about this amazing phenomenon.

5 Put the verbs in brackets into the correct form of the *present simple* or the *present continuous*. Then, answer the questions about yourself, as in the example.

1 *Do you know* **(you/know)** what to do in the event of an earthquake?
   Yes, I do./No, I don't.

2 .... **(your friends/enjoy)** watching talent shows?
   ....

3 .... **(your teacher/let)** you go home early tomorrow?
   ....

4 .... **(it/hurt)** when someone slams a door on your finger?
   ....

5 .... **(you/read)** anything interesting these days?
   ....

6 .... **(you/think)** volcano chasers have an exciting job?
   ....

Past Simple

Form
The **past simple** affirmative of regular verbs is formed by adding **-ed** to the verb. Some verbs have an irregular past form (see list of Irregular Verbs).

AFFIRMATIVE
I/You/He/She/It/We/They **stayed/ran**.

NEGATIVE	
Long Form	**Short Form**
I/you/he/she/it/we/they **did not stay/run**.	I/you/he/she/it/we/they **didn't stay/run**.

INTERROGATIVE	SHORT ANSWERS
Did I/you/he/she/it/we/they **stay/run**?	**Yes**, I/you/he/she/it/we/they **did**. **No**, I/you/he/she/it/we/they **didn't**.

Spelling
- We add **-d** to verbs ending in **-e**. *I live – I lived*
- For verbs ending in **consonant + y**, we drop the **-y** and add **-ied**. *I try – I tried*
- For verbs ending in **vowel + y**, we add **-ed**. *I enjoy – I enjoyed*
- For verbs ending in one stressed vowel between two consonants, we double the last consonant and add **-ed**. *I admit – I admitted*

Use
We use the **past simple** for:
- actions which happened at **a specific time in the past**. *Sue came home at 7 pm. (When? At 7 pm)*
- **past habits**. *Mum often took me to the park when I was little.*
- past actions which happened **one immediately after the other**. *Brad, had breakfast, read the morning paper and left for work.*

> **Time expressions used with the *past simple*:** yesterday, yesterday morning/evening, etc, last night/week, etc, two weeks/a month ago, in 2010, etc.

Past Continuous

AFFIRMATIVE	NEGATIVE
I/He/She/It **was walking**. We/You/They **were walking**.	I/He/She/It **wasn't walking**. We/You/They **weren't walking**.

INTERROGATIVE	SHORT ANSWERS
Was I/he/she/it **walking**?	**Yes**, I/he/she/it **was**. **No**, I/he/she/it **wasn't**.
Were we/you/they **walking**?	**Yes**, we/you/they **were**. **No**, we/you/they **weren't**.

We use the **past continuous** for:
- an action which was **in progress** at a stated time in the past. We do not know when the action started or finished. *Tom was watching a film at 9 pm last night.*
- a **past action** which was **in progress** when another action **interrupted** it. We use the past continuous for the action in progress (longer action) and the past simple for the action which interrupted it (shorter action). *He was sleeping when a loud noise woke him up.*
- two or more actions which were happening at the same time in the past **(simultaneous actions)**. *We were taking notes while the teacher was talking.*
- to give **background information** in a story. *The sun was shining and the birds were singing when Emma got up that morning.*

> **Time expressions used with the *past continuous*:** while, when, as, all day/night/morning, yesterday, etc.

Past Simple vs Past Continuous

PAST SIMPLE	PAST CONTINUOUS
actions which happened at a **stated time** in the past *The accident **happened** at 4:30 pm.*	actions **in progress** at a stated time in the past *He **was watching** a hockey game at 8 in the evening.*
actions which happened **one after the other** in the past *They **paid** the bill and **left** the restaurant.*	two or more actions which were happening **at the same time** in the past *Ellie **was checking** her recipe while she **was preparing** the dish.*

Used to/Would/Past Simple

AFFIRMATIVE	I/You/He/She/It/We/They **used to** play football.
NEGATIVE	I/You/He/She/It/We/They **didn't use to** play football.
INTERROGATIVE	**Did** I/you/he/she/it/we/they **use to** play football?
SHORT ANSWERS	**Yes**, I/you/he/she/it/we/they **did**.
	No, I/you/he/she/it/we/they **didn't**.

- We use ***used to/past simple*** to talk about past habits or actions that happened regularly in the past, but they no longer happen. *He **used to drive/drove** to work. (He doesn't do that any more.)*
- We use ***would/used to*** for repeated actions or routines in the past. We don't use ***would*** with stative verbs. *She **used to wake up/would wake up** early every day.* **BUT** *She **used to have** long hair. (NOT: She would have long hair.)*
- We use the **past simple** for an action that happened at a definite time in the past. *He **went** to work early yesterday. (NOT: He used to go to work early yesterday.)*

Past Simple – Past Continuous

6 Match the sentences (1-7) with the correct description (A-G), as in the example.

1 *E* It was a cold day. A freezing wind **was blowing** and snow **was falling** all morning.

2 ☐ Edna **was watching** her favourite soap opera at 6:00 pm yesterday.

3 ☐ A terrible explosion **happened** last Monday at noon causing a lot of damage.

4 ☐ Peter **was ice skating** when he **slipped** and **broke** his arm.

5 ☐ Jason **finished** his essay, **saved** his work and **turned off** his computer.

6 ☐ We always **had** roast beef on Sundays when I **was** a child.

7 ☐ The sales assistant **was talking** on the phone while she **was serving** customers.

A past habit

B past action which was in progress when another action interrupted it

C action which was in progress at a specific time in the past

D past actions which happened immediately one after the other

E background information to a story

F actions which were happening at the same time in the past

G action which happened at a specific time in the past

7 Put the verbs in brackets into the correct form of the *past simple* or the *past continuous*.

1 A: A terrible earthquake *hit* (hit) Japan yesterday.
 B: I know. I .... (read) about it in the paper when you .... (come) in.

2 A: When .... (you/sprain) your ankle?
 B: Last week, when I .... (fall off) my bike.

3 A: What .... (you/do) when you heard the tsunami warning?
 B: I .... (grab) my family and we .... (drive) to higher ground.

4 A: I hope you .... (not/sleep) when I .... (call) last night.
 B: No, we .... (watch) CSI.

8 Put the verbs in brackets into the correct form of the *past simple* or the *past continuous*.

To: Carlos
From: Alex

Hey Carlos,
I **1)** *was listening* (listen) to the news as I **2)** ....
(drive) to work and I **3)** .... (hear)
that the mine in your town **4)** ....
(collapse) earlier today. What **5)** ....
(happen)? Why **6)** .... (the mine/
collapse)? **7)** .... (you/work)
at the time? I hope people **8)** ....
(not/get) trapped down there.
Anyway, please email me as soon as you can so I'll
know that you're safe and sound. I **9)** ....
(try) to call you earlier, but your line **10)** ....
(be) constantly busy.
Alex

Used to

9 Write sentences about what Drake *used to/ didn't use to do* **when he was younger. When can we use** *would*?

1 watch cartoons ✓
2 travel abroad ✗
3 go windsurfing ✗
4 live in a flat ✓
5 have a car ✗
6 ride a bike ✓

1 *He used to/would watch cartoons.*
2 ....
3 ....
4 ....
5 ....
6 ....

10 Complete the sentences with your own words.

1 As I was riding my bike, *I fell down and sprained my ankle.*

2 First our teacher gave us our tests back, then he ....

3 My friend was talking on the phone while ....

4 Last week, I went to the shopping centre and ....

5 When I was little, I used to................................. ....

Present Perfect

Form: *have/has* + past participle

AFFIRMATIVE	NEGATIVE
I/You/We/They **have/'ve** passed.	I/You/We/They **have not/ haven't** passed.
He/She/It **has/'s** passed.	He/She/It **has not/hasn't** passed.

INTERROGATIVE	SHORT ANSWERS
Have I/you/we/they **passed**? **Has** he/she/it **passed**?	**Yes**, I/you/we/they **have**. **No**, I/you/we/they **haven't**. **Yes**, he/she/it **has**. **No**, he/she/it **hasn't**.

Use

We use the **present perfect**:
- for actions which **started in the past** and **continue** up to the **present** especially with stative verbs such as *be*, *have*, *like*, *know*, etc. *Eddie **has lived** on this street for ten years.* (= He moved to this street ten years ago and he's still living here.)
- to talk about **a past action** which has **a visible result** in the **present**. *Someone **has crashed** into my car and it has a big dent in the door.*
- for actions which happened at an **unstated time** in the **past**. The action is more important than the time it happened. *She **has quit** her job.* (When? We don't know; it's not important.)
- with ***today***, ***this morning/afternoon/week***, ***so far***, etc when these periods of time are not finished at the time of speaking. *Nathan **has called** you three times today.* (The time period – today – is not over yet. He may call again.)
- for **recently completed actions**. *Mum **has** just **served** dinner.* (The action is complete. The dinner is now served.)
- for **personal experiences/changes** which have happened. *I **have never done** anything as exciting.*

Time expressions used with the *present perfect*: just, already, yet, for, since, ever, never, etc.

Have gone (to)/Have been (to)/Have been in

- *Lisa **has gone to** the shop.* (She's on her way to the shop or she's there now. She hasn't come back yet.)
- *Linda **has been to** Hawaii.* (She went to Hawaii but she isn't there now. She's come back.)
- *We **have been in** Los Angeles for three weeks.* (We are in Los Angeles now.)

Present Perfect Continuous

Form: *have/has* + *been* + verb *-ing*

AFFIRMATIVE	NEGATIVE
I/You/We/They **have/'ve been working**.	I/You/We/They **have not/ haven't been working**.
He/She/It **has/'s been working**.	He/She/It **has not/hasn't been working**.

INTERROGATIVE	SHORT ANSWERS
Have I/you/we/they **been working**? **Has** he/she/it **been working**?	**Yes**, I/you/we/they **have**. **No**, I/you/we/they **haven't**. **Yes**, he/she/it **has**. **No**, he/she/it **hasn't**.

Use

We use the **present perfect continuous**:
- to place **emphasis** on the **duration of an action** which started in the past and continues up to the present. *She **has been waiting** for her friends for over an hour.*
- for an action that **started in the past** and lasted for some time. It may still be continuing, or have finished, but it has left **a visible result in the present**. *It **has been raining** all day and the streets are flooded.*

Time expressions used with the *present perfect continuous*: since, for, how long (to place emphasis on duration)

Present Perfect vs Past Simple

PRESENT PERFECT	PAST SIMPLE
an action which happened at an **unstated time** in the past *She **has bought** a car.* (We don't know when.)	an action which happened at a **stated** time in the past *Sarah **went** to Spain last year.* (When? Last year. The time is mentioned.)
an action which started in the past and is still continuing in the present *Pete **has had** the same car for ten years.* (He still has the same car.)	an action which started and finished in the past *He **worked** in a bank for three years.* (He doesn't work in a bank anymore.)

Present Perfect – Present Perfect Continuous

11 Put the verbs in brackets into the correct form of the *present perfect simple* or the *present perfect continuous*.

1 A: *Have the rescuers found* **(rescuers/find)** the missing climbers yet?
  B: No, although they .... **(look)** for the last two days.

2 A: .... **(you/seen)** the new cooking show on Channel 3?
  B: No, I .... **(not/have)** any free time to watch TV lately.

3 A: The volcanic eruption in Chile .... **(force)** the authorities to evacuate 22 villages.
  B: What eruption? I .... **(not/hear)** anything.

4 A: I .... **(try)** to get in touch with you all morning.
  B: I .... **(run)** around town all day doing some errands.

12 Complete the sentences with the correct form of *have gone (to)*, *have been (to)*, *have been (in)*.

1 Paul *has been in* Amsterdam for just two days, so he hasn't done much sightseeing yet.
2 They .... Iceland twice.
3 Martin and his friends ....
mountain climbing. They'll be back on Tuesday.
4 What is Anna cooking? She ....
the kitchen for hours!
5 Michael .... the shops.
Do you want to wait for him?
6 Why don't we go to Italy this summer? We .....
.... not .... there for years.

13 Put the verbs in brackets into the correct form of the *present perfect* or the *past simple*.

1 A: *Has Joe come back* (Joe/come back) from school yet?
B: Yes, about an hour ago. He ....
(have) a bite to eat and ....
(head) straight for his room.
2 A: Kelly .... **(just/email)**
me some amazing pictures.
B: The ones she .... **(take)**
in Chile last month? They're great!
3 A: These terrible floods ....
(leave) hundreds of people homeless.
B: I know, I .... **(see)** the
story on the news last night.
4 A: .... **(Liam/go)** to this
morning's meeting?
B: I'm not sure, I ....
(not/speak) to him since last night.
5 A: How long .... **(the
earthquake/last)** yesterday?
B: Just a few seconds, but there ....
(be) dozens of aftershocks since then.
6 A: You .... **(not/seen)** my
reading glasses, I suppose?
B: I remember you .... **(put)** them
in your handbag before you ....
(leave) for the cinema this afternoon.
7 A: They .... **(take)** David to the
hospital last week.
B: I know, I ....
(already/visit) him twice.

14 Put the verbs in brackets into the correct form of the *present perfect simple*, the *present perfect continuous* or the *past simple*.

Thanks to my work, I **1)** have had **(have)** the chance to view some truly amazing sights over the years. I **2)** .... **(work)** as a freelance nature and wildlife photographer for over two decades, and my job **3)** .... **(take)** me to the four corners of the Earth. I **4)** .... **(photograph)** everything from strange underwater creatures in the Pacific Ocean to rare bird species in the heart of the Amazon Rainforest. The change in my career **5)** .... **(come about)** in 1999, when Mount Etna **6)** .... **(erupt)**. I was in Sicily visiting friends at the time, and the magnificent sight I **7)** .... **(witness)** was the reason why I **8)** .... **(make)** the decision to stop photographing animals and landscapes and go after the forces of nature.
Since then, I **9)** .... **(shoot)** stunning images of the 2004 tsunami disaster in Asia, the 2010 volcanic eruption in Iceland as well as several other events.
So far I **10)** .... **(not/have)** the opportunity to photograph tornados. It's next on my list though and sure to be a challenge. Is my work dangerous? Absolutely! My wife **11)** .... **(ask)** me to go back to wildlife photography for the last two years now, because she fears for my safety. But I can't give up the excitement this kind of photography **12)** .... **(bring)** into my life yet!

15 In pairs, act out dialogues, as in the example.

1 be in hospital **(why)**
   A: Have you ever been in hospital?
   B: Yes, I have.
   A: Why did you go?
   B: Because I had a broken arm.
2 watch a talent show **(when)**
3 travel abroad **(where)**
4 taste something strange **(what)**
5 ask a celebrity for an autograph **(who)**
6 burn yourself **(how)**
7 argue with your best friend **(why)**
8 cook for someone else **(what)**

Past Perfect

Form: subject + **had** + past participle

AFFIRMATIVE	NEGATIVE
I/You/He, etc **had eaten**.	I/You/He, etc **had not/ hadn't eaten**.

INTERROGATIVE	SHORT ANSWERS
Had I/you/he, etc **eaten**?	**Yes**, I/you/he, etc **had**. **No**, I/you/he, etc **hadn't**.

We use the **past perfect**:
- for an action which **finished before another past action** or **before a stated time in the past**. *The children **had finished** all their chores before their mother got home.* (past perfect: **had finished** before another past action: **got home**) *The meeting **had ended** by 11 o'clock.* (before stated time in the past: **by 11 o'clock**)
- for an action which finished in the past and whose result was visible at a later point in the past. *He **had missed** his bus so he was really late.*

> **Time expressions used with the *past perfect*:** before, after, already, just, for, since, till/until, when, by the time, never, etc.

Past Perfect Continuous

Form: subject + **had** + **been** + main verb **-ing**

AFFIRMATIVE
I/You/He/She/It/We/They **had been playing**.

NEGATIVE
I/You/He/She/It/We/They **had not/hadn't been playing**.

INTERROGATIVE	SHORT ANSWERS
Had I/you/he, etc **been playing**?	**Yes**, I/you/he/she/it/we/they **had**. **No**, I/you/he/she/it/we/they **hadn't**.

We use the **past perfect continuous**:
- to put emphasis on the duration of an action which started and finished in the past, before another action or stated time in the past, usually with **for** or **since**. *I **had been looking** for my camera for half an hour, when I remembered I had loaned it to a friend.*
- for an action which lasted for some time in the past and whose result was visible in the past. *They **had been walking** around the town all day and they were tired.*

> **Time expressions used with the past perfect continuous:** for, since, how long, before, until, etc.

Quantifiers

	COUNTABLE	UNCOUNTABLE
AFFIRMATIVE	a lot (of)/lots (of)/ (a) few/some	a lot (of)/lots (of)/ (a) little/some
NEGATIVE	not many	not much
INTERROGATIVE	(how) many/any	(how) much/any

- **A lot/lots of** are used with both plural countable and uncountable nouns. They are normally used in affirmative sentences. The **of** is omitted when **a lot/lots** are not followed by a noun. *Are there **lots of books** in the library? Yes, there are **lots**.*
- **Much** is used with uncountable nouns and **many** is used with countable nouns. They are usually used in negative or interrogative sentences. *I haven't got **much** time. Are there **many** paintings in the exhibition?*
- **How much/many** are used in interrogative sentences. **Much** is used with uncountable nouns and **many** is used with countable nouns. **How much** milk do you need? **How many** visitors does she expect?
- **A few** means **not many**, but enough. It is used with plural countable nouns. *There are **a few** apples in the fridge. I can make an apple pie.*
- **A little** means **not much**, but enough. It is used with uncountable nouns. *He put **a little** money aside so as to go on holiday this summer.*

Note: *few/little* means **hardly any**, **not enough** and can be used with **very** for emphasis. *(Very) few people go to work by bike. We've got (very) little time left. Hurry up!*

- **A couple of**, **several**, **a few**, **many**, **both**, **a (large/great/ good) number of** are followed by a **countable noun**. *There were **several** people at the meeting.*
- **(Too) much**, **a little**, **a great/good deal of**, **a large/small amount/quantity of** are followed by an **uncountable noun**. *She has made **a good deal of** progress in her studies.*
- **A lot of**, **lots of**, **hardly any**, **some**, **no**, **plenty of** are followed by a **countable** or **uncountable noun**. *She has bought **a lot of** dresses. We've had **plenty of** rain this year.*

Both – Either/Neither – All – None – Every – Each – Whole

- **Both** refers to **two** people or things. It has a **positive meaning** and takes a verb in the **plural**. It is the opposite of **neither/not either**. *Mark and Bob are businessmen. **Both** Mark and Bob are businessmen. They are **both** businessmen. **Both of them** are businessmen. **Both** men are businessmen.*
- **Either** (= any one of two) / **Neither** (= not the one and not the other) refers to **two** people or things and are used before **singular countable** nouns. *Neither car is cheap enough for me to buy.* **Neither of/Either of** take a verb either in the singular or plural. *Neither of the boys **like/likes** football.*
- **All** refers to **more than two** people or things. It has a **positive meaning** and takes a verb in the **plural**. It is the opposite of **none**. *All the students passed the exam. **All of them** passed the exam. They **all** passed the exam.* **All + that-clause** (= the only thing) takes a **singular** verb. *All that she did **was** complain about everything.*
- **None** refers to **more than two** people or things. It has a **negative** meaning and isn't followed by a noun. *"Is there any juice left?" "No, **none**."* **None of** is used before nouns or object pronouns followed by a verb **either in the singular** or **plural**. It is the opposite of **all**. *None of the students/them **has/have** finished the project.*

Note: *no + noun.* *There's **no time** to study.*
- ***Every*** is used with **singular countable** nouns. It refers to a **group** of people or things and means **all**, or **each**. *She has to pay a rent **every** month.*
- ***Each*** is used with **singular countable** nouns. It means **one by one**, considered individually (it usually means **only two**). ***Each** member of the winning team was awarded a medal.*

Note: ***Every one*** and ***each (one)*** have **of** constructions. ***Every one of/Each (one) of** the students was invited to the graduation ceremony.*

- ***Whole*** (= complete) is used with **countable** nouns. We always use *a*, *the*, *this*, *my*, etc + *whole* + **countable** noun. *the **whole** day = all day*
- ***Both ... and ...*** + plural verb *Both Julie and Debbie **are** nurses*
- ***Either ... or ... / Neither ... nor / Not only ... but also ...*** + **singular** or **plural** verb depending on the subject which follows *nor*, *or*, *but also*. ***Neither** Mary **nor** Jessica **is** a teacher. **Either** Tom **or** his parents **are** meeting you tonight.*

Past Perfect – Past Perfect Continuous

16 **Underline the correct item.**

1 Patrick **hadn't attended**/hadn't been attending a live concert before.
2 Jessica **had been lying**/had lain in the sun for hours and her skin was starting to go red.
3 Her phone **had been ringing**/had rung for a few minutes before she finally answered it.
4 John **had grown**/had been growing a beard and looked really different.
5 They **had evacuated**/had been evacuating the village hours before the tsunami hit.

17 **Put the verbs in brackets into the *past simple*, the *past perfect* or the *past perfect continuous*.**

1 A: Why *did Chris faint* (Chris/faint)?
   B: Because he was exhausted after he .... (hike) for hours.
2 A: .... (you/have) a chance to talk to Sam at the party?
   B: No, he .... (leave) long before I .... (get) there.
3 A: Do you know why Harry .... (not/show up) for work yesterday?
   B: Because he .... (not/get) any sleep the night before and he was really tired.
4 A: .... (Ben and Jerry/finally/settle) their differences?
   B: Yes, but they .... (argue) for hours before that .... (happen)!

Quantifiers – Both – Either/Neither – All – None – Every – Each – Whole

18 **Underline the correct item.**

1 It was only a small earthquake, so there was **very little**/very few damage to the buildings.
2 The blizzard caused **lots/several** problems in the area.
3 We haven't got **much/many** information about the state of the trapped miners yet.
4 A great **amount/number** of people rushed to help the hurricane victims.
5 You should hurry; we only have **a little/little** time before we board the plane.

19 **Underline the correct item.**

1 I invited Kelly and Elaine to the dinner party but **none/neither** of them accepted.
2 James is a fussy eater; **all/both** that he likes is pasta.
3 I've never met **either/neither** of the twins, but I've heard they look exactly alike.
4 There's **none/no** reason to worry.
5 **Each/Every** of the two actors starring in this film has won an award.
6 The rescuers spent the **all/whole** day trying to pull a boy from the rubble.

20 **Rewrite the sentences using the words in brackets.**

1 You can text me the details or else you can email them to me. **(either ... or)**
   You can either text or email me the details.
2 This soap opera is boring and has a predictable plot. **(not only ... but also)**
   ....
3 Ian had never seen a tornado before. Tom hadn't either. **(neither ... nor)**
   ....
4 One by one, the students presented their projects in class. **(each)**
   ....
5 Ball lightning and fire tornadoes are very rare phenomena. **(both ... and)**
   ....

Will

Form: subject + *will* + main verb

AFFIRMATIVE	NEGATIVE
I/You/He/She/It/We/They **will/'ll stay**.	I/You/He/She/It/We/They **will not/won't stay**.
INTERROGATIVE	**SHORT ANSWERS**
Will I/you/he/she/it/we/they **stay**?	**Yes**, I/you/he/she/it/we/they **will**. **No**, I/you/he/she/it/we/they **won't**.

Use

We use the **future simple**:

- for **on-the-spot decisions**. *I like these shoes. I'll buy them.*
- for **future predictions based on what we believe or imagine will happen.** (usually with the **verbs**: *hope, think, believe, expect, imagine*, etc; with the **expressions**: *I'm sure, I'm afraid*, etc; with the **adverbs**: *probably, perhaps*, etc.) *I think they will be able to solve the problem. Perhaps Frank will change his mind about it.*
- for **promises**. (usually with the verbs *promise, swear,* etc.) *I promise I'll take you to the museum tomorrow.*, **threats** *Lie to me again and it will be the end of our friendship.*, **warnings** *Drive more carefully or you'll have an accident.*, **hopes** *He hopes they will choose him for the job.*, **offers** *I'll make you some coffee.*
- for actions/events/situations which will **definitely happen** in the future and which **we cannot control.** *It will be spring soon.*

Time expressions used with the *future simple*: tomorrow, the day after tomorrow, next week/month/ year, tonight, soon, in a week/month/year, etc.

Be going to

Form: subject + verb *to be (am/is/are)* + *going to* + bare infinitive of the main verb

AFFIRMATIVE	I am He/She/It **is** We/You/They **are**	} going to swim.
NEGATIVE	I am not He/She/It **is not** We/You/they **are not**	} going to swim.
INTERROGATIVE	Am I **Is** he/she/it **Are** we/you/they	} going to swim?
SHORT ANSWERS	**Yes**, I am./**No**, I'm not. **Yes**, he/she/it **is**./No, he/she/it **isn't**. **Yes**, we/you/they **are**./ **No**, we/you/they **aren't**.	

Use

We use *be going to*:

- to talk about our **future plans** and **intentions**. *Paul is going to travel abroad next month.* (He's planning to ...)
- to make **predictions based on what we see or know.** *Look out! You're going to fall into the pool.*
- to talk about **things we are sure about** or **we have already decided to do** in the near future. *Sally is going to look for a new job.* (She has already decided to do this.)

Present Simple/Present Continuous (future meaning)

- We can use the **present simple** to talk about **schedules** or **timetables**. *His plane lands at 7:00 am.*
- We use the **present continuous** for **fixed arrangements** in the near future. *The Millers are coming to dinner tonight. I invited them last week.*
- We use the **present continuous** for changing or gradually developing situations. *More and more students are applying to colleges abroad.*

Future Continuous

Form: subject + *will* + *be* + verb *-ing*

AFFIRMATIVE	NEGATIVE
I/You/He/She/It/We/They **will be sleeping**.	I/You/He/She/It/We/They **will not/won't be sleeping**.
INTERROGATIVE	**SHORT ANSWERS**
Will I/you/he/she/it/we/they **be sleeping**?	**Yes**, I/you/he/she/it/we/they **will**. **No**, I/you/he/she/it/we/they **won't**.

We use the **future continuous** for actions which will be in **progress** at a **stated future time**. *This time on Friday I'll be driving my new car.*

Will – Be going to – Present Simple/Present Continuous Future Continuous

1 **Match the tenses in bold to their use.**

1	A	Watch your spending or you **will fall** into debt.
2		Terry **is taking** her dog to the vet this afternoon.
3		I **am going to work** for an overseas charity in summer.
4		Look out! You **are going to spill** your tea all over your new shirt.
5		I think computers **will run** our homes in the future.
6		This time tomorrow, I **will be having** a meeting with my interior designer.
7		I like these brown boots. I think I **will buy** them.
8		Mike's plane **leaves** at 7:00 am.

- A a threat or warning
- B a fixed arrangement in the near future
- C an action that will be in progress at a stated time in the future
- D an action we are sure about
- E a prediction based on what we think/imagine
- F an on-the-spot decision
- G a schedule or timetable
- H a prediction based on what we see or know

2 Underline the correct item.

1 You can't carry all those shopping bags on your own. I'**ll be helping**/'**ll help** you.
2 Watch out! You **will knock**/'**re going to knock** over those bottles!
3 Fiona **will be**/**is being** a famous fashion designer one day.
4 The last bus from the city centre **leaves**/**is leaving** at 11:30 pm.
5 I'll meet you outside the florist's at 10:00. I **won't be**/'**m not** late this time!
6 Now that I've saved up some money I'**m buying**/**am going to buy** Kylie a birthday present.

3 Complete the sentences with the *future continuous* of the verbs from the list.

• run • use • wait • have • take

1 I'*ll be waiting* for you outside the train station when you get there.
2 In just one week, I .... my own business.
3 I can't meet you at 8:00. I .... my brother to school.
4 It would be better if you didn't call us at 7:00. We .... dinner then.
5 I can't let you borrow my laptop this afternoon. I .... it.

4 Fill in the gaps with the correct *future forms* of the verbs in brackets.

1 A: I can't believe how much this camcorder costs!
   B: Have a look online. I think you '*ll find* **(find)** it cheaper.
2 A: Would you like chocolate or cherry syrup on your waffle?
   B: I .... **(have)** some cherry syrup, please.
3 A: The summer sales .... **(start)** in August.
   B: I can't wait to go shopping!
4 A: Do you have any plans for this afternoon?
   B: Yes. I .... **(go)** shopping with Mary.
5 A: Mark and Heather .... **(get)** married this time next weekend.
   B: Wow! That's wonderful news!

5 Complete the dialogue with the correct *future form*.

Nick: Hi, Pete. I heard you and Lisa 1) *are going* **(go)** to Paris next week.
Pete: Yes, we 2) .... **(spend)** a couple of weeks there.
Nick: That 3) .... **(be)** exciting!
Pete: Definitely! We 4) .... **(do)** some shopping and lots of sightseeing.
Nick: You'd better take some comfortable shoes with you. It's 5) .... **(be)** pretty tiring.
Pete: Yes, I bet I 6) .... **(come back)** exhausted!
Nick: And when 7) .... **(you/leave)**?
Pete: We 8) .... **(fly)** to Paris this time next Monday!
Nick: That's wonderful! I 9) .... **(see)** you when you get back then.

6 What will life be like in 100 years' time? Make sentences using *will* or *won't* in *future simple*.

1 People/commute to work in flying cars (✓)
   People will commute to work in flying cars.
2 People /do all their shopping online. (✓)
   ....
3 People/use fossil fuels (✗)
   ....
4 People/wear spray-on clothes. (✓)
   ....
5 Voice-activated computers/help run our houses (✓)
   ....
6 People/pay for things in cash (✗)
   ....

7 Put the words in the correct order to form questions. Then answer them about you.

1 meet/you/going/are/to/your/friend/the/at/mall?
   ....
   ....
2 what/doing/you/weekend/at/are/the?
   ....
   ....
3 be/tomorrow/working/you/this/will/time?
   ....
   ....

Comparatives/Superlatives

- We use the **comparative** to compare one person or thing with another. We use the **superlative** to compare one person or thing with the others of the same group.
  *This box is **heavier than** that one. It's **the heaviest of all**.*
- We often use **than** after a comparative.
  *Ben is **younger than** Jim.*
- We normally use **the** before a superlative. We can use **in** or **of** after superlatives. We often use **in** with places.
  *I think Ben Stiller is **the funniest of** all actors.*
  *This is **the biggest** park **in** our city.*

Formation of comparatives and superlatives

Adjectives

- With **one-syllable adjectives**, we add **-(e)r** to form the comparative and **-(e)st** to form the superlative.
  *old – old**er** – **the** old**est***
- **Note:** For one-syllable adjectives ending in **vowel + consonant**, we double the consonant.
  *sad – sad**der** – **the** sad**dest***
- With **two-syllable adjectives**, we form the comparative with **more** + **adjective** and the superlative with **most** + **adjective**. *famous – **more** famous – **the most** famous*
- **Note:** For two-syllable adjectives ending in **consonant + y**, we replace **-y** with **-i** and add **-er/-est**.
  *happy – happ**ier** – the happ**iest***
- With **adjectives having more than two syllables**, comparatives and superlatives are formed with **more/the most**. *interesting – **more** interesting – **the most** interesting*
- **Note:** *clever, common, cruel, friendly, gentle, narrow*, pleasant, *polite, quiet, shallow, simple, stupid* form their comparatives and superlatives either with **-er/-est** or with **more/the most**. *simple – simpl**er**/**more** simple – **the** simpl**est**/**the most** simple*

Adverbs

- With adverbs that have **the same form** as their adjectives (*hard, fast, free, late, high, low, deep, long, near, straight*), we add **-er/-est**. *fast – fast**er** – **the** fast**est***
- Adverbs formed by adding **-ly** to the adjective take **more** in the comparative and **most** in the superlative form.
  *slowly – **more** slowly – **the most** slowly*

IRREGULAR FORMS		
Adjective/Adverb	Comparative	Superlative
good/well	*better*	*best*
much/many	*more*	*most*
far	*farther/further*	*farthest/furthest*
bad/badly	*worse*	*worst*
little	*less*	*least*

Note: We can use **elder/eldest** for people in the same family.
*Her **elder/eldest** sister is a doctor.*

Study the examples:
- **very** + **adjective/adverb**: *Jason is a **very kind** man.*
- **much** + **comparative form of adjective/adverb**: *Liz is **much taller** than her sister.*
- **(not) as** + **adjective/adverb** + **as**: *Their house is **as big as** ours. Lions aren't **as fast as** cheetahs.*
- **a bit/a little/far/slightly** + **comparative form of adjective/adverb**: *I feel **a bit better** now that I've had some rest.*

- **by far** + **superlative form of adjective/adverb**: *Steven is **by far the kindest** person I've ever met.*

Comparatives/Superlatives

8 **Complete the table with the correct comparative and superlative forms of the adjectives.**

Adjective	Comparative	Superlative
cheap	*cheaper*	*the cheapest*
		the most expensive
	better	
		the least
trendy		
stylish		
	worse	
thin		

9 **Write the *comparative* and *superlative* forms of the following adverbs.**

1 quietly *more quietly* *the most quietly*
2 late ....
3 calmly ....
4 beautifully ....
5 hard ....

10 **Put the *adjectives/adverbs* in brackets into the correct form, adding any necessary words.**

1 A: Do you think Jane would make a good fashion designer?
  B: Yes. She is by far *the most artistic* **(artistic)** girl I know.
2 A: It's boiling hot today!
  B: I know. It's much .... **(hot)** than it was yesterday.
3 A: Did you like Jill's new dress?
  B: Actually, I didn't think it looked as .... **(smart)** as her other clothes.
4 A: You'll feel a bit .... **(confident)** about singing in public if you take lessons.
  B: Yes and it'll be .... **(helpful)** than practising on my own.
5 A: What do you think of Helen's new short story?
  B: I'm afraid I didn't find it very .... **(interesting)**.
6 A: The rolls from this bakery are far .... **(tasty)** than those we get at the supermarket.
  B: I know. They're delicious!

11 Fill in: *of*, *than*, *in* or *the*.

1 Life in the 21st century is more fast-paced *than* 100 years ago.
2 Shinsengae Centum City department store is .... largest department store in the world.
3 Casual clothes are more comfortable .... formal clothes.
4 Lola Lamour is one of the most successful 1940s singers .... England.
5 Kate is the friendliest .... all the cashiers in the store.
6 Some people feel life in the 50s was happier .... it is now.
7 Helen is .... most efficient employee in the company.
8 The Smiths have the best-kept garden .... our street.

12 Fill in the correct *comparative/superlative* form of the *adjectives/ adverbs* in brackets.

Dear Sir/Madam,

I am writing to complain about the **1)** *worst* **(bad)** *service I have ever received from your company. I bought a computer game from Top Games Stores on 17th November. Unfortunately, I experienced a number of problems when I contacted the store about the game.*

I ordered the **2)** *................................* **(recent)** *version of Friends of the Earth computer game and, despite the promise that your company has one of the* **3)** *.............................* **(fast)** *delivery times in the area, it did not arrive until 27th November, ten days* **4)** *........................* **(late)***. To make matters* **5)** *........................* **(bad)***, when I eventually received the game it was badly scratched. When I tried to contact the company, the person who dealt with my call was one of the* **6)** *....................* **(rude)** *people I have ever spoken to. She told me that I had misused the game and the company could not be held responsible.*

As a regular customer of yours I feel very disappointed with the way I have been treated. Therefore, I would appreciate it if you could replace the computer game or give me a refund.

I look forward to your reply as **7)** *......................* **(soon)** *possible.*

Yours faithfully,
Diane Webbs

13 Underline the correct item.

1 Community farms are **less/least** expensive to run than individual farms.
2 My MP3 player works **much/very** better now that I have new earphones for it.
3 Buying products that come in **slightly/less** packaging is good for the environment.
4 They recycle as much of their household waste **than/as** possible.
5 Sally thinks paying by credit card is **more/far** convenient than using cash.
6 Jeans are **by far/far** the most popular item of clothing for teens.

14 **a)** Look at the table and compare the three places.

shopping centre

supermarket   grocer's

	supermarket	grocer's	shopping centre
popular with teens	★★	★	★★★
far from the centre	★★	★	★★★
noisy	★★	★	★★★
quiet	★★	★★★	★

The shopping centre is the most popular place with teens.
The supermarket isn't as popular with teens as the shopping centre.
The grocer's is the least popular place of all with teens.

b) Write sentences comparing three shops in your area. Use these adjectives:
popular, expensive, friendly service, far, large, cheap, noisy, busy, quiet.

The shopping centre is the most popular place in town.

-ing form

The **-ing form** is used:

- as a **noun**. *Swimming is an enjoyable activity.*
- after certain verbs: *admit, appreciate, avoid, consider, continue, deny, go* (for activities), *imagine, mind, miss, quit, save, suggest, practise, prevent. Have you considered moving to a bigger house?*
- after *love, like, enjoy, prefer, dislike, hate* to express general preference. *She prefers walking to work.* **BUT** for a specific preference *(would like/would prefer/would love)* we use *to-infinitive. She would prefer to take the bus to work today.*
- after expressions such as: *be busy, it's no use, it's no good, it's (not) worth, what's the use of, can't help, there's no point (in), can't stand, have difficulty (in), have trouble,* etc. *It's not worth arguing with him.*
- after *spend, waste,* or *lose* (time, money, etc). *He spends two hours exercising every day.*
- after the preposition *to* with verbs and expressions such as: *look forward to, be used to, in addition to, object to, prefer* (doing sth to doing sth else). *He's looking forward to starting his new job.*
- after other **prepositions**. *He was nervous about meeting his future in-laws.*

Infinitive

The **to-infinitive** is used:

- to express **purpose**. *He's joined a gym to get into shape.*
- after certain verbs that refer to the future (*agree, appear, decide, expect, hope, plan, promise, refuse,* etc). *She agreed to help them.*
- after *would like, would prefer, would love,* etc to express a specific preference.
  We would like to visit the most popular sights.
- after adjectives which describe feelings/emotions (*happy, glad, sad,* etc), express willingness/unwillingness (*eager, reluctant, willing,* etc) or refer to a person's character (*clever, kind,* etc); and the adjectives **lucky** and **fortunate**.
  It was kind of you to lend us your car.
- after **too/enough**. *Are you old enough to drive?*
- in the expressions *to tell you the truth, to be honest, to sum up, to begin with,* etc.
  To be honest, I forgot it was your birthday today.

TENSES OF INFINITIVE

	Active voice	Passive voice
Present	(to) write	(to) be written
Present Continuous	(to) be writing	—
Perfect	(to) have written	(to) have been written
Perfect Continuous	(to) have been writing	—

Forms of the infinitive corresponding to verb tenses

Present simple/will →	**present infinitive**
Present continuous/future continuous → **present continuous infinitive**	
past simple/present perfect/past perfect → **perfect infinitive**	
past continuous / present perfect continuous / past perfect continuous → **present perfect continuous**	

The **infinitive without to** (bare infinitive) is used:

- after **modal verbs**.
  They might go to Rome.
- after the verbs *let, make, see, hear* and *feel*.
  They made him leave the room.
  BUT we use the *to*-infinitive after **be made, be heard, be seen,** etc (passive form). *He was made to leave the room.*
- after **had better** and **would rather**.
  I would rather have a sandwich for lunch.
- **help** can be followed by the **to-infinitive**, but in American English it is normally followed by the **infinitive without to**. *She helped me (to) put away the dishes.*

Difference in meaning between the to-infinitive and -ing form

Some verbs can take either the **to-infinitive** or the **-ing** form with a change in meaning.

- forget + *to*-infinitive = not remember (to do sth)
  She forgot to pick up the dry cleaning.
- forget + *-ing* form = not recall (sth)
  I'll never forget travelling abroad for the first time.
- remember + *to*-infinitive = not forget (to do sth)
  Did you remember to bring me my CD?
- remember + *-ing* form = recall (sth)
  I remember telling you about the party yesterday.
- mean + *to*-infinitive = intend to
  He didn't mean to insult you.
- mean + *-ing* form = involve
  Getting a second job means having less free time.
- regret + *to*-infinitive = be sorry to (normally used in the present simple with verbs such as **say, tell, inform**)
  I regret to inform you that your application was rejected.
- regret + *-ing* form = feel sorry about
  He regrets dropping out of college.
- try + *to*-infinitive = attempt, do one's best
  I tried to tell him the truth, but he wouldn't listen.
- try + *-ing* form = do something as an experiment
  If you can't sleep, try drinking some warm milk.
- stop + *to*-infinitive = stop temporarily in order to do something else
  While he was jogging, he stopped to tie his shoelaces.
- stop + *-ing* form = finish doing something
  Mr Jones stopped working at the age of 65.
- would prefer + *to*-infinitive (specific preference)
  I'd prefer to eat out tonight. It's such a lovely evening.
- prefer + *-ing* form (general preference)
  I prefer eating home-made food to eating junk food.

-ing form, Infinitive

15 Complete the sentences with the correct infinitive.

1 He is very creative.
He appears *to be* very creative.
2 She is working efficiently.
She seems .... efficiently.
3 He has been having a difficult time.
He appears .... a difficult time.
4 He renovated his house.
He seems .... his house.
5 They will be planting a community farm.
They appear .... a community farm.

16 Underline the correct item.

1 A: I can't stand to **wait/waiting** in a queue at the supermarket.
   B: Me neither. I prefer **shopping/to shop** at my local grocer's because it's quieter.
2 A: John doesn't appear **to have made/to be made** much progress this term.
   B: I know, it's a shame his grades have fallen.
3 A: I hate it when my mum makes me **put/to put** away the groceries.
   B: So do I! I think it's ever so boring!
4 A: Can you **help/to help** me pick out an outfit for our end of the year dance?
   B: Sure! How about **going/go** to that new clothes shop in the shopping centre?
5 A: Have you considered **to call/calling** the store about your faulty MP3 player?
   B: Yes, but I seem **to have been having/to be having** trouble getting through to them.

17 Circle the correct item.

1 I suggest ..... these on in a different size.
   A try   **B** trying   **C** to try
2 I would prefer ..... at a cafe at the moment than studying for my exams.
   A sitting   **B** to have sat   **C** to be sitting
3 I would rather ..... organic goods.
   A to buy   **B** buy   **C** buying
4 Tom was lucky ..... with only a broken leg after falling off the roof.
   A escaping   **B** escape   **C** to have escaped

18 Put the verbs in brackets into the *to-infinitive* or the *-ing form*. How do the sentences differ in meaning?

1 a John forgot *to stop* (**stop**) by the post office on his way home.
   b Nick will never forget .... (**be**) wrongly accused of shoplifting.
2 a Stop .... (**complain**) about the service. The waiters are doing their best.
   b Why don't we stop .... (**get**) something to drink? I'm thirsty.
3 a Try .... (**visit**) the shopping centre during the week when it's not so busy.
   b I tried .... (**get**) him to spend less money, but he wouldn't listen.
4 a I regret .... (**spend**) so much on that formal gown.
   b We regret .... (**inform**) you that we are unable to give you a refund.
5 a Remember .... (**bring**) your credit card with you.
   b Do you remember .... (**visit**) that little antique shop in the centre?

19 Put the verbs in brackets into the correct *infinitive* or *-ing* form.

How to become a fashion designer

If you spend most of your time 1) **looking at** (**look at**) clothes and 2) .... (**read**) fashion magazines then how about 3) .... (**consider**) a career in fashion?

Tips:
• You should 4) .... (**get**) a fine arts degree in fashion at college.
• 5) .... (**learn**) how to draw and sew is a must.
• It's a good idea 6) .... (**apply**) for an internship at a fashion house.
• You need 7) .... (**be**) highly creative and passionate about fashion.
Who knows? You might even 8) .... (**create**) your own fashion label one day!

20 Complete the sentences about you.

1 I've decided ....
2 I hope ....
3 I'm keen on ....
4 I have difficulty in ....

Future Perfect

Form: *will* + *have* + **past participle** of the main verb

AFFIRMATIVE	NEGATIVE
I/You/He/She/It/We/They **will have left**.	I/You/He/She/It/We/They **will not/won't have left**.

INTERROGATIVE	SHORT ANSWERS
Will I/you/he/she/it/we/they **have left**?	**Yes,** I/you/he/she/it/we/they **will**. **No,** I/you/he/she/it/we/they **won't**.

We use the **future perfect** for actions that **will have finished** before a stated time in the future. *Jenny **will have moved** house by the end of the week.*

Future Perfect Continuous

Form: *will* + *have been* + main verb + *-ing*

AFFIRMATIVE	NEGATIVE
I/You/He/She/It/We/They **will have been studying**.	I/You/He/She/It/We/They **will not/won't have been studying**.

INTERROGATIVE	SHORT ANSWERS
Will I/you/he/she/it/we/they **have been studying**?	**Yes,** I/you/he/she/it/we/they **will**. **No,** I/you/he/she/it/we/they **won't**.

We use the **future perfect continuous** to emphasise the duration of an action up to a certain time in the future. The **future perfect continuous** is often used with: *by ... for*. *By the time he retires, he **will have been teaching for** twenty years.*

> **Time expressions used with the *future perfect* and *the future perfect continuous*:** before, by, by then, by the time, until/till (only in negative sentences), etc.

Exclamations

Exclamations are words or sentences used to express admiration, surprise, etc. To form **exclamatory sentences**, we can use *how*, *what (a/an)*, *so*, *such (a/an)*, or a **negative question form**.

*   **how** + adjective/adverb
    How expensive these shoes are! How well she sings!
*   **what a/an** (+ adjective) + singular countable noun
    What a boring book! What a day!
*   **what** (+ adjective) + plural/uncountable noun
    What amazing paintings! What stylish furniture!
*   **so** + adjective/adverb
    She is so helpful! He talked to me so rudely!
*   **such a/an** (+ adjective) + singular countable noun
    Mr Adams is such a good teacher!
*   **such** (+ adjective) + plural/uncountable noun
    They are such polite children!
    Laura has such lovely hair!
*   **negative question form**
    Weren't they excellent hosts!
    Isn't that a great suggestion!

Note: Exclamations are not used in formal writing.

Clauses of Concession

Concession is expressed with:
*   *Although/Even though/Though* + **clause**. *Although she studied hard, she failed the exam.* **Though** can also be put at the end of the sentence. *She studied hard. She failed the exam, **though**.*
*   *Despite/In spite of* + **noun/-ing form**. *Despite working hard/his hard work*, he wasn't promoted.
*   *Despite/In spite of the fact (that)* + **clause**. *In spite of the fact that it was raining*, they continued the football game.
*   *While/Whereas/But/On the other hand/Yet* + **clause**. *They did their best, **yet** they lost the match.*
*   *Nevertheless/However* + **clause**. *He has lots of experience; **however**, he didn't get the job.*
*   *However/No matter how* + **adj/adv** + **subject** *(+may)* + **verb**. *However hard he tried*, he didn't finish the race.
*   A comma is used when the **clause of concession** either precedes or follows the main clause. *Even though it was snowing, we went for a walk. We went for a walk, **even though** it was snowing.*

Future Perfect – Future Perfect Continuous

21 **Put the verbs in brackets into the *future perfect* or the *future perfect continuous*.**

1   Jonathan *will have been working* **(work)** on his invention for three hours before he finally goes to bed.
2   By the time the girls return from their shopping trip, I .... **(cook)** dinner.
3   .... **(Jane/finish)** her homework by the time the wildlife documentary begins?
4   Jack .... **(work)** at the post office for 20 years by the time he's 50.
5   I'm afraid Jack .... **(not/recover)** from the accident by the time his football training begins.
6   I .... **(grow)** my own vegetables for two years by the end of the year.
7   .... **(mail)** the invitations before Friday?
8   By November, Harry .... **(sell)** his produce to local stores for two years.
9   We .... **(convert)** the rooftop of our apartment into a garden by the end of the week.
10 By June, Mr Patterson .... **(teach)** music at our school for ten years.
11 Scientists hope they .... **(solve)** the world's food shortage problem by the end of the century.

22 Underline the correct item.

1 Are you sure you**'ll have been cleaning/'ll have cleaned** the living room before the guests arrive?

2 By the time we reach our first stop, we **will have drive/will have been driving** for 4 hours.

3 The shop **will not have been repairing/will not have repaired** my camcorder until the end of the week.

4 By noon, the fire from the powerful explosion **will have been burning/will have burnt** for 12 hours straight.

5 **Will they have published/Will they have been publishing** her new book by summer?

Exclamations

23 Fill in: *what (a/an)*, *how*, *such (a/an)* or *so*.

1 A: Let's go shopping this afternoon!
   B: *What a* great idea!

2 A: .... delicious apples! Where did you buy them?
   B: From farmer Jack. He's got an organic farm.

3 A: That was .... interesting article!
   B: I know. We learnt .... much about the fashion industry from it.

4 A: There was a catastrophic earthquake in Japan.
   B: Oh no! .... terrible for the people there!

24 In pairs rephrase the following, as in the example. Then write the sentences.

1 What a brilliant idea!
   How brilliant an idea it is!
   This idea is so brilliant!
   Isn't this idea brilliant?
   It's such a brilliant idea!

2 This is such a trendy outfit!
   ....
   ....
   ....
   ....

3 How professional he is!
   ....
   ....
   ....
   ....

Clauses of Concession

25 Circle the correct item.

1 Sarah saves her pocket money, ... her sister spends it straightaway.
   Ⓐ whereas   B even though   C despite

2 ..... it was a weekday, Melody decided to go out with her friends.
   A Despite   B In spite   C Although

3 David gashed his leg. ....., he didn't need to have stitches.
   A Even though   B Whereas   C However

4 ..... hard I tried, I couldn't speak to the manager about my faulty camera.
   A No matter how   B While   C Though

5 ..... of having ordered a black mobile, I received a white one.
   A In spite   B Despite   C However

6 He made a mistake, ... he didn't tell anyone.
   A whereas   B yet   C while

26 Rewrite the sentences as in the example.

1 She wants to buy a new ski suit. She can't afford it. (**although, however**)
   a *Although she wants to buy a new ski suit, she can't afford it.*
   b *She wants to buy a new ski suit. However, she can't afford it.*

2 I love fashion shows. I haven't been to one. (**even though/yet**)
   a ....
   b ....

3 Susan has a great singing voice. She doesn't want a career in music. (**despite, even though**)
   a ....
   b ....

4 She gets her flowers from the local florist. She has her own flower garden. (**in spite of, but**)
   a ....
   b ....

5 He always buys organically-grown vegetables. They are more expensive. (**despite the fact that, though**)
   a ....
   b ....

Modals

Can/could, may/might, must/have to, ought to, shall/should, will/would:

- don't take *-s*, *-ing* or *-ed* suffixes.
- are followed by the bare infinitive (infinitive *without to*).
- come before the subject in questions and are followed by *not* in negations.
- don't have tenses in the normal sense. When followed by a present bare infinitive, they refer to an incomplete action or state (i.e. present or future). *You **should tell** them the truth.* When followed by a perfect bare infinitive, they refer to a complete action or state. *You **should have told** them the truth.*

Note how the forms of the infinitive are formed:

Present: (to) go
Present continuous: (to) be going
Perfect: (to) have gone
Perfect continuous: (to) have been going

Obligation/Duty/Necessity *(must, have to, should/ought to)*

- ***Must*** expresses **duty/strong obligation** to do sth, and shows that sth is essential. We generally use ***must*** when the speaker has decided that sth is necessary (i.e. subjective). *If you witness an accident, you **must** report it to the police. You **must** apologise to her for being so rude.* (It is your duty./You are obliged to do sth.)
- ***Have to*** expresses **strong necessity/obligation**. We usually use ***have to*** when somebody other than the speaker has decided that sth is necessary (i.e. objective). *Mum says that we **have to walk** the dog every day.* (It's necessary.)
- ***Had to*** is the past form of both ***must*** and ***have to***.
- ***Should/Ought to*** express **duty, weak obligation**. *You **should** help your little brother with his homework.* (It's your duty. – less emphatic than ***must***)

Absence of necessity *(don't have to/don't need to, needn't)*

- ***Don't have to/Don't need to/Needn't:*** It isn't necessary to do sth in the present/future. *You **don't have to work** late today. She **doesn't need to dress** formally for the party. He **needn't water** the garden today.*
- ***Didn't need to/Didn't have to:*** It wasn't necessary to do sth. We don't know if it was done or not. *They **didn't have to confirm** their reservation.* (We don't know if they confirmed it.)

Permission/Prohibition *(can, may, mustn't, can't)*

- ***Can/May*** are used to **ask for/give permission**. ***May*** is more formal than ***can***. ***Can/May*** *I ask you something? Yes, you **can/may**.* (Is it OK if ...?)
- ***Mustn't/Can't:*** **It is forbidden to** do sth; it is **against the rules/law; you are not allowed to** do sth. *You **mustn't/can't** drive without wearing your seatbelt.*

Possibility *(can, could)*

- ***Can*** + **present infinitive: General/theoretical possibility.** Not usually used for a specific situation. *Our teacher **can be** quite strict.* (general possibility – it is theoretically possible)
- ***Could/May/Might*** + **present infinitive: Possibility** in a specific situation. *We **might** go out in the afternoon, so come in the morning.* (It is possible./It is likely./Perhaps.)

Note: We can use ***can/could/might*** in questions but **not may**. *Who **could** I ask for professional advice?*

- ***Could/Might/Would*** + **perfect infinitive** refer to **sth in the past that was possible but didn't happen**. *I **would have gone** to the beach with them, but I was too busy.*

Ability/Inability *(can, could, was able to)*

- ***Can('t)*** expresses **(in)ability in the present/future**. *She **can** run very fast.* (She is able to ...)
- ***Could*** expresses general repeated **ability in the past**. *He **could** work very long hours before he retired.* (He was able to ...)
- ***Was(n't) able to*** expresses **(in)ability** on a **specific occasion** in the **past**. *He **was(n't) able to** fix his computer.* (He didn't manage/managed to ...)
- ***Couldn't*** may be used to express any kind of inability in the past, repeated or specific. *Emma **couldn't** cook when she was a teen.* (past repeated action) *Emma **couldn't/wasn't able to** cook yesterday, because her stove wasn't working.* (past single action)

Offers/Suggestions *(can, would, shall, could)*

- ***Can:*** ***Can*** *I help you with something?* (Would you like me to ...?)
- ***Would:*** ***Would*** *you like to sit down?* (Do you want to ...?)
- ***Shall:*** ***Shall*** *I return these books to the library for you?* (Would you like me to ...?/Do you want me to ...?)
- ***Can/Could:*** *We **can** go mountain climbing. You **could** take out a loan.* (Let's ...)

Probability *(will, should/ought to)*

- ***Will:*** *He **will** get a promotion.* (100% certain)
- ***Should/Ought to:*** *They **should/ought to** arrive on time tomorrow.* (90% certain; future only; it's probable)

Advice *(should, ought to, shall)*

- ***Should:*** **general advice** *You **should** take up a hobby.* (It's my advice./I advise you to ...)
- ***Ought to:*** **general advice** *You **ought to** be on time for work.* (It's a good idea/thing to do.)
- ***Shall:*** **asking for advice** ***Shall*** *I cut my hair short?* (Do you think it's a good idea to ...?)

Modals

1 Match the modal verbs in bold to their meanings (a-j).

1 D The soup kitchen **might** be open now.

2 ☐ **Can** I leave a message, please?

3 ☐ You **should** listen to the advice of the elderly.

4 ☐ **May** I see your ID, please?

5 ☐ You **have to** move the car; you can't park here.

6 ☐ You **don't have to** help me find a job.

7 ☐ You **can** join the volunteer group.

8 ☐ You **mustn't** cross the road here; use the zebra crossing.

9 ☐ She **can't** be eighty years old; she looks amazing!

10 ☐ You **shouldn't** get into debt.

A It's not necessary.	**F** It's a good idea.
B It's forbidden.	**G** You're obliged to.
C Would it be OK if ...?	**H** You're allowed to.
D It's possible.	**I** Is it OK?
E I'm sure she isn't.	**J** It's not a good idea.

2 Rewrite the sentences using the modals in the list.

- may • could(n't) • can('t) • don't have to
- should • must

1 I **advise you to** try harder to find employment.
You should try harder to find employment.

2 **Perhaps we will** go to the music festival.
....

3 **It is not necessary for you to** give me a lift.
....

4 When I was a child, I **didn't know how to** look after an animal properly.
....

5 He **was able to** get around with the use of a cane.
....

6 **Do you insist** that I show you my identification?
....

7 **You're not allowed** to drop litter in the street.
....

8 **Do you mind if** I sit in here for a moment?
....

3 Rephrase the sentences in as many ways as possible.

1 **It's possible** that we will find a solution to the homeless situation.
We may/might/could find a solution to the homeless situation.

2 **It's necessary** to have a senior citizen's card to get in free.
....

3 **It is forbidden to** transfer festival tickets to another name.
....

4 **I advise you to** get some help from the charity.
....

5 **Would it be OK** if I stayed at your house tonight?
....

6 **It's not a good idea** to walk in the forest alone.
....

7 **We are obliged to** recycle in this town, it's a law.
....

8 **She managed to** pitch her tent before it got too dark.
....

4 Choose the correct item.

1 You ..... get off the street now!
A must **B** shall **C** would

2 He ..... have gone to the homeless shelter; it's very cold.
A would **B** should **C** can't

3 ..... I take the rubbish out later, Mum?
A Would **B** Need **C** Can

4 You ..... be rude to the elderly.
A needn't **B** couldn't **C** mustn't

5 We ..... ban all public transport in the city centre.
A don't need **B** need **C** must

6 We ..... to do what we can for those in need.
A ought **B** should **C** must

7 You ..... bring food; there are food stalls everywhere.
A mustn't **B** needn't **C** should

8 She ..... read and write when she was three.
A would **B** must **C** could

Conditionals: types 0/1/2/3

Conditional clauses consist of two parts: the **if-clause** (hypothesis) and the **main clause** (result).

When the **if-clause** comes before the **main clause**, the two clauses are separated with a comma. *If I go to Paris, I will send you a postcard. – I will send you a postcard if I go to Paris.*

	IF-CLAUSE (hypothesis)	MAIN CLAUSE (result)
0 conditional general truth or scientific fact	if/when + present simple	present simple
	*If you **drop** ice in water, it **floats**.*	
1st conditional real, likely to happen in the present/future	if + present simple	simple future, imperative, **can/must/may**, etc + bare infinitive
	*If it **rains**, we **will stay** home.*	
2nd conditional • imaginary situation in the present/ future • advice	if + past simple	**would/could/ might** + bare infinitive
	*If I **lived** by the beach, I **would go** swimming every day.* **BUT** *I don't live by the beach.* (untrue in the present). *If I **were** you, I **wouldn't believe** those lies.*	
3rd conditional • imaginary situation in the past • regrets • criticism	if + past perfect	**would/could/ might have** + past participle
	*If you **had booked** tickets, we **wouldn't have stayed** home.* (but you didn't) *If you **had been** honest from the start, none of this **would have happened**.*	

- We can use **were** instead of **was** for all persons in the **if-clause** of Type 2 conditionals.
  *If he **weren't/wasn't** so stressed all the time, he **would enjoy** life more.*
- With type 1 conditionals we can use **unless** + affirmative verb or **if** + negative verb.
  *They will not hire you **unless** you have a lot of experience.* (They will not hire you if you don't have a lot of experience.)

Mixed Conditionals

We can form **mixed conditionals**, if the context permits it, by combining an **if-clause** of one type with a main clause of another.

IF-CLAUSE	MAIN CLAUSE
Type 2	Type 3
*If he **were** a fast runner, he **would have won** the race.*	

IF-CLAUSE	MAIN CLAUSE
Type 3	Type 2
*If she **had invited** me, I **would go** to her party tonight.*	

Wishes

We can use **wish/if only** to express a wish.

WISH/ IF ONLY		USE
+ past simple/ past continuous	*He wishes he **was/ were** on holiday now.* (but he isn't) *If only the bus **wasn't/weren't** running so late.* (but it is)	to say that we would like something to be different about a present situation
+ past perfect	*I wish I **had accepted** their offer.* (but I didn't) *If only I **hadn't bought** those books.* (but I did)	to express regret about something which happened or didn't happen in the past
+ subject + would + bare infinitive	*I wish **you would stop** interrupting me all the time. If only Mum **would allow** me to stay out later.*	to express: • a polite imperative • a desire for a situation or person's behaviour to change

If only is used in exactly the same way as **wish** but it is more emphatic or more dramatic. We can use **were** instead of **was** after **wish** and **if only**. *I wish I **weren't/wasn't** so busy.*

Conditionals

5 **Underline the correct item.**

1 If they **have/had** more shelters, there would be fewer people living on the streets.
2 The world's rainforests will disappear within a century if logging **continues/would continue** at this rate.
3 If you **heated/heat** ice, it melts.
4 If he had taken breaks more frequently, he **wouldn't have collapsed/wouldn't collapse** with exhaustion.
5 If I had the chance, I **would volunteer/will volunteer** at a soup kitchen.
6 If the children get an education, they **escaped/ will escape** their lives of poverty.
7 If the volunteer group **had refused/refused** my help, I would have gone back home.
8 If you want to help the poor, you **can contact/ contact** me.
9 If I **were/had been** you, I would take up the teaching position in Brazil.
10 We can drive to Somerset, unless you **want/don't want** to take the train.

6 Put the verbs in brackets into the correct tense to form *conditionals*.

1 If I *were* **(be)** like my friends, I would have travelled round the world on my holiday.
2 If he weren't so concerned about the homeless, he .... **(not/donate)** to the charity.
3 I .... **(take)** a book if I had known the flight would be delayed.
4 If you hadn't been so selfish, you .... **(offer)** to help them.
5 You harm the environment if you .... **(drive)** your car everywhere.
6 He will be hungry if he .... **(not/eat)** breakfast.
7 If I'd known they were looking for people to live on the space station, I .... **(apply)** for the job!
8 I would gladly live on the moon if they ever .... **(colonise)** it.

7 Rewrite the following as *mixed conditional* sentences.

1 Jake didn't accept the job offer. He is still unemployed.
   If Jake had accepted the job offer, he wouldn't still be unemployed.
2 Mary doesn't speak French. She didn't get the job at the school.
   ....
3 The hiker didn't find anything to eat in the jungle. He's feeling hungry now.
   ....
4 I don't know him. I didn't ask for his help.
   ....
5 The children were singing and dancing at the festival all morning. They are tired now.
   ....

8 Complete the sentences about you.

1 If I weren't so tired, *I would go for a jog.*
2 If I had known about the festival, ...
3 If I have time, ...
4 If I were you, ...
5 If I could play a musical instrument, ...
6 If I had a lot of money, ...

Wishes

9 Put the verbs in brackets into the correct tense.

1 A: I wish the little boy *had told* **(tell)** us where his parents are.
   B: Yes, it's so sad to see him living in the streets.
2 A: I wish I .... **(not/yell)** at that elderly man.
   B: Well, if you see him again, you can apologise.
3 A: If only I .... **(have)** more time to volunteer at the animal shelter.
   B: Don't worry. You do a lot more than other people.
4 A: I wish I .... **(not/drop out)** of school.
   B: Well, you can always take a night course.
5 A: If only more rich people .... **(give)** money to those in need.
   B: That would truly make a difference.
6 A: If only the company .... **(not/close down)**.
   B: I know. Hundreds of people were left jobless.

10 Rewrite the sentences using *wishes*, as in the example.

1 I forgot to bring food to the centre.
   I wish/If only I had brought food to the centre.
2 I'm not good at pitching a tent.
   ....
3 The woman can't afford to buy a new outfit.
   ....
4 I would like to give a home to every homeless person in the city, but I can't.
   ....
5 The police didn't catch the thief.
   ....
6 Mike broke my MP3 player.
   ....

11 Complete the sentences about yourself.

1 I wish I were *a teacher, so I could teach poor children how to read.*
2 I wish I had.. .
3 I wish I hadn't ....
4 I wish I wasn't ....
5 I wish I could ....

Relatives – Relative Clauses

Use

- We use **relative pronouns** (who/whose/which/that) and **relative adverbs** (where/when/that/why) to introduce **relative clauses**. We use relative clauses to identify/describe the person/place/thing in the main clause.

Relative Clause

*The man **who won the award** is our neighbour.*

- We use **who/that** to refer to people. *The students **who/that** were late for class had to stay behind an extra hour.*
- We use **which/that** to refer to objects or animals. *The package **which/that** is on my desk arrived for you this morning.*
- We use **where** to refer to places. *That's the shop **where** they serve frozen yoghurt.*
- We use **whose** with people, animals and things to show possession. *She's the woman **whose** sons are in a rock band.*
- We use **why** to give a reason. *Chris won't tell anyone **why** he's upset.*

Defining and Non-defining Relative Clauses

- A **defining relative** clause gives necessary information essential to the meaning of the main sentence. It is not put in commas and is introduced with **who**, **which**, **that**, **whose**, **where**, **when**, or **the reason (why)**. *The girl **who** sits next to me in class is from Thailand.* The relative pronoun can be omitted when it is the object of the relative clause. *The book **(which/that)** I bought yesterday was very cheap.*
- A **non-defining relative clause** gives extra information and is not essential to the meaning of the main sentence. It is put in commas and is introduced with **who**, **whom**, **which**, **whose**, **where**, or **when**. The relative pronoun cannot be omitted. *My brother, **who** is 18, is taking driving lessons.*

Relatives

12 Fill in the correct *relative pronoun* or *adverb*.

1 Kevin McLeod is the man *who* started the tree-planting project.
2 She'll never forget the day .... she saw how people in the slums live for the first time.
3 Helen chose a volunteer programme .... suited her personal schedule.
4 The forest .... illegal logging used to take place is now protected by environmental organisations.
5 The school .... environmental project was the most informative won the competition.

13 Join the sentences, as in the example.

1 The woman gave a talk. **(She works to reduce deforestation.)**
   The woman who works to reduce deforestation gave a talk.
2 The sheep and cows belong to a local framer. **(They were set loose by loggers.)**
   The ....
3 Greenpeace is an environmental organisation. **(Its actions are known all over the world.)**
   Greenpeace ....
4 The reasons are still unknown. **(He ended up on the streets.)**
   The ....
5 This is a collection point. **(People can dispose of old electronic equipment here.)**
   This ....

14 Fill in the gaps with the correct *relative pronoun* or *adverb*.

Animals in Space

In the earlier days of space exploration nobody knew if humans could survive a space trip, so scientists decided to send animals instead of people into space. In 1961, **1)** *when* NASA launched U.S. Mercury spacecraft, American scientists sent Enos, a chimpanzee, into space to see if it could survive the take off and landing. While the chimpanzee was in flight, it ate, drank and performed all the tasks **2)** .... it had been trained to do. At the same time the scientists **3)** .... were on Earth monitored his behaviour. Enos survived the space voyage, **4)** .... involved making two complete orbits of the earth. Other experiments involved sending mice into space. Scientists **5)** .... work involved research into the effect of zero gravity wanted to determine whether weightlessness would confuse the animals. Would floating instead of walking affect them? Surprisingly, within 5 minutes the mice floated happily around their living quarters. They were able to adapt very quickly to the new environment, **6)** .... they ate and groomed themselves just as they did on Earth. These experiments prepared the way for human space flight.

15 **Choose the correct answer.**

1 Fiona is the designer ..... created the costumes for the play.
   A which   **B** where   **C** who

2 The cages ..... the animals are kept are spacious.
   A who   **B** which   **C** where

3 The outfit ..... she is wearing is a designer label.
   A when   **B** where   **C** which

4 Where's the DVD ..... we rented yesterday?
   A who   **B** that   **C** when

5 That's the teacher ..... son is in the same class as me.
   A which   **B** who's   **C** whose

6 I remember the time ..... we hiked in the mountains alone.
   A when   **B** who   **C** where

16 **Fill in the correct *relative pronoun*. Then write *S* for subject or *O* for object. Finally, state if the relatives can be omitted or not.**

1 How old is the man *who/that* first stepped on the Moon? *(S – not omitted)*
2 The spacecraft .... they built belongs to NASA.
3 What's the name of the planet .... was wiped out by a massive explosion?
4 The planet .... is closest to Earth is Venus.
5 The people .... work on the ISS spend months away from home.
6 That's the man .... book was made into a film.
7 The boy .... sprained his ankle had to go to hospital.
8 The hurricane .... hit New Orleans caused great destruction.
9 The bag .... I bought is made of silk.
10 The shop assistant .... I talked to was very helpful.
11 The woman .... Ben is planning to marry is a leading scientist.
12 The MP3 player ....
I ordered from an online store was quite cheap.

17 **Fill in the *relative pronoun* or *adverb*. Put commas where necessary. Write *D* for defining and *ND* for non-defining.**

1 Mr Stafford, *whose* son walked the length of the Amazon, is very proud. *ND*
2 Illiteracy .... is a major world problem affects a person's life on many levels.
3 Peru .... Ed set off from is in South America.
4 The reason .... they were furious was that foreigners were in their territory.
5 My mother .... has very concerned about the environment goes to many fund-raising events.
6 Brazil .... is the world's largest rainforest has the highest deforestation rate on the planet.
7 The date .... many countries celebrate International Earth Day is 22 April.
8 I'd rather see the film .... your brother has recommended.
9 Volcano surfing .... is an extreme sport can be quite dangerous.
10 Jack is the boy .... brother is a news reporter.
11 Jerry is the student .... won the short story competition.
12 The reason .... she's sad is because she lost her bag.

18 **Complete the following sentences using your own ideas and the appropriate *relative pronouns/adverbs*.**

1 I once read a book *which described life on other planets.*
2 I sometimes don't understand the reason ....
....
3 I can still remember the summer ....
....
4 I'd love to travel to a place ....
....
5 I watched a documentary ....
....
6 I sit next to a girl ....
....

The passive

Form: We form the **passive** with the verb **to be** in the appropriate tense and the **past participle** of the main verb.

	ACTIVE	PASSIVE
Present Simple	Ben **plants** a tree.	A tree **is planted** by Ben.
Present Continuous	Ben **is planting** a tree.	A tree **is being planted** by Ben.
Past Simple	Ben **planted** a tree.	A tree **was planted** by Ben.
Past Continuous	Ben **was planting** a tree.	A tree **was being planted** by Ben.
Present Perfect Simple	Ben **has planted** a tree.	A tree **has been planted** by Ben.
Past Perfect Simple	Ben **had planted** a tree.	A tree **had been planted** by Ben.
Future Simple	Ben **will plant** a tree.	A tree **will be planted** by Ben.
Infinitive	Ben **has to plant** a tree.	A tree **has to be planted** by Ben.
Modal Verbs	Ben **might plant** a tree.	A tree **might be planted** by Ben.

We use the **passive**:
- when the person/people doing the action is/are **unknown**, **unimportant**, or **obvious from the context**. *The vase was broken.* (We don't know who broke it).
  *The package **will be delivered** today.* (Who will deliver it is unimportant).
  *Our exam papers **have been corrected**.* (It's obvious that the teacher has corrected our exam papers).
- when the **action** itself is **more important** than the **person/people** doing it, as in **news headlines**, **newspaper articles**, **formal notices**, **advertisements**, **instructions**, **processes**, etc. *Cell phones must **be turned off** during the examination.*
- when we want to **avoid taking responsibility** for an action or when we refer to an unpleasant event and we do not want to say who or what is to blame.
  *They **were cheated** out of their money.*
- to **emphasise** the agent. *The announcement was made **by the Prime Minister himself**.*
- to make statements **more formal** or **polite**. *My book **has been torn**.* (More polite than saying, "You tore my book.")

Changing from the active to the passive:
- The object of the active sentence becomes the subject in the passive sentence.
- The active verb remains in the same tense but changes into passive form.
- The subject of the active sentence becomes the agent, and is either introduced with the preposition **by** or is omitted.

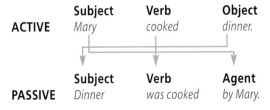

	Subject	Verb	Object
ACTIVE	Mary	cooked	dinner.

	Subject	Verb	Agent
PASSIVE	Dinner	was cooked	by Mary.

- Only transitive verbs (verbs that take an object) can be changed into the passive. *A house **collapsed** in the earthquake.* (intransitive verb; **no passive form**.)

Note: Some transitive verbs (*have*, *fit* (= be the right size), *suit*, *resemble*, etc) cannot be changed into the passive. *The blue shirt **suits** you.* (NOT: ~~You are suited by the blue shirt.~~)

- **Let** becomes **be allowed to** in the passive. *They **let** us leave early. – We **were allowed to** leave early.*
- We can use the verb **to get** instead of the verb **to be** in everyday speech when we talk about things that happen by accident or unexpectedly. *The window **got smashed** in the storm.*
- **By + agent** is used to say who or what carries out an action. **With + instrument/material/ingredient** is used to say what the agent used. *This sculpture was created **by a young artist**. It was made **with recycled materials**.*
- The agent can be **omitted** when the subject is **they**, **he**, **someone/somebody**, **people**, **one**, etc. *A lot of money **was raised** for the charity.* (= They raised a lot of money for the charity.)
- The agent **is not omitted** when it is a **specific** or **important person**, or when it is **essential** to the meaning of the sentence. *Comedies are enjoyed **by people of all ages**.*
- With verbs which can take two objects, such as **bring**, **tell**, **send**, **show**, **teach**, **promise**, **sell**, **read**, **offer**, **give**, **lend**, etc, we can form two different passive sentences.
  *She **sent** me an email.* (active) *I **was sent** an email.* (passive, more common) *An email **was sent** to me.* (passive, less common)
- In passive questions with **who**, **whom**, or **which** we do not omit **by**. *Who **wrote** this song? Who **was** this song **written by**?*
- The verbs **hear**, **help**, **see**, and **make** are followed by a bare infinitive in the active, but a to-infinitive in the passive. *Mum **made** me hoover the rug.* (active)
  *I **was made to hoover** the rug.* (passive)

Impersonal/Personal Passive Constructions

- The verbs **believe**, **consider**, **expect**, **know**, **report**, **say**, **think**, etc have both personal and impersonal constructions in the passive.
  active: *People **expect** that he **will win** the contest.*
  passive: *It **is expected** that he **will win** the contest.* (impersonal construction)
  *He **is expected to win** the contest.* (personal construction)
  active: *They **say** that he **lost** all his money.*
  passive: *It **is said** that he **lost** all his money.* (impersonal construction)
  *He **is said to have lost** all his money.* (personal construction)

The passive

1 **Put the verbs in brackets into the correct *passive form*.**

1 They believe the castle *is haunted* (**haunt**) by the ghost of its owner.
2 A strange creature .... (**spot**) near the village last week.
3 The mystery of the moving stones in Death Valley .... (**not/explain**) yet.
4 The details for the trip to the Cryptozoology Museum .... (**discuss**) right now.
5 The film is about a scientist who believes that in the future, Earth .... (**take over**) by aliens.
6 James was waiting patiently while his takeaway meal .... (**prepare**).
7 Tickets for the London Ghost tour should .... (**book**) in advance.
8 Photos of the supposed alien craft .... (**never/show**) to the public before the newspaper published them.
9 The celebrity asked .... (**give**) a private tour of the museum.
10 A charity bazaar to raise money for the homeless .... (**hold**) in my town every year.

2 **Rewrite the sentences in the *passive*.**

1 The Space Museum will hold an interesting exhibition.
An interesting exhibition will be held by the Space Museum.
2 Did they inform you about the cost of the tour?
....
3 The police is investigating reports of UFO sightings in the area.
....
4 They built Stonehenge thousands of years ago.
....
5 They have filmed a TV mini-series about the Bermuda Triangle.
....
6 They still haven't found the source of the strange humming noise.
....
7 You need to rewrite the first paragraph.
....

3 **Put the verbs in brackets into the correct *passive form*.**

Review of Honeysuckle Cottage
by P.G. Wodehouse

Throughout the centuries countless stories of haunting horror **1)** *have been written* (**write**) exciting readers' imaginations around the world. Though humour **2)** .... (**not/expect**) of ghost stories, author P.G. Wodehouse pleasantly surprises his readers. *Honeysuckle Cottage* tells the story of James Rodman, a young writer of detective stories who finds himself living in a house that **3)** .... (**inhabit**) by a ghost. The problem is that somehow his writing **4)** .... (**affect**) by the spirit of the place, causing him to write romantic stories instead of detective ones. Matters **5)** .... (**complicate**) even more when a real girl **6)** .... (**hit**) by a car outside the cottage and **7)** .... (**force**) to seek James' help. *Honeysuckle Cottage* **8)** .... (**write**) in 1925, yet it **9)** .... (**still/consider**) one of the funniest ghost stories of all time. In 2002, it **10)** .... (**adapt**) into a radio play for BBC Radio, introducing it to a whole new, younger audience. The story can **11)** .... (**find**) in the Wodehouse collection called *Meet Mr. Mulliner*. Ghost enthusiasts **12)** .... (**certainly/thrill**) by the interesting twist at the end of the story.

4 **Fill in the gaps with *by* or *with*.**

1 *Eclipse* was written *by* Stephanie Meyer.
2 The model of the spacecraft for the science show was constructed .... cardboard.
3 Scientists believe that dinosaurs can be recreated .... DNA material found during excavations.
4 A huge sum was given to the charity .... an anonymous donor.
5 The food served at this restaurant is made exclusively .... organically-grown vegetables.
6 A local woman claims she was captured .... aliens when she was a child.
7 Bigfoot is described as a huge creature that is covered .... hair and looks like an ape.
8 The Roswell UFO festival is attended .... visitors from all over the world.

5 Use the words to write questions and answers, as in the example.

1 people/trap/2010 mining disaster/Chile/33?
How many *people were trapped in the 2010 mining disaster in Chile?*
33 people were trapped.

2 Stonehenge/build/between 3100 and 1500 BC?
When ....?
....

3 a big UFO festival/hold/every year/Roswell, USA?
Where ....?
....

4 *The Day of the Triffids*/write/John Wyndham?
Who ....?
....

5 the coelacanth/rediscover/1938?
When ....?
....

6 Greenpeace/found/Bob Hunter?
Who ....?
....

6 Rewrite the newspaper headlines as complete *passive* sentences.

A **MISSING HIKER FOUND AFTER THREE DAYS**

B **FOUR PEOPLE INJURED IN YESTERDAY'S TRAIN CRASH**

C *CITY COUNCIL WILL CREATE MORE SOUP KITCHENS FOR THE HOMELESS*

D **AUTHORITIES HAVE EVACUATED THIRTY VILLAGES**

E **LOCAL RESIDENT REPORTS STRANGE HUMMING NOISE**

F **CITY MIGHT RE-OPEN NATURAL HISTORY MUSEUM**

A *A missing hiker was found after three days.*
B ....
C ....
D ....
E ....
F ....

7 Rewrite the sentences in the *passive*, as in the examples.

1 Our science teacher showed us a film.
We *were shown a film by our science teacher.*
A film *was shown to us by our science teacher.*

2 She has given the charity all her money.
The charity ....
All her money ....

3 The company promised me a replacement product.
I ....
A replacement product ....

4 The police officer read the man his rights.
The man ....
His rights ....

5 They will teach their son Spanish.
Their son ....
Spanish ....

6 They have offered Ian a new job.
Ian ....
A new job ....

7 Someone should tell him the truth soon.
He ....
The truth ....

8 Mina has sent me some photographs.
I ....
Some photographs ....

8 Complete the sentences, as in the example.

1 They don't know what causes the Naga fireballs.
It *is not known what causes the Naga fireballs.*

2 It was reported that an alien craft appeared in the sky.
An alien craft ....

3 People believe that scientists are conducting secret experiments.
Scientists ....

4 He is expected to make an announcement tomorrow.
It ....

5 Some say that a strange creature was hiding in the woods.
A strange creature ....

6 They consider him to be a leading paleontologist.
He ....

7 It is thought that her books lack originality.
Her books ....

8 It is claimed that he has solved the mystery.
He ....

113

9 **Rewrite the news report in the *passive*.**

> Mrs Harris, a local resident, has spotted a mysterious creature in the town park. She says the creature resembles a huge ape, and is sure that it is the Yeti. Yesterday, the authorities called in a team of scientists to investigate the claim. After some investigations, the scientists solved the mystery. What the woman saw was not the Yeti, but a big orang-utan they are keeping at the local zoo. The animal had escaped a few days earlier and the zoo workers had even made an announcement warning people of the fact. Mrs Harris had obviously not heard the announcement.

A mysterious creature has been spotted in the town park by Mrs Harris, a local resident. ....
....
....
....
....
....
....
....

10 **Rewrite the sentences in the *active*.**

1 Japan was hit by a huge earthquake in 2011.
A huge earthquake hit Japan in 2011.

2 The International Cryptozoology Museum is owned by Loren Coleman.
....

3 The house was believed by many people to be haunted.
....

4 The existence of aliens has not been proved by experts.
....

5 Many interesting things can be seen by visitors to the museum.
....

6 Tours around haunted castles are taken by many tourists.
....

7 The recent discovery was being discussed by scientists at yesterday's conference.
....

8 People had been warned of a tsunami approaching the area by the authorities.
....

11 **Circle the correct item.**

1 It ..... that lightning never strikes twice in the same spot.
A says **B** is said **C** has said

2 The man was made ..... that the photograph of the monster was fake.
A to admit **B** admit
C to be admitted

3 All the clothes sold in this shop are made ..... environmentally-friendly fabrics.
A by **B** with **C** for

4 Many books ..... about life on other planets.
A have been written **B** had written
C have been writing

5 Do you think these jeans ..... me?
A get suited **B** are suited **C** suit

6 A man was seen ..... the burning building just before it collapsed.
A to enter **B** he entered **C** enter

12 **Complete the sentences using the word in bold. Use between two and five words.**

1 They didn't let the children go to the UFO festival.
WERE The children *were not allowed to* go to the UFO festival.

2 People think humans will colonise space one day.
THOUGHT It is .... colonised by humans one day.

3 Jason's mother gave him a book for his birthday.
TO A book .... for his birthday.

4 According to the witnesses' reports, the creature looked like Bigfoot.
RESEMBLED It was .... Bigfoot.

5 Did anyone make Liam tell those terrible lies?
MADE Was .... those terrible lies?

6 It is believed that she didn't write the book herself.
HAVE She is .... the book herself.

Question tags

- **Question tags** are short questions at the end of statements. They are mainly used in speech when we want to confirm something (falling intonation) or when we want to find out if something is true or not (rising intonation).
- **Question tags** are formed with an auxiliary verb and the appropriate subject pronoun. They take the same auxiliary as in the statement, or, if there isn't an auxiliary in the statement, they take *do/does* (present simple) or *did* (past simple). *Will plays hockey, **doesn't he**?*
- After affirmative statements, we use a negative question tag and after negative statements, we use a positive question tag. *Andrew is allergic to seafood, **isn't he**? They haven't given you an answer, **have they**?*
- When the sentence contains a word with a negative meaning such as **never**, **hardly**, **seldom** or **rarely**, the question tag is positive. *Pam **never** goes to the opera, does she?*

Note: • ***Let's*** has the tag ***shall we?***
  *Let's have some coffee, **shall we**?*
  • ***Let me/him*** has the tag ***will you/won't you?***
  *Let me explain, **will you/won't you**?*
  • **I have** (possess) has the tag ***haven't I?***
  BUT *I have* (used idiomatically) has the tag ***don't I?***
  *They have a boat, **haven't they**?*
  *She has dinner with her friends every Saturday, **doesn't she**?*
  • ***This/That is*** has the tag ***isn't it?***
  *That's Sam's bike, **isn't it**?*
  • ***I am*** has the tag ***aren't I?*** *I am late, **aren't I**?*
  • A positive imperative has the question tag ***will/won't?*** *Stop complaining, **will/won't you**?*
  • A negative imperative has the question tag ***will you?*** *Don't drive so fast, **will you**?*

Reflexive/Emphatic Pronouns

I – myself, you – yourself, he – himself, she – herself, it – itself, we – ourselves, you – yourselves, they – themselves

We use **reflexive pronouns**:
- with verbs such as ***behave**, **burn**, **cut**, **enjoy**, **hurt**, **introduce**, **kill**, **look at**, **teach***, etc, or with prepositions when the subject and the object of the verb are the same person.
  *He (subject) **introduced himself** (object) to everyone in the room.*
- in the following expressions: ***enjoy yourself*** (have a good time), ***behave yourself*** (be good), ***help yourself*** (you are welcome to take something if you want).
  ***Help yourself** to some cookies; I've made a fresh batch.*

We use **emphatic pronouns**:
- with the preposition ***by*** when we mean alone/without company or without help (on one's own).
  *He lifted the heavy couch **by himself/on his own**.*

- to emphasise the subject or the object of a sentence.
  *Cindy drew this picture **herself**. (Cindy drew the picture. No one else drew it.)*
  *Bob was congratulated by **the president himself**. (The president congratulated Bob, not someone else.)*

Notes: • We do not normally use reflexive pronouns with the verbs **concentrate**, **feel**, **meet**, and **relax**. *If you don't **feel** well, go home. (NOT: If you don't feel yourself well go home.)*
  • Reflexive pronouns are used with the verbs **dress**, **wash**, and **shave** when we want to show that someone did something with a lot of effort. *Despite having a broken arm, Ron managed to **dress himself**.*

Questions tags

13 Underline the correct *question tag*.

1 Don't sit there, **will you/don't you**?
2 Tom has published his book, **hasn't he/didn't he**?
3 Ethan hadn't booked tickets, **hadn't he/had he**?
4 The novel is very well-written, **is it/isn't it**?
5 That's your bike, **isn't that/isn't it**?
6 She really thought she saw Bigfoot, **didn't she/doesn't she**?
7 We are having lunch with the Millers tomorrow, **aren't we/haven't we**?
8 Let's go on the Ghost Tour, **will we/shall we**?
9 I am right about this, **am I/aren't I**?
10 Kate has a dog, **hasn't she/doesn't she**?

14 Match the sentences to the correct *question tag*.

1	D	You can do this,	A will you?
2		You don't believe in ghosts,	B wasn't he?
3		James was wrong,	C have you?
4		They're leaving soon,	D can't you?
5		You're not listening to me,	E aren't they?
6		He rarely spoke to anyone,	F isn't it?
7		Let me help you,	G did he?
8		Jenny works here,	H are you?
9		You haven't read this,	I do you?
10		The museum is closed,	J doesn't she?

115

15 Complete the sentences with the correct *question tags*.

1 The Tower of London tour lasts for an hour, *doesn't it*?

2 No one agreed to his proposal, ...?

3 You wouldn't like to come to the UFO festival with me, ...?

4 They insist that they saw an alien spacecraft, ...?

5 I'm going to have to pay extra, ...?

6 Pete has a book on mysterious places, ...?

7 Stop tapping your foot on the floor, ...?

8 This isn't the way to Joe's house, ...?

Reflexive/emphatic pronouns

16 Complete the sentences with the correct *reflexive/emphatic pronoun*.

1 Helen likes living by *herself*, but it gets lonely at times.

2 My mum says if you want something done right, do it ....

3 Help .... to some cake if you want.

4 Don't say anything to John, I want to tell him the good news ....

5 James and Lilly really enjoyed .... at the party.

6 Alex banged his head on the kitchen cupboard and hurt .... badly.

7 Anne can't stand looking at .... in photographs.

8 Our teacher told us to behave .... while we were at the museum.

17 Fill in the correct *reflexive pronoun* where necessary.

1 A: Wow! That laptop must have cost a lot.
   B: True, but I wanted to give *myself* something nice for my birthday!

2 A: How come Jane didn't come with you?
   B: She isn't feeling .... very well.

3 A: What do you think of your new neighbours?
   B: Actually, we haven't met .... yet.

4 A: George is a fantastic guitar player.
   B: Isn't he? And to think that he taught ....!

5 A: Did you like the London Ghost tour?
   B: Yeah! We enjoyed .... so much that we're planning to take it again.

6 A: Did you hear what happened in Chile?
   B: Yes, some workers found .... trapped when their mine collapsed.

18 Fill in the correct *reflexive/emphatic pronoun*.

Blog of MYSTERIES!

Have you ever found **1)** *yourselves* in a mysterious situation? Share your stories with other readers!

Brian, Edinburgh ▾

My brother and I were at home by **2)** .... , watching TV. At some point, we heard a strange buzzing sound. The sound **3)** .... wasn't scary, but it wouldn't stop and was driving us crazy! After about an hour's search, we discovered that there was a swarm of bees helping **4)** .... to some honey that had somehow spilled on the floor behind the kitchen counter. Mystery solved!

Clark, Kent ▾

That's funny, Brian! Unfortunately, my story isn't so funny. Last summer I was in Florida, and I decided to teach **5)** .... how to surf. I was in the water when this strange, huge creature rose from the water and jumped over my head. I don't know what it was but it looked like nothing I'd ever seen before. A girl surfing nearby saw it too, and she said the same thing **6)** .... Anyway, I was so shocked that I lost my balance and landed on the surf board, breaking both my arms in the process. For a month I couldn't even wash or dress **7)** .... Last I heard, the creature is still out there.

The Indefinite Article *a/an*

- We use *a* before singular countable nouns which begin with a consonant sound (*a dog*, *a uniform*). We use *an* before singular countable nouns which begin with a vowel sound (*an orange*, *an hour*).

The **indefinite article** is used:
- with singular countable nouns. *a pencil*, *an apple*
- when we talk about things in general. *I want to buy an iPad.* (any iPad).
- after the verb *to be* when we want to say what somebody/something is. *She's an engineer. It's a beautiful day!*
- with certain phrases to show how often someone does something. *They go shopping twice a month.*

The **indefinite article** is not used:
- with uncountable or plural countable nouns. We use *some* instead. *some rice*, *some pasta*, *some CDs*
- before an adjective when there is no noun after it. However, when there is a noun after the adjective, we use *a* for adjectives which begin with a consonant sound and *an* for adjectives which begin with a vowel sound. *She a fashion model. She's famous. She's a famous fashion model.*

The Definite Article *The*

We use *the*:
- with **nouns** when talking about **something** specific, that is, when the noun is mentioned for a second time or is already known. *Are the red gloves yours?* (The listener knows what gloves we're talking about. The red ones.)
- with nouns which are **unique** (*the* Moon, *the* Parthenon, *the* London Eye etc).
- before the names of **rivers** (*the* Nile), **seas** (*the* Aegean), **oceans** (*the* Atlantic), **mountain ranges** (*the* Alps), **deserts** (*the* Gobi), **groups of islands** (*the* Canary islands), **countries** when they include words such as 'state', 'kingdom', etc (*the* United States) and nouns with **of** (*the* Tower of London).
- before the names of **musical instruments** (*the* piano, *the* guitar) and dances (*the* tango).
- before the names of **hotels** (*the* Ritz Hotel), **theatres/cinemas** (*the* Royal Opera House), **ships** (*the* Titanic), **organisations** (*the* UN), **newspapers** (*The* Guardian Weekly) and **museums** (*the* British Museum).
- before **nationalities** ending in *-sh* (*the* Turkish), *-ch* (*the* Dutch) or *-ese* (*the* Portuguese) and **families** (*the* Simpsons).
- before **titles when the person's name is not mentioned** (*the* Prince, *the* Prime Minister).
- before the words *morning*, *afternoon* and *evening*. *She starts work at 8 o'clock in the afternoon.*
- with **adjectives** in the **superlative form**. *I'm the oldest in my family.*
- with the words *station*, *shop*, *cinema*, *village*, *world* etc. *She went to the shop to buy new clothes.*
- with **historical periods/events**. *The Middle Ages* **BUT** *World War II*.
- with the words *only*, *last*, *first* (used as adjectives). *She was the first runner to win a medal in the race.*

We don't use *the*:
- with **plural nouns when we talk about them in general**. *Dogs are loving animals.*
- before **proper names**. *Marta is twelve years old.*
- before the names of **countries** (*Italy*), **cities** (*Tokyo*), **streets** (*Wall Street*), **parks** (*Hyde Park*), **mountains** (*Everest*), **islands** (*Hawaii*), **lakes** (*Loch Ness*) and **continents** (*Africa*).
- before the names of **meals**, (*dinner, etc*) **games** and **sports** (*volleyball, football*, etc). *I love having lunch early. / I play tennis at 7 every afternoon.*
- with the words *this/that/these/those*. *This hat is my mum's.*
- with **possessive adjectives** or the **possessive case**. *That isn't your pen. It's Jake's.*
- before **titles** when the **person's name is mentioned**. *Queen Elizabeth, Prince Harry* **BUT** *the Queen, the King*
- with the words *school*, *church*, *bed*, *hospital*, *prison* or *home* when we refer to the purpose for which they exist. *John goes to school every day.* (John is a student.) **BUT** *John's mum wants to go to the school to ask John's teacher about his marks.* (John's mum is a visitor, not a student.)
- with **languages**. *I speak Turkish.* **BUT** *The French language is difficult.*
- with **the names of illnesses**. *He's got pneumonia.* **BUT** *flu/the flu, measles/the measles*

Note: We use *the* + **adjective** to refer to a group of people. Examples include: *poor, rich, sick, old, blind, young*, etc.
The old sometimes feel neglected.

The Indefinite Article *a/an* – The Definite Article *the*

19 Fill in *a*, *an* or *some*.

1 Judy is convinced that there was *an* alien spacecraft hovering over her house.
2 There was .... time when stories about monsters were very popular.
3 .... people believe that one day humans will live on other planets.
4 Brian is watching .... interesting documentary about strange creatures.
5 Experts have proved that the pictures of the lake monster were .... hoax.
6 .... reporter for the local paper claims to have video footage of .... unidentified object crashing into a nearby field.
7 There is .... unexpected twist at the end of the novel.
8 The scientists are running .... tests to determine the age of the dinosaur bones.

20 Fill in *the* where necessary.

1 Lisa stared at *the* strange creature before her in amazement.

2 How long ago did .... dinosaurs become extinct?

3 Ben thought he just had a bad case of .... flu, but his doctor diagnosed him with .... pneumonia.

4 .... Prince Charles is next in line to become .... King of .... England.

5 .... Strait of Gibraltar connects .... Atlantic Ocean to .... Mediterranean Sea.

21 Fill in *a, an* or *the* where necessary.

1 Hundreds of UFO sightings have been reported in *the* USA over *the* last few years.

2 Visitors to .... International Cryptozoology Museum are greeted by .... replica of Bigfoot at .... entrance.

3 George is in .... hospital with .... broken leg.

4 .... Roswell UFO festival is .... annual event.

5 Pawel is reading .... book about .... origins of .... English language.

22 Fill in *a, an* or *the* where necessary.

1 A: Have you ever been to – New Mexico?
   B: Yes. I was there last year. We stayed at .... Guadelope Hotel.

2 A: Who's .... Ed Stafford?
   B: .... first man to walk .... whole length of .... Amazon River.

3 A: There's .... woman on TV who says she has video footage of .... alien spacecraft landing.
   B: Hmm, I don't think .... footage is genuine.

4 A: Did you get .... today's paper?
   B: Yes, ... Herald is on .... my desk.

5 A: I really want to learn how to play .... guitar. I think I'll take some lessons after .... school.
   B: But you already play .... basketball four times .... week, and didn't you also start .... Spanish lessons recently? I don't think you have enough time!

23 Circle the correct item.

1 How many times ..... week does the London Ghost tour take place?
   A the   (B) a   C –

2 Adam has broken his leg badly and will have to stay in ..... bed for a few weeks.
   A –   B the   C a

3 It took us ..... hour to drive to Brighton.
   A –   B a   C an

4 Dinosaur fossils have been found in ..... Sahara desert.
   A a   B the   C –

5 *Breaking Dawn* is ..... fourth book in the *Twilight* series.
   A –   B a   C the

6 ..... Astor Cinema has a special screening of the *Jurassic Park* trilogy this weekend.
   A The   B –   C An

7 ..... Griffins are a very nice family.
   A Some   B The   C –

8 There are ..... very interesting stories about mythical beasts in this book.
   A the   B an   C some

24 Fill in *a, an* or *the* where necessary.

1) *The* local community of Collingwood in 2) .... Sydney is abuzz with news of 3) .... unusual humming sound coming from 4) .... Preston Park. 5) .... sound was first noticed by 6) .... group of children who were playing 7) .... football at 8) .... park. As one of 9) .... children said: "It was 10) .... strangest thing I've ever heard. It sounded like someone humming 11) .... song really, really loudly." Later in the same week, more visitors to 12) .... park heard 13) .... mysterious sound. Eventually, the police was called upon to investigate 14) .... matter. By now, the strange hum had become extremely loud and could be heard all over 15) .... area. "Sometimes it's worse at 16) .... night," said Mrs Jacobs, 17) .... local resident.
Later in 18) .... week, 19) .... team of scientists will come to Collingwood in 20) .... effort to solve 21) .... mystery of the humming noise.

Reported speech

Direct speech is the exact words someone said. We use quotation marks in direct speech.

Reported speech is the exact meaning of what someone said, but not the exact words. We do not use quotation marks in reported speech. The word *that* can either be used or omitted after the introductory verb (*say, tell*, etc).

Say – Tell

- *say* **+ no personal object**
  *Alex **said (that)** he was tired.*
- *say* **+ *to* + personal object**
  *Alex **said to me (that)** he was tired.*
- *tell* **+ personal object**
  *Alex **told me (that)** he was tired.*
- we use **say + *to*-infinitive** but never **say about**. We use *tell sb*, *speak/talk about*.
  *Adam **said to meet** him outside the cinema.*
  *She **told us/spoke/talked about** her future plans.*

SAY	hello, good morning/afternoon, etc, something/nothing, so, a few words, no more, for certain/sure, sorry, etc.
TELL	the truth, a lie, a story, a secret, a joke, the time, the difference, one from another, somebody one's name, somebody the way, somebody so, someone's fortune, etc.
ASK	a question, a favour, the price, about somebody, the time, around, for something/somebody, etc.

Reported statements

- In reported speech, personal/possessive pronouns and possessive adjectives change according to the meaning of the sentence.
  *Sarah said, "I've lost **my** keys." (direct statement)*
  *Sarah said (that) **she** had lost **her** keys. (reported statement)*
- We can report someone's words either a long time after they were said (out-of-date reporting) or a short time after they were said (up-to-date reporting).

Up-to-date reporting
The tenses can either change or remain the same in reported speech.

Direct speech: *Tony said, "I **went** to the theatre."*
Reported speech: *Tony said that he **went/had gone** to the theatre.*

Out-of-date reporting
The introductory verb is in the past simple and the tenses change as follows:

DIRECT SPEECH	REPORTED SPEECH
Present simple → Past simple	
*"I **like** cooking."*	*She said (that) she **liked** cooking.*
Present continuous → Past continuous	
*"He **is reading** a book."*	*He said (that) he **was reading** a book.*
Present perfect → Past perfect	
*"I **have changed** schools."*	*She said (that) she **had changed** schools.*
Past simple → Past perfect	
*"We **won** the game."*	*They said (that) they **won/had won** the game.*
Past continuous → Past Perfect continuous	
*"I **was surfing** the Net."*	*She said (that) she **had been surfing** the Net.*
Will → Would	
*"I **will close** the door."*	*He said (that) he **would close** the door.*

- Certain words and time expressions change according to the meaning as follows: now → then, immediately; today → that day; yesterday → the day before, the previous day; tomorrow → the next/following day; this week → that week; last week → the week before, the previous week; next week → the week after, the following week; ago → before; here → there

Reported speech (Statements)

1 **Fill in the gaps with *say* or *tell* in the correct form.**

1 A: What did our teacher *say* about the Duke of Edinburgh's award?
  B: He .... us it helps develop character.
2 A: Ted .... to me that he was going bowling.
  B: Really? That's not what he .... me! He .... he'd be at the library.
3 A: Is it true that Adam .... to Jim that their friendship was over?
  B: Yes, apparently Jim .... a lie about Adam to their boss.
4 A: My parents keep .... me to study harder.
  B: Mine too! I think all parents .... the same things!
5 A: When did you .... the library books are due back?
  B: Yesterday! Don't .... me you haven't returned them yet!
6 A: Jane .... that the guided tour cost £50.
  B: I know. But she also .... me that it was worth every penny.

2 Fill in the gaps with the correct *pronouns* or *possessive adjectives*.

1 Jack said: "I am so pleased that you passed your finals."

Jack said that *he* was so pleased that .... had passed .... finals.

2 She said: "My brother wants me to help him fill in the application form."

She said that .... brother wanted .... to help .... fill in the application form.

3 Nancy said to me: "I can't find your calculator on your desk."

Nancy told me that .... couldn't find .... calculator on .... desk.

4 Ron said: "We've signed up for Kung Fu classes at a martial arts centre near our house."

Ron said that .... had signed up for Kung Fu classes at a martial arts centre near .... house.

3 Underline the correct item. What were the speakers exact words?

1 A: How is Melody going to finance her studies?

B: She told me she **would win/had won** a scholarship.

"I have won a scholarship."

2 A: Is your brother staying in a hall of residence?

B: No, he said he **would stay/had stayed** off campus.

....

3 A: Is Jane taking a gap year after graduating from high school?

B: Yes, she said she **travelled/was going to travel** around Europe for a year.

....

4 A: Did Kevin receive an award for his participation in the DofE programme?

B: Yes, he told me he **was getting/got** a silver award.

....

5 A: Are you going to help Jake with his project?

B: No, he told me he **hasn't needed/didn't need** any help.

....

4 Turn the following sentences into *reported speech*.

1 "I'm thinking of enrolling at an online university this September," she said.

She said she was thinking of enrolling at an online university that September.

2 "My dog was barking all night," he said.

....

3 "It takes discipline and patience to master the art of Kung Fu," said the instructor.

....

4 "I hope I'll pass my driving test this time," said Janet.

....

5 "We're having a karate class tomorrow," he said.

....

6 "I don't understand why some students borrow books from the library and don't return them on time," said Fiona.

....

7 "I haven't seen Patrick since last week," she said.

....

5 Choose the correct *direct speech*.

1 He said that he was applying for an online course soon.

   a "I was applying for an online course soon."

   (b) "I'm applying for an online course soon."

2 Jane said that she hadn't visited her grandparents since the week before.

   a "I haven't visited my grandparents since last week."

   b "I didn't visit my grandparents since the week before."

3 They told us they had always wanted to see the Australian outback.

   a "We have always wanted to see the Australian outback."

   b "We always want to see the Australian outback."

4 We told them we would have to leave early the following day.

   a "We would have to leave early tomorrow."

   b "We'll have to leave early tomorrow."

Reported questions

- Reported questions are usually introduced with the verbs *ask*, *inquire*, *wonder*, or the expression *want to know*.
- When the direct question begins with a question word (*who*, *where*, *how*, *when*, *what*, etc), the reported question is introduced with the same question word.
  "What did you put in the salad?" he asked. (direct question)
  He asked what I had put in the salad. (reported question)
- When the direct question begins with an auxiliary (*be*, *do*, *have*) or a modal verb (*can*, *may*, etc), then the reported question is introduced with *if* or *whether*.
  "Do you like jazz?" he asked her. (direct question)
  He asked her if/whether she liked jazz. (reported question)
- In reported questions, the verb is in the affirmative. The question mark and words/expressions such as *please*, *well*, *oh*, etc are omitted. The verb tenses, pronouns and time expressions change as in statements.
  "Can you do the dishes, please?" he asked her. (direct question)
  He asked her if she could do the dishes. (reported question)

Indirect questions

- **Indirect questions** are used to ask for advice or information. They are introduced with: **Could you tell me ...?**, **Do you know ...?**, **I wonder ...**, **I want to know ...**, **I doubt ...**, etc and the verb is in the affirmative. If the indirect question starts with **I want to know ...**, **I wonder ...** or **I doubt ...**, the question mark is omitted.

  Direct question   *"How far is it to the beach?"*
  Indirect question   *Do you know how far it is to the beach?*

Reported commands/requests/ suggestions/orders

- **Reported commands/requests/suggestions** are introduced with a special introductory verb (*advise*, *ask*, *beg*, *suggest*, etc) followed by a *to-infinitive*, an *-ing* form, or a *that*-clause, depending on the introductory verb.
  "Put your things over there," he told us. → *He told us to put our things over there.* (command)
  "Return to your seat, please," she said. → *She asked me to return to my seat.* (request)
  "Let's go to the cinema," he said. → *He suggested going to the cinema.* (suggestion)
  "You'd better wear something warmer," she said. → *She suggested that I (should) wear something warmer.* (suggestion)
- To report **orders** or **instructions**, we use the verbs *order* or *tell* + sb + (not) *to*-infinitive.
  "Stop talking," she told them. (direct order)
  She told them to stop talking. (reported order)
  "Don't move," the policeman told the thief. (direct order)
  The policeman ordered the thief not to move. (reported order)

Modal verbs in reported speech

Note how the following modal verbs change in reported speech when the reported sentence is out of date. will/shall → **would**, can → **could** (present reference)/**would be able to** (future reference), may → **might/could**, shall → **should** (asking for advice/asking for information)/offer (expressing offers), must → **must/had to** (obligation) (*must remains the same when it expresses possibility or deduction), needn't → **didn't need to/didn't have to** (present reference)/ **wouldn't have to** (future reference). **Would, could, used to, mustn't, should, might, ought to** or **had better** remain unchanged in reported speech.

DIRECT SPEECH		REPORTED SPEECH
He said, "I **will** call you later."	→	He said (that) he **would** call me later.
He said, "I **can't** do this."	→	He said (that) he **couldn't** do that. (present)
He said, "I **can** come next week."	→	He said (that) he **would be able to** come the following week. (future)
He said, "I **may** leave early."	→	He said (that) he **might** leave early.
He said, "Where **shall** I put this?"	→	He asked me where he **should** put that. (information)
He said, "**Shall** I offer to help her?"	→	He asked (me) if he **should** offer to help her. (advice)
He said, "**Shall** I help you carry the bags?"	→	He **offered** to help me carry the bags. (offer)
He said, "You **must** be here at 10."	→	He said (that) I **had to** be there at 10. (obligation)
He said, "They **must** be at work."	→	He said (that) they **must** be at work. (deduction)
He said, "He **had better** tell the truth."	→	He said (that) he **had better** tell the truth.
He said, "You **needn't** walk the dog today."	→	He said (that) I **didn't need to/didn't have to** walk the dog that day.
He said, "I **needn't** go to school tomorrow."	→	He said (that) he **wouldn't have to** go to school the next/following day. (future)
He said, "I **should** apologise to her."	→	He said (that) he **should** apologise to her.

Reported speech (Questions/ Commands/Requests/Suggestions/Orders)

6 **A judo instructor is having a class. Turn the following sentences *into reported speech*.**

1 "Let's do some warm-up exercises!"
  The judo instructor suggested doing some warm-up exercises.

2 "Bow to your partners, please."
  ....

3 "Stand still with your legs bent."
  ....

4 "Now take several deep breaths."
  ....

5 "Move forward on your hands and knees."
  ....

6 "Let's take a ten-minute break."
  ....

121

7 Rewrite the following questions in *reported speech*.

1 "Do you want to join a yoga class with me?" Sue asked Kim.
Sue asked Kim if/whether she wanted to join a yoga class with her.

2 "Why is your assignment late?" the teacher asked Paul.
....

3 "Did you have interactive whiteboards in your last school?" I asked them.
....

4 "What time does our geography class start?" Joan asked me.
....

5 "When will you sign up for the extracurricular activities?" Heather asked us.
....

6 "Have you taken a first-aid class?" the camp leader asked them.
....

8 Reporter Francis Fowler interviewed a student after he won the young scientist award. Turn the following into *indirect questions* using the verbs in brackets.

1 When did you first become interested in science? **(Could you tell me …)**
Could you tell me when you first became interested in science?

2 How does it feel to be the winner of the young scientist award? **(want to know)**
....

3 How will your invention improve people's lives? **(wonder)**
....

4 How long did it take you to perfect your invention? **(want to know)**
....

5 Did you work on the invention on your own? **(Could you tell me…)**
....

6 Who encouraged you to take part in the competition? **(wonder)**
....

7 What will your next invention be? **(Do you know)**
....

Modal verbs in reported speech

9 Turn the sentences into *reported speech*.

1 "You can work together on this project," Mrs Jameson said to us.
Mrs Jameson told us we could work together on that project.

2 "Mark should put more effort into his homework," the English teacher said.
....

3 "Shall I come back later?" Ian asked.
....

4 "You needn't book a place for tomorrow's tour," the guide told me.
....

5 "You needn't train any more today," the coach told them.
....

6 "I may win a scholarship," Jason said.
....

7 "Your parents must sign this form," Mr Halls said to his class.
....

8 "Hillary might write a report on illiteracy," said Phillip.
....

10 Turn the following sentences into *reported speech*.

1 "I'm graduating from college this year," he said.
He said that he was graduating from college that year.

2 She said, "Shall we watch the lecture online?"
....

3 Don't use your calculators during the maths test!" The teacher said to us.
....

4 "Please help me edit my essay," Melissa said to Jeremy.
....

5 "Where is the student cafeteria?" she asked.
....

6 "Could you lend me that book?" Kim said to Lisa.
....

7 "You might be elected class president," she said to me.
....

SPECIAL INTRODUCTORY VERBS

Introductory Verb	Direct Speech		Reported Speech
+ *to*-inf			
agree	"Yes, I'll give you a lift."	→	He **agreed to give** me a lift.
demand	"Show me some proof!"	→	He **demanded to be shown** some proof.
offer	"Would you like me to make you some coffee?"	→	He **offered to** make me some coffee.
promise	"I'll come on time."	→	He **promised to come** on time.
refuse	"No, I won't play with you."	→	He **refused to play** with me.
threaten	"Leave or I'll call the police."	→	He **threatened to call** the police if I didn't leave.
claim	"I saw her break into the house."	→	He **claimed to have seen** her break into the house.
+ sb + *to*-inf			
advise	"You should get more sleep."	→	He **advised me to get** more sleep.
allow	"You can stay at your friend's."	→	He **allowed me to stay** at my friend's.
ask	"Please, turn off the TV."	→	He **asked me to turn off** the TV.
beg	"Please, please stop making fun of me."	→	He **begged me to stop** making fun of him.
command	"Get out of my office!"	→	He **commanded me to get out** of his office.
encourage	"Go ahead, try it."	→	He **encouraged me to try** it.
forbid	"You mustn't stay out late."	→	He **forbade me to stay out** late.
instruct	"Type in your password."	→	He **instructed me to type** in my password.
invite sb	"Would you like to go to the beach with us?"	→	He **invited me to go** to the beach with them.
order	"Go to your room!"	→	He **ordered me to go** to my room.
permit/allow	"You may sit here."	→	He **permitted/allowed me to sit** there.
remind	"Don't forget to lock the door."	→	He **reminded me to lock** the door.
urge	"Be careful."	→	He **urged me to be** careful.
warn	"Don't run around the pool."	→	He **warned me not to run** around the pool.
want	"I'd like you to take extra lessons."	→	He **wanted me to take** extra lessons.
+ *-ing* form			
accuse sb of	"You ruined my jacket!"	→	He **accused me of ruining/having ruined** his jacket.
apologise for	"I'm sorry I was rude."	→	He **apologised for being/having been** rude.
admit (to)	"Yes, I broke the vase."	→	He **admitted (to) breaking/having broken** the vase.
boast about	"I cook better than all of you."	→	He **boasted about cooking** better than all of us.
complain to sb about	"You never take my side."	→	He **complained to me about my never taking** his side.
deny	"No, I didn't lie."	→	He **denied lying/having lied**.
insist on	"You must leave now."	→	He **insisted on me/my leaving** immediately.
suggest + *-ing* form	"Let's have some juice."	→	He **suggested having** some juice.
+ *that*-clause			
agree	"Yes, it is a good solution."	→	He **agreed that** it was a good solution.
boast	"I'm an excellent driver."	→	He **boasted that** he was an excellent driver.
claim	"I came first in the race."	→	He **claimed that** he had come first in the race.
complain	"You never do any chores."	→	He **complained that** I never did any chores.
deny	"I never said that."	→	He **denied that** he had ever said that.
exclaim	"It's fantastic!"	→	He **exclaimed that** it was fantastic.
explain	"It is a very easy recipe."	→	He **explained that** it was a very easy recipe.
inform sb	"Your request was rejected."	→	He **informed me that** my request had been rejected.
promise	"I'll do the shopping."	→	He **promised that** he would do the shopping.
suggest	"You should leave early."	→	He **suggested that** I leave early.
explain to sb + how	"This is how you make an espresso."	→	He **explained to me** how to make an espresso.
wonder *where/what/why/how* + clause (when the subject of the introductory verb is not the same as the subject in the reported question)	He asked himself, "Where is Tom?" He asked himself, "What is she doing?" He asked himself, "Why are they here?" He asked himself, "How did she do that?"	→ → → →	He **wondered where** Tom was. He **wondered what** she was doing. He **wondered why** they were there. He **wondered how** she had done that.
wonder + whether + *to*-inf or clause	He asked himself, "Should I hire her?"	→	He **wondered whether** to hire her.
wonder *where/what/how* + *to*-inf (when the subject of the infinitive is the **same** as the subject of the verb)	He asked himself, "Where should I go?" He asked himself, "What can I eat?" He asked himself, "How can I fix this?"	→ → →	He **wondered where** to go. He **wondered what** to eat. He **wondered how** to fix that.

Reported speech (Special introductory verbs)

11 Complete the gaps with the appropriate introductory verbs from the list below.

- boast - demand - agreed - refuse - allow

1 "Yes, I'll lend you my lecture notes." he said.
   He *agreed* to lend me his lecture notes.
2 "I made the best presentation in class," she said.
   She .... that she had made the best presentation in class.
3 "You can go to Ryan's party."
   Mum .... me to go to Ryan's party.
4 "No, I won't do your science homework!" my brother told me.
   My brother .... to do my science homework.
5 "Give me an explanation for why you haven't done your assignment," the teacher told me.
   The teacher .... to be told why I hadn't done my assignment.

12 Match the sentences (1-5) to the correct introductory verb (a-e). Then report the sentences.

1	b	"You need to follow the instructions carefully," the IT teacher said to us.
2		"You never clean up after yourselves," said Martha.
3		"I'd like you to do some more research on your projects," Mr Sykes said to the students.
4		"Please, please give me back my mobile phone," Sandra said to me.
5		"Don't forget to hand in your essays this afternoon," the teacher said to us.

a want   c complain   e beg
b explain   d remind

1 *The IT teacher explained that we needed to follow the instructions carefully.*
2 ....
   ....
3 ....
   ....
4 ....
   ....
5 ....
   ....

13 Complete the sentences using the appropriate introductory verb.

1 "How can I explain this physics problem to them?" the teacher asked himself.
   The teacher *wondered how he could explain the physics problem to them.*
2 "Your exam results will be announced tomorrow." the head teacher said.
   The head teacher ....
   ....
3 "I run the fastest of all my team-mates," Sandy said.
   Sandy ....
   ....
4 "Go ahead, sign up for the Duke of Edinburgh's award!" my friend said.
   My friend ....
   ....
5 "Don't forget to feed the dog before you go to school," Mum said.
   Mum ....
   ....
6 "You scratched my DVD!" Tim said to Luke.
   Tim ....
   ....
7 "You should revise more systematically for your tests." Mr Lakes said.
   Mr Lakes ....
   ....
8 "I'm sorry for interrupting the lesson." Sarah said.
   Sarah ....
   ....
9 "Don't let Bill bully you!" she said to me.
   She ....
   ....
10 "I didn't download music from the Internet." she said.
   She ....
   ....
11 "Yes, I took your notebook by mistake." he said.
   He ....
   ....
12 "You must let me pay for the damage I've caused." Harry said.
   He ....
   ....

Clauses of time

- **Clauses of time** are introduced by: *after*, *as*, *as long as*, *as soon as*, *before*, *by the time* (= before, not later than), *every time*, *immediately*, *just as*, *once*, *the moment (that)*, *until/till* (= up to the time when), *when*, *while*, etc.
  *They waited for three hours **before** the bus finally arrived.*

- When the verb of the **main clause** is in a **present** or **future** form, the verb of the **time clause** is in the **present** form. When the verb of the **main clause** is in a **past** form, the verb of the **time clause** is in a **past form**. We don't use *will/would* in a clause of time.
  *I'll call you **as soon as** I get home. (NOT: as soon as I will get)*

- When the time clause precedes the main clause, a comma is used. When the time clause follows, no comma is used.
  ***When** you see him, tell him to call me.*
  BUT
  *Tell him to call me **when** you see him.*

Linking Words

Linking words show the logical relationship between sentences or parts of a sentence.

Positive Addition
and, both ... and, too, besides (this/that), moreover, what is more, in addition (to), also, as well (as this/that), furthermore, etc.
*She is **both** creative **and** imaginative.*

Negative Addition
neither ... nor, nor, neither, either
***Neither** Mum **nor** Dad can use a computer.*

Contrast
but, although, in spite of, despite, while, whereas, even though, on the other hand, however, yet, still, etc.
*Beth is hardworking, **but** not very social.*

Giving Examples
such as, like, for example, for instance, especially, in particular, etc. – *I like all James Bond films, **especially** Never Say Never Again.*

Cause/Reason
as, because, because of, since, for this reason, due to, so, as a result (of), etc.
*They were late **because** their car broke down.*

Condition
if, whether, only if, in case (of), provided (that), providing (that), unless, as/so long as, otherwise, or (else), on condition (that), etc.
*I'll lend you my car **provided** you drive carefully.*

Purpose
to, so that, so as (not) to, in order (not) to, in order that, etc.
*I went to bed early **so that** I wouldn't be tired during the exam.*

Effect/Result
such/so ... that, so, consequently, as a result, therefore, for this reason, etc.
*It snowed all day, **therefore** we didn't go out of the house.*

Time
when, whenever, as, as soon as, while, before, until/till, after, since, etc. *I'll leave **when** I'm ready.*

Place
where, wherever
*I'd like to live in a place **where** it's quiet and remote.*

Exception
except (for), apart from
*Everyone attended the meeting, **apart from** Dennis.*

Relatives
who, whom, whose, which, what, that
*The woman over there is the one **who** lives across the street.*

Listing Points/Events
To begin: **initially, first, at first, firstly, to start/begin with, first of all,** etc. – ***First**, heat the oil.*
To continue: **secondly, after this/that, second, afterwards, then, next,** etc.
***Then**, pour the ingredients into the hot oil.*
To conclude: **finally, lastly, in the end, at last, eventually,** etc. – ***Finally**, serve the food.*

Summarising
in conclusion, in summary, to sum up, on the whole, all in all, altogether, in short, etc.
***All in all**, I enjoyed the film, although I found the plot hard to follow.*

Clauses of Time

1 Underline the correct item.

1 **Once/While** we've saved some money, we can go on holiday to Spain.
2 We'll throw him a party **as/after** he graduates.
3 I made sure I'd turned off my computer **after/before** I went to work.
4 Wait **until/when** the language program downloads and then you can install it.
5 **Whenever/As** Tara is in town, she meets up with her friends.

2 Put the verbs in brackets into the correct form.

1 We will inform you as soon as we *make* **(make)** the reservation.
2 Whenever Tina .... **(not/approve)** of something, she raises her eyebrows.
3 .... **(you/send)** me a message as soon as your rehearsal is over?
4 Do you wrinkle your nose when you .... **(not/like)** something?
5 We had dinner after the girls .... **(get)** home.

3 **Put the verbs in brackets into the correct tense.**

1 A: What did you do yesterday afternoon?
B: Nothing special. I had to take care of my sister until my parents *came* **(come)** home.

2 A: How do you think Petra looks now that she's had a facelift?
B: Nice, but I think she looked beautiful before she .... **(have)** surgery too.

3 A: As soon as that new girl ....
.... **(arrive)** she started making trouble!
B: I know. She's so aggressive!

4 A: How did you manage to lose so much weight?
B: I went on diet when my doctor ....
.... **(tell)** me I had a back problem last May.

5 A: Diane looked exhausted!
B: Yes, she fell asleep the moment she ....
.... **(lie)** down.

6 A: Do you drive to your dance class?
B: No, I always walk, especially when the weather .... **(be)** fine.

4 **Underline the appropriate *time conjunctions* and put the verbs in brackets into the correct form.**

1 Fiona woke up **until/the moment** the alarm clock *went off* **(go off)**.

2 **The first time/Every time** I met her, I ....
.... **(realise)** she was a big drama queen.

3 It's important that you see your supervisor **as soon as/since** you ....
(come) to the lab tomorrow.

4 I have to finish this assignment **before/when** my class .... **(start)**.

5 Don't worry about your computer; I'm sure the technician .... **(fix)** it **as/by** the end of the week.

6 **As/Once** she ....
(walk) down the street, she met her old ballet teacher.

Linking Words

5 **Choose the correct item.**

1 Gerald took his father's car **in spite/despite/although** his father had told him not to.

2 Flamenco dancing keeps you fit. **Furthermore/Although/For instance**, it's a great way to socialise.

3 George has shaved his head, **while/since/besides** Fred has grown a beard.

4 Could you call me **until/as soon as/while** you arrive at the hotel?

5 Drama queens exaggerate everything that happens to them. **For example/Because of/Due to**, they may get the flu and act as if they had severe pneumonia.

6 My brother is a know-it-all. **Whenever/Whereas/Where** a problem comes up, he insists that his solution is the best.

6 **Replace the words in bold with appropriate synonyms from the list.**

• while • as • in order to • apart from
• at last • only if • at first • all in all

1 **Initially**, local companies funded the dance academy.
At first, local companies funded the dance academy.

2 She was running **because** she was late for her job interview.
....

3 **Finally**, after being stuck in traffic for 2 hours, they arrived home!
....

4 **On the whole**, the play was a success.
....

5 Sally likes to read, **whereas** Brett doesn't.
....

6 He sent the company a letter **so as to** complain about the faulty MP3 player.
....

7 Everyone volunteered for the food drive **except for** Helen, who was ill.
....

8 I'll do the extra work **provided** you help me.
....

Causative form

- We use **have** + **object** + **past participle** to say that we have arranged for someone to do something for us. *Mr Benson* **had** *his house* **painted**. (He didn't paint it himself.)
- Questions and negations in the causative are formed with **do/does** (present simple) or **did** (past simple) + **have** + **object** + **past participle**.
  When **did** *you* **have** *your hair cut?*

	ACTIVE	CAUSATIVE
Present Simple	*He* **paints** *his room.*	*He* **has** *his room* **painted**.
Present Continuous	*He* **is painting** *his room.*	*He* **is having** *his room* **painted**.
Past Simple	*He* **painted** *his room.*	*He* **had** *his room* **painted**.
Past Continuous	*He* **was painting** *his room.*	*He* **was having** *his room* **painted**.
Present Perfect Simple	*He* **has painted** *his room.*	*He* **has had** *his room* **painted**.
Past Perfect	*He* **had painted** *his room.*	*He* **had had** *his room* **painted**.
Simple Future	*He* **will paint** *his room.*	*He* **will have** *his room* **painted**.

Note:
- We also use **the causative form** to say that something unpleasant or unexpected happened to somebody. *Steven* **had his laptop stolen** *last week*.
- We can use **get** instead of **have** only in informal conversation. *You should* **get** *those jeans shortened*.

Logical Assumptions/Deductions (*must, may/might, can't*)

- **Must** = almost certain that this is/was true *This diamond ring* **must** *be very expensive. Jim isn't home; he* **must** *have left for football practice.* (I'm sure/certain that sth is true.)
- **May/Might/Could** = possible that this is/was true *I have the day off tomorrow, so I* **might** *visit some friends. He* **may** *have sent the invitation to the wrong address; you'd better check.* (It is possible./It is likely./Perhaps.)
- **Can't/Couldn't** = almost certain that this is/was impossible *This* **can't** *be Joe's car; he sold his a month ago. She* **couldn't** *have made this delicious cake; she's hopeless at baking.* (I'm sure that sth isn't true, real, etc.)

Study these examples:

I'm sure she knows him well. *I'm sure he won't be late.*	**Present Infinitive**	*She must* **know** *him well.* *He can't* **be** *late.*
I'm certain he's working late. *I'm certain she won't be working tomorrow.*	**Present continuous Infinitive**	*He must* **be working** *late.* *She can't* **be working** *tomorrow.*
I'm sure she didn't study hard. *I'm sure he has studied hard.* *I'm certain John hadn't studied hard.*	**Perfect Infinitive**	*She can't* **have studied** *hard.* *He must* **have studied** *hard.* *John can't* **have studied** *hard.*
I'm certain she was sleeping. *I'm sure she hasn't been working hard lately.* *I'm sure Jane had been hiding.*	**Perfect continuous Infinitive**	*She must* **have been sleeping**. *She can't* **have been working** *hard lately.* *Jane must* **have been hiding**.

Causative

7 **Rewrite the sentences using the *causative*.**

1 Mrs Holmes is making their costumes.
   They *are having their costumes made by Mrs Holmes.*
2 When will the hairdresser dye Ann's hair?
   When ....?
3 Would you like somebody to pierce your ears?
   Would ....?
4 Barbara's dentist checked her teeth yesterday.
   Barbara ....
5 Andrea has asked the receptionist to reschedule her appointment.
   Andrea ....
6 A plastic surgeon had already fixed Janet's nose before her photo shoot.
   Janet ....

8 **Something bad happened to each of these people. Make sentences saying what happened to them. Use the *causative*.**

1 Barry (**his arm/burnt**) in the fire.
   Barry had his arm burnt in the fire.
2 Jo (**leg/break**) in an accident.
   ....
3 The hairdresser (**her salon/burgle**) last night.
   ....
4 Edward (**his car stereo/steal**) last week.
   ....

9 Complete the exchanges with the *causative form* of the verbs in brackets.

1 A: Your hair's a lovely colour!
   B: Thanks. I *had it dyed* **(it/dye)** by my hairdresser yesterday.

2 A: .... **(your eyes/test)** yet?
   B: Yes, I went to the eye specialist yesterday.

3 A: When will we see the photos from the performance?
   B: John ....
   (the photos/develop) this week.

4 A: Has the new fashion catalogue been posted yet?
   B: Yes. We .... **(it/deliver)** last week.

5 A: Do you wash your car by yourself?
   B: No, I .... **(it/clean)** every fortnight.

6 A: Did you paint your nails today?
   B: No, I .... **(them/paint)** yesterday.

10 Read the situations, then write sentences using the *causative form*.

1 A dressmaker will take in Pamela's dress this week. What will she do?
   She will have her dress taken in.

2 The manager has asked a psychologist to interview the applicants. What has he done?
   ....

3 Ken had someone draw a sketch of his dog. What did he do?
   ....

4 Nichole's jewellery was stolen yesterday. What happened to her?
   ....

5 A professional will train the Harrisons' dog. What will they do?
   ....

6 A beauty therapist was plucking Helen's eyebrows at 2:00. What was she doing?
   ....

7 A local designer made Mary a stunning outfit. What did she do?
   ....

8 The manager will ask someone to renovate the concert hall. What will he do?
   ....

11 Write the sentences in the *causative*.

1 The dietician is writing out a diet plan for Sue.
   Sue is having a diet plan written out.

2 Ms Smith asked her assistant to make reservations for dinner.
   ....

3 Will she ask someone to manicure her nails?
   ....

4 Harry had not asked the hotel to reserve a double room.
   ....

5 Ben's telephone service was disconnected because he hadn't paid his bill.
   ....

6 A beauty therapist was applying cream on Tina's face.
   ....

Logical assumptions/deductions

12 Rewrite the sentences using *must*, *can't* or *may*.

1 I'm sure she is a model.
   She *must be a model*.

2 I'm sure she isn't applying her own make-up.
   She ....

3 Perhaps a makeup artist is doing her make-up.
   A make up artist ....

4 I'm sure she didn't style her own hair.
   She ....

13 Complete the sentences using *must* or *can't*.

1 I'm sure she's talking about me behind my back.
   She *must be talking about me behind my back*.

2 I'm certain Mike lied about the accident.
   Mike ....

3 I'm sure Fiona hasn't had a facelift.
   Fiona ....

4 I'm sure Shelly didn't get her nose pierced.
   Sally ....

5 I'm certain she made up an excuse.
   She ....

6 I'm sure Fred has stopped bullying his classmates.
   Fred ....

7 I'm certain Clare has been looking for a new job.
   Claire ....

Clauses (purpose/result/reason/manner)

Clauses of Purpose

Clauses of purpose are used to explain why somebody does something.
We can express **positive purpose** using:

- **to + infinitive** *He's studying **to be** an architect.*
- **in order to/so as to + infinitive** (formal)
  *She left early **so as to** (be) on time.*
- **so that/in order that + can/will** (present/future reference)
  *I'll write down my PIN **so that/in order that** I will remember it at all times.*
- **so that/in order that + could/would** (past reference)
  *I drove my car to work **so that/in order that** I could be on time for the meeting.*
- **in case + present tense** (present/future reference)
  *Take some cash with you **in case** you need it.*
- **in case + past tense** (past reference)
  *She took an umbrella **in case** it rained.*

Note: **in case** is never used with **will** or **would**.
  *I'll pack some juice for the picnic, **in case** we **are** thirsty later. (NOT: ... ~~we will be~~)*

- **for + noun** (expresses the purpose of an action)
  *I've bought a new camera **for photography class**.*
- **for + -ing** form (expresses the purpose of something or its function)
  *This cream is used **for polishing** silver.*
- **with a view to + -ing** form
  *They started saving up **with a view to** buying a car.*

We can express **negative purpose** using:

- **in order not to/so as not to + infinitive**
  *He asked for a ride **in order not to/so as not to** be late.*

Note: We never use **not to** to express negative purpose.

- **prevent + noun/pronoun (+ from) + -ing** form
  *They put up notices to **prevent people (from)** walking on the grass.*
- **avoid + -ing** form
  *He bought a GPS **to avoid getting** lost.*
- **so that + can't/won't** (present/future reference)
  *I'll call her **so that** she **won't** feel lonely.*
- **so that + couldn't/wouldn't** (past reference)
  *She took a taxi **so that she wouldn't** be late for the meeting.*

Notes: Clauses of Purpose should not be confused with **clauses of result**.

- **Clauses of Purpose** are introduced with **so that/in order that** ...
  *He studied hard **so that** he would pass the exam.* (this shows purpose)
- **Clauses of Result** are introduced with **so/such ... that**
  *It was **such** nice day **that** we decided to have a picnic.*

Clauses of Purpose follow the rule of the sequence of tenses the same way that **Time Clauses** do.
*I'**ll turn** the lights on **so that** I **can** see clearer.*
*I **took** a jacket with me **so that** I **wouldn't** get cold.*

Clauses of Result

Clauses of result are used to express result. They are introduced with the following words/phrases:

- **as a result/therefore/consequently/as a consequence**
  *He was ill. **As a result/Therefore/Consequently/As a consequence**, he didn't go to work.*
- **such a/an + adjective + singular countable noun ... that**
  *He's **such a rude person that** nobody likes him.*
- **such + adjective + plural/uncountable noun ... that**
  *They lived in **such terrible conditions that** the local community decided to build them a house.*
  *We were having **such bad weather that** we decided to postpone the picnic.*
- **such a lot of + plural/uncountable noun ... that**
  *There were **such a lot of people** at the restaurant **that** we couldn't get a table. There was **such a lot of** snow **that** he couldn't move his car.*
- **so + adjective/adverb ... that**
  *The book was **so boring that** I couldn't keep my eyes open. She sings **so beautifully that** I listen to her for hours.*
- **so + adjective + a(n) + noun ... that**
  *It was **so bad a day** that we stayed in.*
- **so much/little + uncountable noun ... that**
  *He spends **so little** time studying **that** he'll fail his exams. He had **so much luggage that** he couldn't carry it.*
- **so many/few + plural noun ... that**
  *There are **so many applicants for the job that** I don't think I'll get the job.*
  *There are **so few tickets** left **that** we'll be lucky to find any.*

Clauses of Reason

Clauses of reason are used to express the reason for something. They are introduced with the following words/expressions: **because, as/since, the reason for/why, because of/on account of/due to, now (that), for,** etc.

- **because** *I didn't invite him **because** I don't like him.*
- **as/since** (= because) *We can't visit Stella **as/since** she's away on holiday.*
- **the reason for + noun/-ing** form
  __The reason for his delay/for his being__ late was the stormy weather.
  *__the reason why__ + clause The accident on the motorway was **the reason why** he was late.*
- **because of/on account of/due to + noun** *Some power lines fell down **because of/on account of/due to** strong winds.*
- **because of/on account of/due to the fact that + clause**
  *They couldn't concentrate **because of/on account of/due to the fact that** there was a lot of noise.*
- **now (that) + clause** *Now (that) we have graduated, we can get a job.*
- **for** (= because) (formal written style) A clause of reason introduced with **for** always comes after the main clause.
  *She was very quiet all day, **for** she had a lot on her mind.*

Clauses of Manner

Clauses of manner are introduced with **as, how, as if/as though, (in) the way (that), (in) the same way (as)** and are used to express the way in which something is done/said, etc.

- We use **as if/as though** after the verbs **act, appear, be, behave, feel, look, seem, smell, sound, taste** to say how somebody or something looks, behaves, etc.
  *The air is humid. It **feels as if/as though** it's going to rain.*
  We also use **as if/as though** with other verbs to say how somebody does something.
  *She sounds **as if/as though** she's really hurt by what you said.*

- We use **as if/as though** + **past tense** although we refer to the present when we are talking about an unreal present situation. **Were** can be used instead of **was** in all persons.
  *He acts **as if/as though** he knew everything.* (but he doesn't)
  *He behaves **as if/as though** he were a child.* (but he isn't)

- We can also use **as** in **clauses of manner** to mean 'in the way that'.
  *Try to do it **as** I've showed you.*

Note: We can use **like** instead of **as if/as though** in spoken English.
  *You look **like** you need a holiday.* (informal spoken English)

Clauses of Purpose

14 **Choose the correct item.**

1 She met up with me **to/so that** tell me all the latest gossip.
2 I didn't argue with the know-it-all **so as/so that** he would get bored and go away.
3 She acts like a drama queen **in order to/so that** attract attention.
4 Ignore her **so that/so as** she will stop talking about herself.
5 He did what she wanted **so that/so as** not to make her even angrier.
6 Take a book with you on the train **in case/so that** you get bored.
7 He walked away from her **in order/so that** not to gossip.
8 They do the Haka dance **so as to/so that** scare off their enemies.
9 They have put up signs to **avoid/prevent** people from entering the building.
10 An espresso maker is used **for/to** making Italian-style coffee.

15 **Rewrite the sentences using the words in brackets.**

1 The Maori tribe performed their dance with the purpose of welcoming their visitors. **(in order to)**
   The Maori tribe performed their dance in order to welcome their visitors.

2 They got tattoos on their bodies in the hope of looking more ferocious. **(so as to)**
   ....
   ....

3 He went to New Zealand because he wanted to learn more about the country's culture. **(so that)**
   ....
   ....

4 They use their dance movements as a way of frightening others. **(to)**
   ....
   ....

5 Ants use their antennae to communicate with other ants. **(so that)**
   ....
   ....

16 **Underline the correct item.**

Nileen was not a happy person as she wasn't pleased with the way she looked. She went to a cosmetic surgeon **1) so that/to** he would make her look like the person she wanted to be. First, she had her nosed fixed **2) in order to/so** to make it smaller and straighter. Then, she had a facelift **3) so as not to/because of** look her age. Finally, she had her eyebrows lifted **4) for/in order to** make her eyes look larger. In all, Nileen had 53 cosmetic surgeries and why? **5) To/So that** look like Queen Nefertiti, the Egyptian ruler!

Clauses of Result

17 Fill in: *so, such, such a/an.*

1 There was *such* noise in the room that I decided to leave.
2 It was .... terrible gossip that I told her to stop talking.
3 He acts .... aggressively that I can't stand to be around him.
4 She is .... ambitious person that she'd do anything to succeed.
5 He had .... curious tattoo on his arm that many people stared at it.
6 The cosmetic surgery was .... difficult that it took three hours to complete.
7 She is .... bully that none of the children will play with her.
8 She had .... few worries that she spent most of her time enjoying herself.

18 Join the sentences using the words in brackets.

1 She is a drama queen. She cries when she stubs her toe. **(such)**
She is such a drama queen that she cries when she stubs her toe.
2 They had an argument. They stopped speaking to each other. **(as a result)**
....
3 There was a lot to do. I became completely disorganised. **(such a)**
....
4 There aren't many people who like her. She'll be lucky to be invited to the party. **(so few)**
....
5 He kept throwing loud parties. He was asked to vacate the flat. **(consequently)**
....
6 She wore a lot of make-up. I couldn't see her face! **(so much)**
....
7 There were many people waiting in the queue. I decided to leave. **(so many)**
....

Clauses of Reason

19 Underline the correct item.

1 I don't like him **as/due to** he's always lying.
2 He asked for directions **for/because** he was lost.
3 **Due to/Since** the many complaints the company withdrew the faulty product from the market.
4 No one knows **the reason for/the reason why** people scratch their head when they are confused.
5 He was fired from his job **on account of/because** his irresponsible behaviour.
6 The psychologist asked her the question again **because/for** he knew she wasn't telling the truth.
7 **Since/For** so many people tell lies, you have to be very careful.
8 **On account of/Now that** he has apologised to me, we're friends again.
9 The electricity was cut off **because of/since** the lightning storm.
10 She blushed, **due to/for** she was telling a lie.

20 Fill in: *on account of, as, for, the reason why, the reason for, because of, because, now that, since* **or** *due to.* **Sometimes more than one answer is possible**

1 She didn't have any friends *on account of/due to* the fact that she was a terrible gossip.
2 .... his being happy is that he has solved her problem.
3 They aren't inviting him to the party ....
.... he bullies the other children.
4 .... I don't trust you is that you have lied to me many times.
5 .... we're all here, the psychologist will begin the test.
6 He won't believe her .... she never tells the truth.
7 I had to drop out of the study ....
an illness.
8 .... it was getting cold, Clark turned on the heating.
9 He decided to stay home .... the fact that he was ill.
10 You'd better tell her the truth, ...
she'll never trust you again.

21 **Combine the sentences using the words in brackets.**

1 She is a snob. We don't like her. **(as)**
We don't like her as she is a snob.

2 Pamela visited a psychologist. She had a big problem. **(due to)**
....

3 I can't tell you my secret. I don't trust you. **(since)**
....

4 She wants to know why we argued. She's a nosy parker. **(the reason why)**
....

5 There were so many dolphins that needed help. She made dolphins her life's work. **(due to the fact)**
....

6 There was a flock of sheep blocking the road. I couldn't get through. **(because of)**
....

7 The plane didn't take off. There was a mechanical problem. **(because of)**
....

8 The party is over. Now I'm going to clean up. **(now that)**
....

Clauses of Manner

22 **Fill in:** *as if/though*, *as*, *the same way as* **or** *the way (that)*.

1 Nelly felt *as if/though* she could swim for kilometres.

2 We simply love .... you've given your life to helping the dolphins.

3 They danced in .... Maoris had danced hundreds of years ago.

4 I feel .... I've been tricked!

5 Don't lie to me, just do .... you're told and go to your room.

6 He acted .... he were better than the rest of us.

23 **Put the verbs in brackets into the correct tense.**

1 She talks so much that it feels as if my ears *are going to fall off*! **(fall off)**

2 He stared at Nileen as though he .... **(never/see)** a woman who had had cosmetic surgery before.

3 You look wonderful! It looks as if you .... **(have)** a facelift.

4 Look at her face. It's as if it .... **(be made)** of plastic, but it isn't, of course!

5 She sat in the corner of the room. She looked as if she .... **(be)** lonely.

6 What's the matter? You look as if you .... **(cry)**.

7 I find that hard to believe. It sounds as if you .... **(not/tell)** the truth.

8 Melissa isn't very smart, but she acts as if she .... **(be)** a genius!

9 Kevin had a big problem. He looked as if he .... **(not/sleep)** for several weeks.

10 He acted as if he .... **(meet)** a lot of famous people, though I know for a fact that he hasn't.

11 Grant behaves as if he .... **(be)** the boss here, but he's not.

24 **Circle the correct word.**

1 She had cosmetic surgery ..... look like the famous Egyptian Queen Nefertiti.
(A) so as to **B** in order that **C** so that

2 She loves all creatures. ..... , she has made helping them her life's work.
A As the result **B** As the consequence
C As a consequence

3 There are ..... people who can stand her bossiness that she is never invited anywhere.
A so few **B** so many **C** so little

4 I don't like having a conversation with her ..... I can never get a word in edgeways!
A because of **B** due to **C** as

5 I went to New Zealand ..... studying the ways of the Maoris.
A in case **B** in order to **C** with a view to

6 She knows dolphins ..... well that she can write books about them.
A such **B** so **C** so much

Inversion

modal/auxiliary verb + subject + main verb

We use **inversion**:
- in questions.
  Can you come to the meeting?
- after the following words or expressions, when they come at the beginning of a sentence:

Seldom	Only in this way
Rarely	Only then
Little	Hardly (ever) … when
Barely	No sooner … than
Nowhere (else)	Not only … but (also)
Never (before)	Not until
Not (even) once	In no way
On no account	In/Under no circumstances
Only by	So/Such
	Not since, etc.

Never (before) have I watched such an interesting film.
Not only did I write the report but I (also) sent it to the manager.
Seldom does this restaurant get so crowded.
BUT
This restaurant seldom gets so crowded. (There is no inversion because the word seldom does not come at the beginning of the sentence.)

Note: When the expressions *only after*, *only by*, *only if*, *only when*, *not until/till* come at the beginning of a sentence, the inversion is in the main clause.
Only after I waved to him did he speak to me.
Only if you speak English will he understand you.

- with *so*, *neither*, *nor*, as to express agreement.
  "I love fresh fruits." "So do I." (We use 'so' to agree with an affirmative statement.)
  She was an excellent singer, as was her mother/and so was her mother.
  "Neither/Nor can I." (We use "neither/nor" to agree with a negative statement.)
  "I don't speak Spanish well. "Neither/Nor do I."
- with **should**, **were**, **had** when they come at the beginning of an if-clause instead of 'if'.
  Type 1: *Should he call, tell him to come here.* (= If he should call …)
  Type 2: *Were I you, I would go to the doctor.* (= If I were you …)
  Type 3: *Had I been invited, I would have gone to the wedding reception.* (= If I had been invited …)

main verb + subject

It is used in the following cases:
- after verbs of movement or adverbial expressions of place when they come at the beginning of a sentence.
  Inside the house ran the little boy.
  On the sofa slept the cat.
  Here comes the bride.
  There goes the last bus.

If the subject is a pronoun, there is no inversion.
Here he is. (NOT: Here is he.)
Off you go. (NOT: Off go you.)
- in direct speech when the subject of the introductory verb is a noun.
  "I love comedies," **said Jenny**.
  (**or** *… Jenny said.*)
  "Open your notebooks," **said the teacher**.
  (**or** *… the teacher said.*)
  BUT *"What can I do for you?"* **she asked**.
  (NOT: ~~asked she~~, because the subject of the introductory verb is a pronoun.)

Inversion

25 Fill in the gaps, as in the example.

1 I am having my hair cut tomorrow.
  So *am* I. My fringe's getting very long.

2 I didn't go shopping last week.
  Nor .... I. I didn't have any money to spare.

3 I've got some great news!
  So .... I. I've been accepted at university.

4 I have never won an award.
  Neither .... I. It's a little disappointing.

5 I'd like to help out at the homeless shelter this week.
  So .... I. Could we go together?

6 We'll be visiting the Natural History Museum this week.
  So .... we. We're going on a field trip for our science lesson.

7 I don't have a dance class tonight.
  Nor .... I. Our dance instructor is ill.

8 I'm not friends with Kylie anymore.
  Neither .... we. She's a bit of a snob.

9 I liked that documentary on reviving dinosaurs.
  So .... I. It was very interesting.

10 I'll send Kate a message.
  So .... I. I hope she can come to my party this weekend.

11 I need to see a dentist.
  So .... George. He had a bad toothache yesterday.

12 I wasn't expecting to see you here.
  Neither .... I. I'm so glad you came, though.

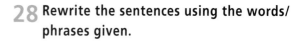
26 Rewrite the sentences, beginning with the words/phrases in bold.

1 The snow came **down**.
  Down came the snow.
2 My school is **opposite my house**.
  ....
3 The dancers came **onto the stage**.
  ....
4 The Shaolin monk climbed **up the wall**.
  ....
5 The dolphin jumped **through the hoop**.
  ....
6 The bee flew **from one flower to another**.
  ....
7 The town crier would walk **down the street**.
  ....
8 The robbers ran **out of the bank**.
  ....
9 The balloon flew **away**.
  ....
10 Your chance to let her know how you feel is **now**.
  ....

27 **Fay Davis is an animal trainer. She is talking to trainee students about training dolphins. Put the verbs in brackets into the correct form.**

The most important part of dolphin training is to establish trust between the animal and the trainer. Here are a few important things to remember: Dolphins should be taught to look above the water at a trainer. Only in this way 1) *can we teach* **(we/can/teach)** them to respond to certain sounds or hand signals. Not until they've been trained for months 2) .... **(they/will/be able)** to perform tricks. Under no circumstances 3) .... **(you/must/be)** aggressive with the dolphins. Never 4) .... **(we/punish)** the animals; instead we give them treats when they perform well. As you have already seen, not only 5) .... **(dolphin training/require)** patience but determination as well.

28 Rewrite the sentences using the words/phrases given.

1 I have seldom seen such a stunning performance.
  Seldom *have I seen such a stunning performance*.
2 She had no sooner left the house than she realised that she'd left her notes at home.
  No sooner ....
3 We not only saw a bottlenose dolphin, but we also got to swim with one.
  Not only ....
4 I have never heard such a frightening story before.
  Never ....
5 We realised only then that the house was haunted.
  Only then ....
6 There have seldom been so many homeless in this city.
  Seldom ....
7 Harry has not once donated to charity.
  Not once ....
8 You should not enter the laboratory under any circumstances.
  Under no circumstances ....
  ....
9 I understood what the lecture was about only after I had listened to it several times.
  Only after ....
  ....
10 Jane didn't know that she had won the first prize.
  Little ....
11 I haven't been to the theatre since last month.
  Not since ....
12 If I had known about Anna's graduation, I would have gone.
  Had ....
13 We haven't seen such natural beauty anywhere else.
  Nowhere ....
14 If I were you, I'd apply to lots of universities.
  Were ....
15 He had barely entered his house when the earth started shaking violently.
  Barely ....
  ....

Use of English
Part 1

1 For questions 1-12, read the text below and decide which answer (*A, B, C* or *D*) best fits each gap. There is an example at the beginning (0).

Example:

0 (A) couple   B set   C few   D duet

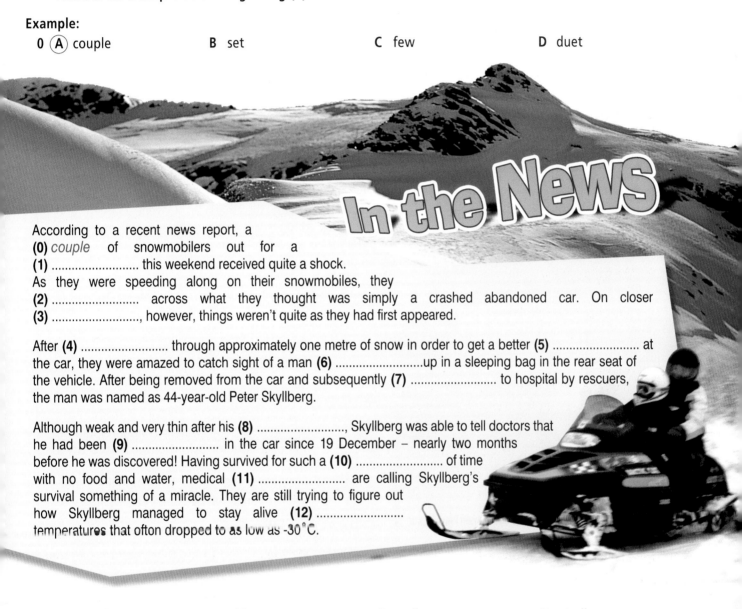

In the News

According to a recent news report, a **(0)** *couple* of snowmobilers out for a **(1)** .... this weekend received quite a shock. As they were speeding along on their snowmobiles, they **(2)** .... across what they thought was simply a crashed abandoned car. On closer **(3)** ...., however, things weren't quite as they had first appeared.

After **(4)** .... through approximately one metre of snow in order to get a better **(5)** .... at the car, they were amazed to catch sight of a man **(6)** ....up in a sleeping bag in the rear seat of the vehicle. After being removed from the car and subsequently **(7)** .... to hospital by rescuers, the man was named as 44-year-old Peter Skyllberg.

Although weak and very thin after his **(8)** ...., Skyllberg was able to tell doctors that he had been **(9)** .... in the car since 19 December – nearly two months before he was discovered! Having survived for such a **(10)** .... of time with no food and water, medical **(11)** .... are calling Skyllberg's survival something of a miracle. They are still trying to figure out how Skyllberg managed to stay alive **(12)** .... temperatures that often dropped to as low as -30°C.

1	**A** march	**B** ride	**C** cruise	**D** stroll
2	**A** went	**B** got	**C** came	**D** put
3	**A** examination	**B** investigation	**C** analysis	**D** inspection
4	**A** mining	**B** digging	**C** clawing	**D** scratching
5	**A** look	**B** scene	**C** view	**D** glimpse
6	**A** packed	**B** wrapped	**C** folded	**D** closed
7	**A** relocated	**B** wheeled	**C** transported	**D** carried
8	**A** ordeal	**B** trial	**C** agony	**D** torture
9	**A** trapped	**B** caught	**C** captured	**D** seized
10	**A** height	**B** width	**C** length	**D** depth
11	**A** personnel	**B** officers	**C** agents	**D** employers
12	**A** since	**B** although	**C** despite	**D** however

2 For questions 1-12, read the text below and decide which answer (*A*, *B*, *C* or *D*) best fits each gap.
There is an example at the beginning (0).

Example:

0 A exist   **(B)** live   **C** breathe   **D** survive

Shop 'Til you DROP!

If you **(0)** *live* to shop, then London is the place for you – it's a shopper's paradise! No **(1)** .... your budget, London has something for everyone. For those with little cash to **(2)** ...., there are the markets. Covent Garden and Camden Lock Markets are open daily and sell everything from clothes to jewellery to furnishings – all at **(3)** .... bottom prices.

If you're one of the lucky **(4)** .... for whom 'money is no object', you might want to stop by the world-renowned Harrods **(5)** .... located near Knightsbridge Tube Station. Occupying a huge 20,000 sq metre site and boasting over 330 departments full of brand name goods, Harrods is a **(6)** .... for those in need of a few hours of high-quality shopping **(7)** ....!

And, of course, no shopping spree in London would be **(8)** .... without a visit to Oxford Street in the city's West End. **(9)** .... as Europe's busiest shopping street, Oxford Street is **(10)** .... with shop after shop selling the widest range of designer **(11)** .... and luxury goods imaginable. Be honest, can you think of a better way to round **(12)** .... a day of shopping in England's capital?

1	**A** concern	**B** trouble	**C** problem	**D** matter
2	**A** give	**B** donate	**C** spare	**D** afford
3	**A** rubble	**B** boulder	**C** stone	**D** rock
4	**A** exceptional	**B** rare	**C** unusual	**D** few
5	**A** conveniently	**B** easily	**C** usefully	**D** helpfully
6	**A** need	**B** must	**C** should	**D** would
7	**A** treatment	**B** therapy	**C** remedy	**D** cure
8	**A** finished	**B** ended	**C** complete	**D** done
9	**A** Regarded	**B** Said	**C** Believed	**D** Thought
10	**A** encircled	**B** lined	**C** walled	**D** enclosed
11	**A** tags	**B** stickers	**C** tickets	**D** labels
12	**A** in	**B** on	**C** off	**D** up

3 For questions 1-12, read the text below and decide which answer (A, B, C or D) best fits each gap. There is an example at the beginning (0).

Example:

0 A known   **(B)** aware   **C** read   **D** informed

Answers from the

Ice Age

We are all too well **(0)** *aware* that the extinction of animal and plant species is one of the biggest and most horrifying threats **(1)** .... our planet these days. Having said that, there has recently been some good **(2)** .... out of Russia regarding something called regeneration – a(n) **(3)** .... solution to this ever-growing problem.

Regeneration involves **(4)** .... tissue from a plant or animal that has become extinct and 'bringing it back **(5)** .... life. In recent Russian experiments, scientists took fruit and seeds from the underground burrow of a long-dead Siberian squirrel and **(6)** .... to regenerate a beautiful flower called the Silene stenophylla. To **(7)** ...., it is the oldest plant to be produced from the innovative regeneration **(8)** ....

Understandably, experts are over the **(9)** .... about their success as it shows once and for **(10)** .... that tissue can survive ice conservation for thousands of years. Those who participated in the regeneration of the flower are pleased and are now **(11)** .... to find pre-historic squirrel tissue or perhaps even **(12)** .... tissue from the great woolly mammoth, which could lead to the resurrection of those two species.

1	**A** facing	**B** challenging	**C** heading	**D** confronting
2	**A** reports	**B** information	**C** news	**D** statements
3	**A** probable	**B** expected	**C** possible	**D** likely
4	**A** taking	**B** moving	**C** pulling	**D** bringing
5	**A** in	**B** for	**C** to	**D** at
6	**A** conducted	**B** managed	**C** directed	**D** succeeded
7	**A** time	**B** date	**C** month	**D** year
8	**A** action	**B** process	**C** practice	**D** manner
9	**A** moon	**B** galaxy	**C** star	**D** sun
10	**A** any	**B** both	**C** every	**D** all
11	**A** imagining	**B** hoping	**C** wishing	**D** dreaming
12	**A** freezing	**B** iced	**C** frozen	**D** icy

4 For questions 1-12, read the text below and decide which answer (*A, B, C or D*) best fits each gap. There is an example at the beginning (0).

Example:

0 **A** talking   **B** speaking   **C** saying   **D** telling

THE FRILLED Lizard

It goes without **(0)** saying, that our world is a truly weird and wonderful place. The Earth's forests, deserts and seas contain countless **(1)** .... of creatures – all diverse and all amazing in their own unique way. Let's take a **(2)** .... at a strange little reptile from 'The Land Down Under' commonly **(3)** .... to as the Frilled Lizard.

The Australian Frilled Lizard can grow to as much as one metre **(4)** .... length and weigh about half a kilo. It gets its **(5)** .... from the large frill of skin located between its head and neck. The **(6)** .... of the frill is to scare off enemies – it's constructed in such a **(7)** .... that when the lizard becomes frightened the frill flares out showing **(8)** .... its brightly-coloured scales.

(9) .... from the Frilled Lizard's unusual appearance, its movements too are rather curious. **(10)** .... the lizard usually gets around on all four of its legs, when it is alarmed it rises onto its **(11)** .... legs and flees to the nearest tree. It then quickly climbs up into the top branches of the tree and takes **(12)** .... until the danger has passed.

1 **A** numbers	**B** amounts	**C** quantities	**D** masses
2 **A** glimpse	**B** glance	**C** look	**D** stare
3 **A** considered	**B** called	**C** known	**D** referred
4 **A** in	**B** at	**C** for	**D** of
5 **A** name	**B** brand	**C** label	**D** make
6 **A** goal	**B** aim	**C** use	**D** purpose
7 **A** means	**B** method	**C** way	**D** mode
8 **A** off	**B** up	**C** into	**D** through
9 **A** Aside	**B** Besides	**C** Addition	**D** Except
10 **A** Despite	**B** However	**C** While	**D** As
11 **A** behind	**B** end	**C** rear	**D** hind
12 **A** safety	**B** cover	**C** protection	**D** security

5 For questions 1-12, read the text below and decide which answer (A, B, C or D) best fits each gap. There is an example at the beginning (0).

Example:

0 A argument   **B** disapproval   **(C)** controversy   **D** discussion

Education at Sea

Amid much **(0)** *controversy*, 16-year-old Laura Dekker, and her boat Guppy, have completed what many are calling a record-breaking solo global navigation. Unfortunately, however, Guinness World Records say they no **(1)** .... have a record for the youngest sailor. They, like the Dutch authorities who tried to **(2)** .... Laura's 27,000-mile trip around the world, feel **(3)** .... record-breaking attempts are far too risky for such a young **(4)** ....

Dutch school officials were also against Laura's endeavour as they were of the **(5)** .... that she should be in the classroom learning, not on a small boat sailing the high **(6)** .... However, unlike Abby Sutherland and Jessica Watson – two other teenagers who have sailed the globe – Laura **(7)** .... at ports all along the way to sleep, repair her 38-foot boat, and **(8)** .... up on homework.

While it may be **(9)** .... that Laura hasn't spent as much time in formal education as **(10)** .... her age, she has studied weather, tides, navigation and naval regulations extensively. **(11)** ...., she gave ten percent of all donations she received to the wildlife protection agency Sea Shepherd Netherlands – and that is a lesson in caring and generosity that we should all **(12)** ....

1	**A** higher	**B** longer	**C** wider	**D** deeper
2	**A** block	**B** close	**C** plug	**D** check
3	**A** so	**B** what	**C** how	**D** such
4	**A** player	**B** participant	**C** contestant	**D** opponent
5	**A** view	**B** idea	**C** mind	**D** opinion
6	**A** seas	**B** waters	**C** oceans	**D** lakes
7	**A** docked	**B** parked	**C** landed	**D** embarked
8	**A** make	**B** keep	**C** catch	**D** hold
9	**A** honest	**B** real	**C** true	**D** truthful
10	**A** others	**B** those	**C** them	**D** another
11	**A** Furthermore	**B** Although	**C** Therefore	**D** Despite
12	**A** discover	**B** notice	**C** learn	**D** spot

6 For questions 1-12, read the text below and decide which answer (A, B, C or D) best fits each gap. There is an example at the beginning (0).

Example:

0 **A** note   **B** message   **C** text   **(D)** letter

Bad Body Language

Today is one of those red **(0)** *letter* days. You've got a big job interview and you really want to get the position that you're applying **(1)** .... Your interview has been arranged for ten o'clock in the morning so you **(2)** .... bright and early to make sure you get there on time.

You go into the building where the meeting is to be held and take the lift to the fourteenth floor. You enter a very **(3)** .... office where a well-dressed secretary asks you politely to have a **(4)** .... You feel relaxed. You cross your legs and sit with your hands clasped loosely on your **(5)** ....

Then, your name is **(6)** .... and you are ushered into the inner office. Suddenly, you **(7)** .... out in a cold sweat. You feel nervous and you've got **(8)** .... in your stomach. You shake the interviewer's hand and you know your palm is **(9)** .... You sit facing the interviewer with your arms **(10)** .... tightly in a defensive pose. You are on **(11)** .... and your body language clearly indicates this fact. Deep **(12)** .... you know you are never going to get this job.

1	**A** on	**B** in	**C** for	**D** from
2	**A** set off	**B** pull away	**C** leave out	**D** go up
3	**A** clever	**B** smart	**C** keen	**D** brisk
4	**A** chair	**B** sofa	**C** seat	**D** place
5	**A** hip	**B** chest	**C** lap	**D** knee
6	**A** screamed	**B** yelled	**C** roared	**D** called
7	**A** break	**B** bend	**C** twist	**D** sprain
8	**A** bees	**B** worms	**C** moths	**D** butterflies
9	**A** sweaty	**B** damp	**C** soggy	**D** humid
10	**A** crossed	**B** hugged	**C** packed	**D** covered
11	**A** rim	**B** end	**C** edge	**D** limit
12	**A** behind	**B** down	**C** back	**D** over

Use of English
Part 2

1 For questions 1-12, read the text below and think of the word which best fits each gap. Use only one word in each gap. There is an example at the beginning (0).

Supervolcanoes

Ordinary volcanoes are formed by a column of very hot molten rock, known **(0)** *as* magma, rising to the earth's surface from deep within the Earth's core. This type **(1)** .... volcano usually erupts from the top of a cone shaped mountain, such as the famous volcano, Vesuvius, near Naples in Italy. However, there is **(2)** .... kind of volcano, called a supervolcano. It is one of the **(3)** .... destructive forces in nature but also one of the least understood. One thing that is known, though, is that if a supervolcano occurs, it **(4)** .... lead to mass extinction of species, and one species in particular **(5)** .... will be under threat is the human race.

So what is a supervolcano exactly and **(6)** .... often do they occur? A supervolcano is basically a huge reservoir, or lake, of boiling magma that lies close to the Earth's surface. They **(7)** .... found in six different regions of the planet. One of the most famous supervolcano regions is in Yellowstone Park in Wyoming, USA. This park is **(8)** .... area of outstanding natural beauty but it is also a sleeping giant that could wake **(9)** .... at any time. The last time the area erupted was **(10)** .... than 600, 000 years ago and a new eruption is now overdue. When it does erupt, because **(11)** .... day it will, it will virtually destroy the USA. And the dust cloud it creates will block **(12)** .... the sun causing the Earth's temperature to plummet threatening the whole planet with mass extinction.

2 For questions 1-12, read the text below and think of the word which best fits each gap. Use only one word in each gap. There is an example at the beginning (0).

Breakfast Time

There has been some controversy lately **(0)** *about* the poor nutritional value of most breakfast cereals. Manufacturers have been accused **(1)** .... not doing enough to reduce the amount of sugar in cereals as recent research has indicated that sugar levels are too high, especially **(2)** .... the cereals marketed at children. In fact, research suggests that some cereals have sugar levels that are **(3)** .... high that they should be labelled **(4)** .... sweets instead. So, what are consumers to do?

First of all, consumers should take **(5)** .... time to read the nutritional information on the cereal packets. It is better to choose whole grain cereals which are high in fibre and contain **(6)** .... added sugar or salt. Most research shows that those **(7)** .... eat more whole grains are **(8)** .... likely to suffer from heart disease or diabetes. And if you do feel the need to add something sweet to your cereal, just add nuts and fresh **(9)** .... dried fruit. Diet experts maintain that eating cereal is fine as **(10)** .... as consumers make the right choices **(11)** .... shopping. With a little care about the ingredients you use you **(12)** .... have a delicious balanced breakfast that will help give you the energy you need for the day.

3 For questions 1-12, read the text below and think of the word which best fits each gap. Use only one word in each gap. There is an example at the beginning (0).

space junk

The ever-growing amount **(0)** *of* rubbish on Earth has become a leading environmental issue, **(1)** .... what about rubbish in space? Debris, such as dust, floating rocks and ice, has **(2)** .... been present in space. Since the onset of the space programme in the 1960s, man has made great progress in space exploration but not without leaving **(3)** .... a trail of rubbish.

Space Junk, as it is commonly referred to, is everything **(4)** .... loose screws and marble-sized pieces of metal to parts of abandoned rockets and whole satellites. The vast majority of the debris is very small fragments, less **(5)** .... 1 centimetre in size. However, NASA estimates that there are potentially millions of objects, **(6)** .... small and large, orbiting the Earth in a giant cloud of junk!

All that rubbish may **(7)** .... be considered much of a problem as it's in outer space, but it can actually be very dangerous. This waste flies around earth .... to 28,000 km per hour and colliding objects create even more rubbish. Most space stations and crafts are equipped with "meteor bumpers" to deflect debris and minimise damage caused **(9)** .... this fast moving waste. Occasionally, some objects have fallen to Earth without burning **(10)** .... on re-entry into the Earth's atmosphere, bringing to light the possible dangers of space junk to Earth. Research into ways of collecting space rubbish is underway. Ideas like launching large magnetic nets or giant umbrellas to catch large amounts of debris **(11)** .... being examined. There is even talk of sending bin lorries to collect or vacuum up the litter. Whatever the solution, **(12)** .... thing is clear: the time has come to clean up space!

4 For questions 1-12, read the text below and think of the word which best fits each gap. Use only one word in each gap. There is an example at the beginning (0).

The Strange Portrait

For **(0)** many years the owners and visitors of Heale house in Devon were aware of a mysterious presence in the mansion. **(1)** .... single night, a female figure would appear in a haze of blue and drift **(2)** .... the fifteen-room house. The lady wore Edwardian clothes and terrified witnesses claimed she was always accompanied by the sound **(3)** .... piano music.

The owners of the old house could **(4)** .... explain this haunting as no one knew who the ghost could **(5)** .... Then one day, the owner, Alan Smith, was approached by a junk dealer **(6)** .... gave him an old painting that she believed belonged to the house. Mr Smith was shocked to see **(7)** .... the picture of a woman sitting at a piano, the same piano still in his drawing room, bore a striking resemblance **(8)** .... the mysterious ghost in his home.

Now very curious **(9)** .... the woman, Mr Smith began to dig deeper into the history of the house and its previous occupants. He eventually discovered that the woman in the picture was a lady called Mrs Bell, who **(10)** .... lived in the house at the beginning of the 20th century. Unfortunately, she soon got into money difficulties and lost **(11)** .... her possessions. Mrs Bell died not long after these sad events.

Strangely, as soon as Mr Smith returned the portrait to its rightful place on his drawing room wall, the ghost of Mrs Bell vanished and has not **(12)** .... seen since.

5 For questions 1-12, read the text below and think of the word which best fits each gap. Use only one word in each gap. There is an example at the beginning (0).

CHINESE MARTIAL ART

Martial arts, (0) whose proper name in China is Wushu, is often called Kung Fu (1) .... the West. Legend has it that martial arts were first developed about four thousand years (2) .... but the first recorded reference to martial arts is from the fifth century BC. Undoubtedly, Wushu developed (3) .... the centuries out of the need for self-defence, hunting techniques (4) .... military training. So a tradition of hand-to-hand combat and weapons practice grew from these needs. Wushu was even an important part of Buddhist monastic life. The monks of Shaolin are some of the (5) .... famous practitioners of Wushu and travel (6) .... over the world to give demonstrations of (7) .... skill and daring.

Martial arts, as well as (8) .... popular sports in China, are also an integral part of popular culture. The Hong Kong film industry (9) .... been making martial arts films (10) .... the 1920s. Not only have these films enjoyed widespread popularity across China, but they also came (11) .... the attention of international cinema-goers in the 1970s. It was the Bruce Lee film Enter The Dragon that first brought Kung Fu to other parts of the world. Even recently, the martial arts film Crouching Tiger, Hidden Dragon gained world wide acclaim and Chinese martial arts stars such (12) .... Jackie Chan and Jet Li are very well known in the West.

6 For questions 1-12, read the text below and think of the word which best fits each gap. Use only one word in each gap. There is an example at the beginning (0).

Changing Appearance

In today's world a (0) lot of attention is paid to body image and ways of helping people change their appearance are big business. There are plenty of ways people can change (1) .... looks. Some can be quite drastic and expensive, while (2) .... are less extreme and easily affordable by most people.

The most drastic way to change (3) .... you look is with cosmetic surgery. Cosmetic surgery to alter a person's figure or combat the signs of ageing (4) .... mainly used by women, although nowadays there are growing numbers of men turning (5) .... cosmetic procedures, too.

Another industry dedicated to improving looks is the diet and fitness industry. People join clubs or go to see a dietician in (6) .... to shed weight and get fit. This is sometimes easier said (7) .... done as most people have got used to not exercising enough and eating (8) .... much. It can be quite an effort to change the habits of a lifetime. Those (9) .... do manage will be healthier, though.

For those who just want to make the most of what they've got, there is the 'make-over'. This means learning about how (10) .... improve their appearance by wearing clothes that suit them and other style tricks. If they can afford a stylist, he or she will help them pick (11) .... clothes that flatter their figure. They will also learn about hairstyles or what kind of make-up to wear. Most Hollywood stars use a stylist to make (12) .... they always look their best.

Key Word Transformations

Complete the second sentence so that it has a similar meaning to the first sentence, using the word in bold. Use two to five words.

1 Carol found it difficult at first to drive on the right hand side of the road.
USED It took Carol a while .... on the right hand side of the road.

2 The film society has given Carol Berkley an award for her work.
PRESENTED Carol Berkley .... an award for her work by the film society.

3 I don't think he'll manage to get that promotion he wants.
SUCCEED I'm not sure he'll .... that promotion he wants.

4 You waited too long to get the concert tickets, which is why we don't have them now.
HAD If you .... long, we would have the concert tickets now.

5 Frank prefers reading books to watching TV.
RATHER Frank .... watch TV.

6 The trip was cancelled because of bad weather.
CALLED The trip was .... to bad weather.

7 Sally doesn't intend to leave her job.
INTENTION Sally has .... her job.

8 This is the best match I've ever seen.
BETTER I've .... match than that.

9 'What are you doing for Easter, John?' asked Lisa.
KNOW Lisa .... what John was doing for Easter.

10 I arranged for a courier to deliver your books today.
HAVING I'm .... a courier today.

11 It's been three years since I last saw Bea.
SEEN I .... three years.

12 It was wrong of Mr Fearne to shout at you like that.
SHOULD Mr Fearne .... at you like that.

13 Tanya was released from the hospital yesterday.
LET Tanya was .... the hospital yesterday.

14 It would be a good idea not to make the dog angry.
BETTER You .... the dog angry.

15 Amy doesn't fancy going out for pizza tonight.
PREFER Amy would .... out for pizza tonight.

16 'Whose camera is this?' she demanded angrily.
TO 'Who ....? ....' she demanded angrily.

17 I dislike the way you treat the staff.
APPROVE I .... the way you treat the staff.

18 It's a pity Daisy lost my favourite book.
HAD If .... lost my favourite book.

19 Your book report should describe the plot very well.
FULL Your book report should .... of the plot.

20 They say he bakes the best cakes in Lancashire.
SAID He .... the best cakes in Lancashire.

21 Her doctor advised her to get more exercise.
WERE 'If I .... get more exercise,' advised her doctor.

22 Please don't put your feet on the table.
MIND Would .... your feet on the table.

23 This spring's fashions have not changed since last year.
SAME This spring's fashions .... last year's.

24 She left university before graduating.
DROPPED She .... university before graduating.

25 The manager believes the team can win the cup.
CAPABLE The manager believes the team .... the cup.

26 The number of unemployed has increased steadily in the past few years.
RISE   There has been ....
.... the number of
unemployed in the past few years.

27 Peter won't win the race because he is slow.
TOO   Peter ....
.... the race.

28 Becky isn't friends with Stacy anymore.
LONGER   Becky ....
.... with Stacy.

29 That's the most gorgeous dress I've ever seen.
NEVER   I've ....
.... gorgeous dress than that.

30 Pamela said that she was sorry that she had hurt Bill's feelings.
APOLOGISED Pamela ....
.... Bill's feelings.

31 The price of the holiday includes three meals a day.
ARE   Three meals a day ....
.... the price of the holiday.

32 You should jump at the opportunity to go to Rome.
ADVANTAGE You should ....
.... the opportunity
to go to Rome.

33 This bag is the same as that one.
DIFFERENCE There ....
.... the two bags.

34 Peter went to the cricket game rather than the cinema.
INSTEAD   Peter went to the cricket game .....
.... the cinema.

35 Listening to very loud music caused him to go deaf.
RESULT   He went deaf ....
.... listening to very loud music.

36 Tony wants you to give him a call this afternoon.
TOUCH   Tony wants you to ....
.... him this afternoon.

37 We haven't been out to dinner in a long time.
AGES   It's ....
.... out to dinner.

38 Ben hasn't been successful as a lawyer.
NO   Ben ....
.... as a lawyer.

39 It isn't very sensible to allow the children to stay up so late
SHOULD   We ....
...... the children to stay up so late.

40 Louise booked her ticket online to make sure she got a good seat.
ORDER   Louise booked her ticket online ....
.... a good seat.

41 My grandfather likes to go for a walk every morning.
HABIT   My grandfather is ....
.... for a walk every morning.

42 Nobody, apart from Chris, had remembered to bring a map for the journey.
ONE   Chris was ....
..... to bring a map for the journey.

43 Paula isn't trying to pass her exams at all.
EFFORT   Paula ....
.... pass her exams.

44 It's too dark to read in here.
LIGHT   There's ....
.... to read in here.

45 I don't want to go into the town centre today.
FEEL   I don't ....
.... into the town centre today.

46 "I know you've taken cash from the till, Lola," said Mr Reilly.
ACCUSED   Mr Reilly ....
.... cash from the till.

47 It's been more than five years since I last saw James.
SEEN   I ....
.... more than five years.

48 John had never visited an art gallery before.
TIME   It ....
...... John had visited an art gallery.

49 Even though Tom can't speak Greek, he is very interested in Greek culture.
UNABLE   Despite ....
.... Greek, Tom
is very interested in Greek culture.

50 The band decided not to play at the concert at the last moment.
BACKED   The band ....
.... the concert at
the last moment.

51 My son is interested in studying for a career as an architect.
   LIKE   My son ....
   .... for a career as an architect.

52 It was impossible for the ferry to leave the port because of the high winds.
   PREVENTED   The high winds ....
   .... the port.

53 "Is it OK if I borrow your car, dad?" asked Ian.
   LEND   Ian asked his dad ....
   .... his car.

54 As soon as I met Finlay I immediately liked him.
   TOOK   I ....
   .... to Finlay.

55 He doesn't realise the risks involved in skydiving.
   AWARE   He ....
   ...... the risks involved in skydiving.

56 I'm certain you were really happy to get a pay rise.
   BEEN   You ....
   .... very happy to get a pay rise.

57 I'm sure he didn't intend to break the window.
   NO   I'm sure he had ....
   .... the window.

58 A famous architect is designing the new museum.
   DESIGNED   The new museum ....
   .... by a famous architect.

59 She closed the door to prevent the heat from escaping.
   SO   She closed the door ....
   .... not escape.

60 I think the new restaurant in town is fine.
   WRONG   There ....
   .... the new restaurant in town.

61 There's no chance of getting to the airport in time.
   POSSIBLE   It won't ....
   .... to the airport in time.

62 The band are selling their new album at the festival.
   SALE   The band's new album will............
   .... at the festival.

63 You really should learn some computer skills.
   HIGH   It's ....
   .... some computer skills.

64 Carol was the only one who didn't like the food.
   APART   Everyone ....
   .... Carol.

65 Tom advised Mary to see a doctor.
   WOULD   "If I ....
   .... see a doctor," Tom told Mary.

66 It might snow so wrap up well before you go out.
   CASE   Just ....
   ...., you had better
   wrap up well before you go out.

67 Could you look after the cat while we're away?
   CARE   Would you mind ....
   .... the cat while we're away?

68 You can be sure that Phil will help out if needed.
   RELY   You can ....
   .... out if needed.

69 Speaking in public comes naturally to Glen.
   USED   Glen ....
   .... in public.

70 Don't worry, I'll make breakfast this morning.
   NEED   Don't worry, you ....
   .... breakfast this morning.

71 The sports commentators were in complete agreement about the referee.
   COMPLETELY The sports commentators ....
   .... other about the referee.

72 You'll have no difficulty locating the restaurant.
   EASY   You'll find ....
   .... the restaurant.

73 You should have booked your tickets online.
   BETTER   It ....
   you had booked your tickets online.

74 She spent a while adjusting to the new system.
   TOOK   It ....
   .... to adjust to the new system.

75 Alice called me last night.
   CALL   I received ....
   .... last night.

76 It's your responsibility to keep the kitchen clean.
   RESPONSIBLE You ....
   .... the kitchen clean.

77 Joan asked how much the entrance fee was.
   COST   Joan wanted to ....
   .... the entrance fee.

78 My neighbours don't like me playing loud music at night.
   OBJECT   My neighbours ....
   .... loud music at night.

MUDDY MAYHEM

1 Complete the sentences with the word derived from the words in bold. There is an example at the beginning (0).

When we think of a volcano, we tend to think of molten lava; but did you know there is such a thing as a mud volcano? Unlike their **0)** *fiery* **(FIRE)** counterparts, mud volcanoes don't spit out lava, but instead produce a(n) **1)** .... **(ERUPT)** of hot mud! One such volcano can be found in Indonesia. It erupted in 2006, expelling 180 million litres of mud onto the district of Porong. **2)** .... **(BELIEVABLE)**, the mud has been flowing **3)** .... **(CONTINUOUS)** since then. It has now buried over seven square kilometres of terrain, leaving 60,000 people **4)** .... **(HOME)**. It has also become the largest mud volcano in the world, but unlike most volcanoes that occur **5)** .... **(NATURAL)**, this one was caused by human error! In fact, it is the **6)** .... **(DISASTER)** result of drilling a well in search of oil and gas. Experts believe that when the drill was removed from the ground, the pressure inside the well caused it to crack. Local **7)** .... **(RESIDE)** are furious at the drilling company, and although they have received **8)** .... **(COMPENSATE)** for the loss of their homes, they will be **9)** .... **(ABLE)** to return to the area for some time. It is estimated that the mud will continue to flow for another 26 years, and there is even the **10)** .... **(POSSIBLE)** of further outbreaks in the future.

Man-made Meat

2 Complete the sentences with the word derived from the words in bold. There is an example at the beginning (0).

Did you know that meat can be grown in a laboratory? Well, that's **0)** *precisely* **(PRECISE)** what some Dutch scientists have managed to do! Their goal is to **1)** .... **(ARTIFICIAL)** create a hamburger in order to reduce the need for farming. Meat produced the **2)** .... **(TRADITION)** way on farms has a massive impact on the planet. In fact, it is thought that livestock is responsible for 18% of greenhouse gas **3)** .... **(EMIT)**; a bigger share than transport! Many experts believe that farming is no longer **4)** .... **(SUSTAIN)**, which is why they have turned to lab-grown meat as a(n) **5)** .... **(EFFECT)** solution to the problem. Not only does it eliminate the need for farmland, but it is also **6)** .... **(ENVIRONMENT)** friendly! However, what will a synthetically grown hamburger taste like? Well, it will probably taste quite bland at first; but scientists are **7)** .... **(OPTIMIST)** that the flavour can be improved at a later stage. They even plan to ask a(n) **8)** .... **(FAME)** celebrity chef to cook their burger, who will **9)** .... **(HOPE)** transform it into a mouth-watering delight! So what do you think? Are you tempted by a test-tube hamburger, or do you find the thought of it rather **10)** .... **(APPEALING)**?

Word Formation

3 Complete the sentences with the word derived from the words in bold. There is an example at the beginning (0).

Lift-off!

While space **0)** *colonisation* **(COLONISE)** is unlikely to happen any time soon, Japanese **1)** .... **(ENGINE)** are busy working on the next best thing: a space lift that is 36,000 km high! This **2)** .... **(REVOLUTION)** lift will take passengers on a week-long journey into outer space! The final destination is a space station, where **3)** .... **(VISIT)** will be able to enjoy a(n) **4)** .... **(ORDINARY)** view of the Earth! So when will this **5)** .... **(MONUMENT)** lift be open to the public? Well, its **6)** .... **(CREATE)** predict that it will be built within the next forty years! However, don't get your hopes up too soon. The cost of this **7)** .... **(AMBITION)** venture has been estimated at over £6 billion and the funding has not yet been secured. Unless the **8)** .... **(CONSTRUCT)** company can acquire these crucial funds, this **9)** .... **(FUTURE)** lift will be nothing more than a dream. Still, the idea of taking a lift into space is extremely **10)** .... **(ATTRACT)**, and this project could mark the beginning of mankind's first steps towards living on another world!

4 Complete the sentences with the word derived from the words in bold. There is an example at the beginning (0).

Lost at Sea

On 7th November 1872, the *Mary Celeste* set sail on a **0)** *doomed* **(DOOM)** voyage across the Atlantic Ocean. The ship, manned by seven **1)** .... **(RELY)** and experienced crewmen, was loaded with cargo destined for Genoa, Italy. However, one month later, it was found abandoned, drifting **2)** .... **(AIMLESS)** in the middle of the ocean. The crew had completely **3)** .... **(APPEAR)**, leaving behind their entire cargo, which was almost perfectly intact! Not only that, but the ship was in **4)** .... **(EXCEPTION)** condition with all of the crew's **5)** .... **(BELONG)** still on board! Once the ship was returned to dry land, a(n) **6)** .... **(LENGTH)** investigation was launched to determine what had happened to the missing crew. However, after many months, investigators could not find a(n) **7)** .... **(LOGIC)** explanation for what had happened. There are many rumours surrounding the mystery, including **8)** .... **(SPECULATE)** that the crew encountered monsters out at sea! But the **9)** .... **(MYSTERY)** case has remained unsolved for centuries, and the **10)** .... **(LUCKY)** crew were never seen again.

5 Complete the sentences with the word derived from the words in bold. There is an example at the beginning (0).

Masters of MAGIC!

Have you ever thought about becoming a wizard? Then enrol at the *Grey School of Wizardry*; the world's only **0)** *officially* **(OFFICIAL)** recognised wizard academy! This **1)** .... **(CONVENTIONAL)** school offers classes in wand-making and even spell-casting! All classes are **2)** .... **(OPTION)**, but in order to obtain a degree in wizardry, students must **3)** .... **(SUCCESS)** complete seven years of study. For less dedicated **4)** .... **(MAGIC)**, the school offers summer camps that are a brief introduction into the peculiar and **5)** .... **(INTRIGUE)** world of magic. This unique **6)** .... **(ESTABLISH)** was founded by former school teacher Oberon Zell-Ravenheart. Oberon's goal was to make wizardry **7)** .... **(ACCESS)** to young people. His school is aimed at children aged between 11-18, but bizarrely, the **8)** .... **(MAJOR)** of his students are actually adults! Well, with **9)** .... **(MEMBER)** costing only a mere £18 per year, it's no wonder people are flocking to become **10)** .... **(PROFESSION)** wizard masters!

6 Complete the sentences with the word derived from the words in bold. There is an example at the beginning (0).

For most people, there is nothing more **0)** *disgraceful* **(DISGRACE)** than being known as a liar. However, for Glen Boylan, it is a badge of honour! Now, before you jump to **1)** .... **(CONCLUDE)**, Glen is not actually a(n) **2)** .... **(HONEST)** man. Rather, he is the proud winner of the World's Biggest Liar competition, where **3)** .... **(CONTEST)** compete to tell the most convincing lies to a panel of judges! The **4)** .... **(HUMOUR)** competition is held in honour of Will Ritson, a landlord who was famous for his **5)** .... **(RIDICULE)** stories. These stories became a(n) **6)** .... **(GLOBE)** sensation, and so, the World's Biggest Liar was established! The event is a fun-filled evening of light-hearted **7)** .... **(ENTERTAIN)**. Today's competition was no exception. When Glen finally took to the stage, the audience roared with **8)** .... **(LAUGH)** at his outlandish, but nonetheless believable story about a snail race! Then, when the night came to an end, Glen's **9)** .... **(IMPRESS)** fib won him the respected title of 'world's biggest liar'; and that's the **10)** .... **(TRUE)**!

Phrasal Verbs

1 Choose the correct particle.

1 Why don't you drop **by/out** for a coffee this morning?
2 These days computer skills are necessary to get **ahead/across** in most jobs.
3 Kelly did **up/over** her living room with antique furniture.
4 George never backs **over/down** from a fight.
5 I'll be there to back you **up/away** if you need any help.
6 Sam carried **out/on** running despite feeling exhausted.
7 They called **back/off** the concert due to rain.
8 Once you've signed the contract, you can't back **up/out** of the deal.
9 Rick didn't like his science project so he did it **up/over** again.

2 Fill in the correct particle(s).

1 You haven't handed .... your assignment yet.
2 They signed .... at the new health club down the street.
3 They were handing .... programmes as we entered the theatre.
4 Please back .... from the train doors to allow passengers to exit.
5 The doctor needs to run some tests .... the patient.
6 Fred forgot to back .... his files on his computer and lost all of them.
7 Shelly dropped .... of the course because she didn't like the teacher.
8 He tried to get his point .... but nobody would listen.
9 The bank robber handed the money .... to the police.

3 Choose the correct particle.

1 Ed picked **out/up** the newspaper and read it.
2 Most of the neighbourhood joined **up/in** the search for the missing boy.
3 The bodyguard kept the screaming fans **away/on** from the film star.
4 Jack's parents felt let **out/down** when he lied about his grades.
5 Mark is a bully and picks **on/out** younger children.
6 Mary loves to spend her weekends hanging **on/out** with her friends.
7 I was let **out/down** of the hospital this morning.
8 Tracy doesn't get **ahead/along** with her co-workers and often causes problems at work.
9 Alex kept **on/off** trying until he finally fixed his computer.

4 Fill in the correct particle.

1 Stacy couldn't pass .... the chance to go shopping.
2 A bus picks .... passengers for the airport every 15 minutes .
3 She felt dizzy and passed .... from the gas fumes.
4 Why don't you stick .... for the show later?
5 Tom needs some time to think the offer ....
6 Mike found the course difficult but stuck .... it until he passed.
7 She walks so fast that nobody can keep .... with her.
8 She picked .... several dresses she wanted to buy.
9 Please keep .... the pavement until the cement dries.

5 Choose the correct particle.

1 Please fill **out/up** this application form.
2 She is on the other line; could you please hang **out/on** for a moment?
3 Sadly, she passed **up/away** in the hospital last night.
4 Lea tried **on/out** the coat but it was too small.
5 Masked men held **up/on** the jewellery shop last night.
6 We need to think **over/up** a great theme for the spring dance.
7 Would you like to try **on/out** this laptop to see if you like it?
8 Jane filled **up/out** her car at the petrol station.
9 John tried **out/on** for the swim team at school.

Verbs/Adjectives/Nouns with Prepositions

A

abide by (v)
absent from (adj)
abstain from (v)
accompanied by (adj)
according to (prep)
account for (v)
accuse sb of (v)
accustomed to (adj)
acquainted with (adj)
addicted to (adj)
adequate for (adj)
adjacent to (adj)
advantage of (n) (**BUT** there's an **advantage in** – (have) an **advantage over** sb)
advice on/against (n)
afraid of (adj)
agree to/on sth (v)

agree with sb (v)
ahead of (prep)
aim at (v)
allergic to (adj)
amazed at/by (adj)
amount to (v)
amused at/with (adj)
angry at what sb does (adj)
angry with sb about sth (adj)
angry with sb for doing sth (adj)
annoyed with sb about sth (adj)
(in) answer to (n)
anxious about sth (adj)
(be) anxious for sth to happen (adj)
apologise to sb for sth (v)
appeal to/against (v)
(make an) appeal to sb for sth (n)
apply in writing (v)

apply to sb for sth (v)
approve of (v)
argue with sb about sth (v)
arrange for sb to do sth (v)
arrest sb for sth (v)
arrive at (a small place) (v)
arrive in (a town) (v)
ashamed of (adj)
ask about/for (v) (**BUT ask sb a question**)
assure (sb) of (v)
astonished at/by (adj)
attached to (adj)
attack on (n)
attack sb for sth (v)
attend to (v)
available to (adj)
(un)aware of (adj)

B

bad at (adj) (**BUT** He was very **bad to** me.)
ban sb from sth (v)
base on (v)
basis for (n)
beg for (v)
begin by/with (v)

believe in (v)
belong to (v)
benefit from (v)
bet on (v)
beware of (v)
(put the) blame on sb (n)
blame sb for sth (v)

blame sth on sb (v)
boast about/of (v)
bored with/of (adj)
borrow sth from sb (v)
brilliant at (adj)
bump into (v)
busy with (adj)

C

call at/on (phr v)
campaign against/for (v)
capable of (adj)
care about (v)
care for sb (v) (= like)
care for sth (v) (= like to do sth)
(take) care of (n)
careful about/of/with (adj)
careless about/with (adj)
cause of (n)
certain of (adj)
change into (v)
characteristic of (n/adj)
charge for (v)
charge sb with (v)
check for (v)
choice between/of (n)
clever at (adj) (**BUT** It was very **clever of** you to buy it.)
cling to sb/sth (v)
close to (adj)
coax sb into (v)
coincide with (v)
collaborate with (v)
collide with (v)

comment on (v)
communicate with (v)
compare to (v) (show the likeness between sb/sth and sb/sth else)
compare with (v) (how people and things are alike and how they are different)
comparison between (n)
compete against/for/with (v)
complain of (v) (= suffer from)
complain to sb about sth (v) (= be annoyed at)
compliment sb on (v)
comply with (v)
conceal sth from sb (v)
concentrate on (v)
(have) confidence in sb (n)
confident in (adj)
confine to (v)
confused about/by (adj)
confusion over (n)
congratulate sb on sth (v)
connection between (n) (**BUT in connection with**)
connect to/with (v)

conscious of (adj)
consider sb for sth (v)
consist of (v)
contact between (n) (**BUT in contact with**)
content with (adj)
contrary to (adj)
contrast with (v)
contribute to (v)
convert to/into (v)
cope with (v)
correspond to/with (v)
count against/towards (v)
count on sb (phr v)
covered in/with (adj)
cover in/with (v)
crash into/through (v)
(have) a craving for sth (n)
crazy about (adj)
crowded with (adj)
cruel to (adj)
cruelty towards/to (n)
cure for (n)
curious about (adj)

D

damage to (n)
date back to (v)
date from (v)
deal with (v)
dear to (adj)
decide on/against (v)
decrease in (n)
dedicate to (v)
deficient in (adj)
definition of (n)
delay in (n)
delighted with (adj)
delight in (v)
demand for (n)
demand from (v)
depart from (v)
departure from (n)
dependent on (adj)

depend on/upon (v)
deputise for (v)
descended from (adj)
describe as (v)
describe sb/sth to sb else (v)
description of (n)
die from/of (v)
die in an accident (v)
(have) difference between/of/in (n)
differ from (v)
different from (adj)
difficulty in/with (n)
disadvantage of (n) (**BUT** there's a **disadvantage in** doing sth)
disagree with (v)
disappointed with/about/by (adj)
disapprove of (v)
discharge sb from (v)

discouraged from (adj)
discussion about/on (n)
disgusted by/at (adj)
dismiss from (v)
dispose of (v)
disqualified from (adj)
dissatisfied with (adj)
distinguish between (v)
divide between/among (v)
divide into/by (v)
donate sth to sb/sth (v)
do sth about (v)
doubtful about (adj)
dream about (v)
dream of (v) (= imagine)
dressed in (adj)

E

eager for (adj)
economise on (v)
efficient at (adj)
(put) effort into sth (n)
emphasis on (n)
engaged to sb/in sth (adj)
engagement to sb (n)
enthusiastic about (adj)
envious of (adj)
equal to (adj)
escape from/to (v)

example of (n)
excellent at (adj)
exception to (n) (**make an exception of sth/sb** = treat sth/sb as a special case – **take exception to sth** = object to sth)
exchange sth for sth else (v)
excited about (adj)
exclaim at (v)
excuse for (n)
excuse sb for (v)

exempt from (adj)
expel from (v)
experienced in/at (adj)
experiment on/with (v)
expert at/in (sth/doing sth) (n) (= person good at)
expert on (n) (= person knowledgeable about a subject)
expert with sth (n) (= good at using sth)

F

face up to (phr v)
fail in an attempt (v)
fail to do sth (v)
failure in (an exam) (n)
failure to (do sth) (n)
faithful to (adj)
fall in (n)
familiar to sb (adj) (= known to/by sb)

familiar with (adj) (= have knowledge of)
famous for (adj)
fed up with (adj)
fill sth with sth else (v)
finish with (v)
fire at (v)
flee from (v)
fond of (adj)

forget about (v)
forgive sb for (v)
fortunate in (adj)
free from/of/for (adj)
friendly with/to (adj)
frightened of (adj)
full of (adj)
furious with sb about/at sth (adj)

G

generosity to/towards (n)
genius at (n)
glance at (v)
glare at (v)

good at (adj) (**BUT** He was very **good to** me.)
grateful to sb for sth (adj)
grudge against (n)

guess at (v)
guilty of (adj) (**BUT** He felt **guilty about** his crime.)

H

happen to (v)
happy about/with/for (adj)
harmful to (adj)
head for (v)
hear about (v) (= be told)
hear from (v) (= receive a letter)

hear of (v) (= learn that sth or sb exists)
heir to (n)
hinder from (v)
hint to sb about sth (v) (**BUT hint at** sth)

hope for (v)
hopeless at (adj)
(no) hope of (n)
hope to do sth (v)

I	idea of (n) identical to (adj) ignorant of/about (adj) ill with (adj) impact on (n) important to sb (adj) impressed by/with (adj) (make an) impression on sb (n) improvement in/on (n) incapable of (adj) include in (v) increase in (n)	independent of/from (adj) indifferent to (adj) indulge in (v) inferior to (adj) information about/on (n) (be) informed about (adj) inject sth into sb/sth (v) inoculate against (v) insist on (v) instead of (prep) insure against (v) intelligent at (adj)	(have no) intention of (n) intent on (adj) interested in (adj) interest in (n) interfere with/in (v) interpretation of (n) invasion of (n) invest in (v) invitation to (n) invite sb to (v) involve in (v) irritated by (adj)
J	jealous of (adj)	join in (v)	joke about (v)
K	keen on sth (adj) keen to do sth (adj) key to (n)	kind to (adj) knock at/on (v) know about/of (v)	knowledge of (n)
L	(be) lacking in sth (adj) lack of (n) laugh at (v) lead to (v) lean on/against (v)	learn about/by (v) leave for (v) (= head for) lend sth to sb (v) listen to (v) live on (v)	long for (v) look at (v) look for (v) (= search for)
M	married to (adj) marvel at (v)	mean to (adj) mention to (v)	mistake sb for (v) mix with (v)
N	name after (v) necessary for (adj) need for (n) neglect of (n)	nervous about (adj) new to (adj) nice to (adj) nominate sb (for/as sth) (v)	(take) (no) notice of (n) notorious for doing sth (adj)
O	obedient to (adj) objection to (n) object to (v) obliged to sb for sth (adj)	obsessed with (adj) obvious to (adj) occur to (v) (take) offence at (n)	operate on (v) opinion of/on (n) opposite of/to (n) optimistic about sth (adj)
P	packed with (adj) part with (v) patient with (adj) pay by (cheque) (v) pay for (v) (**BUT pay a bill**) pay in (cash) (v) peculiar to (adj) persist in (v) (**BUT insist on**) (take a) photograph of (n) picture of (n) pity for (n) (take) pity on sb (exp) pleasant to (adj)	pleased with (adj) (take) pleasure in (n) (have the) pleasure of (n) point at/to/towards (v) (im)polite to (adj) popular with (adj) praise sb for (v) pray for sb/sth (v) (have a) preference for (n) prefer sth to sth else (v) prepare for (v) present sb with (v) prevent sb/sth from (v)	(take) pride in (n) pride oneself on sth/on doing sth (v) profit from (v) prohibit sb from doing sth (v) prone to (adj) protect against/from (v) protection against/from (n) protest about/against (v) proud of (adj) provide sb with (v) provide sth for sb (v) punish sb for (v) puzzled about/by (adj)
Q	qualified for (adj) qualify as/in (v)	quarrel about sth/with sb (v/n) quick at (adj)	quotation from (n)

R

rave about (v)
reaction to (n)
react to (v)
ready for (adj)
reason for (n)
reason with (v)
rebel against (v)
receive from (v)
(keep) a record of (n)
recover from (v)
reduction in (n)
(in/with) reference to (n)
refer to (v)
refrain from (v)
regard as (v)

regardless of (prep)
related to (adj)
relationship between (n) (**BUT** a **relationship with** sb)
relevant to (adj)
rely on (v)
remind sb of/about (v)
remove from (v)
replace sth with sth else (v)
reply to (n/v)
report on (n/v)
reputation for/of (n)
research on/into (n)
respected for (adj)
respect for (n)

respond to (v)
responsibility for (n)
responsible for (adj)
result from/in (v) (= be the consequence of)
result in (v) (= cause)
resulting from (adj)
result of (n)
rhyme with (v)
rich in (adj)
(get) rid of (phr)
rise in (n)
(make) room for (n)
roll across (v)
rude to (adj)

S

safe from (adj)
same as (adj)
satisfied with/by (adj)
save sb from (v)
save sth for sb (v)
scared of (adj)
search for (v/n)
(be in) search of (n)
sensible of sth (adj) (= aware of sth)
sensitive to (adj)
sentence sb to (v)
separate from (v)
serious about (adj)
settle for/on (v)
share in/of sth (n)
shelter from (v)
shocked at/by (adj)
shoot at (v)
short of/on (adj)
shout at (v)
shy of (adj)

sick of (adj)
silly to do sth (adj) (**BUT** it was **silly of** him)
similar to (adj)
skillful/skilled at (adj)
slam into (v)
slow in/about doing sth/to sth (adj)
smell of (n/v)
smile at (v)
solution to (n)
sorry about (adj) (= feel sorry for sb) (**BUT** I'm **sorry for** doing sth)
speak to/with sb about (v)
specialise in (v)
specialist in (n)
spend money on sth (v)
spend time in/doing sth (v)
split into/in (v)
spy on (v)
stare at (v)

strain on (n)
stranded on/in/by (adj)
study for (v)
subject to (adj/v)
submit to (v) (**BUT submit sth for** publication)
subscribe to (v)
succeed in (v)
suffer from (v)
sufficient for sth/sb (adj)
suitable for (adj)
superior to (adj)
sure of/about (adj)
surprised at/by (adj)
surrender to (v)
surrounded by (adj)
survive on (v)
suspect sb of (v)
suspicious of (adj)
sweep sb/sth away (v)
sympathetic to/towards (adj)
sympathise with (v)

T

take sth to sb/sth (v)
talent for sth (n)
talk to sb about sth (v)
(have) taste in (n)
taste of (v)
terrible at (adj)
terrified of (adj)
thankful for (adj)

thank sb for (v)
think about/of (v)
threaten sb with sth (v)
threat to sb/to sth/of sth (n)
throw at (v) (in order to hit)
throw to (v) (in order to catch)
tired of (adj) (= fed up with)
tire of (v)

translate from ... into (v)
tread on (v)
trip over (v)
trouble with (n)
turn into/to (v)
typical of (adj)

U

unaware of (adj)
understanding of (n)
uneasy about (adj)

upset about/over sth (adj)
used to (adj)
useful for/to (adj)

(make) use of (n)

V	valid for (length of time) (adj) valid in (places) (adj)	value sth at (v) vote against/for (v)	vouch for (v)
W	wait for (v) warn sb against/about/of (v) waste (time/money) on (v) weak in/at (adj)	wink at (v) wonder about (v) work as/in/at sth (v) worry about (v)	worthy of (adj) write about (v) write to sb (v) wrong about (adj)

1 Fill in the correct preposition.

1 All incomplete assignments will count .... your final mark for the course.
2 The story is based .... an actual event.
3 Martin is very efficient .... cutting costs and saving money.
4 Anna doesn't really care .... ice-skating; she prefers skiing instead.
5 How did the murderer dispose .... the evidence?
6 None of the employees at the bank could account .... the missing money.
7 They congratulated me .... my win.
8 Tanya really delights .... gossiping about others.
9 Two students were caught cheating and were expelled .... school.
10 Beware .... snakes while walking in the desert.

2 Choose the correct preposition.

1 Carbon emissions are harmful **to/at** the environment.
2 My professor was really impressed **by/from** my knowledge of the subject.
3 It's the manager's job to deal **with/about** any problems customers may have.
4 Are you acquainted **with/about** the shop's returns policy?
5 Elaine is a genius **at/on** maths.
6 Mike is very faithful **to/by** his friends and would never betray them.
7 He has an extensive knowledge **of/on** dinosaurs.
8 During the sales, the shops are crowded **with/from** frantic shoppers.
9 She needs some advice **on/for** how to study more effectively.
10 The conference began **with/from** a speech by the president.

3 Fill in the correct preposition.

1 The council nominated him .... the new position.
2 Tim has an interest .... politics.
3 He was unfairly dismissed .... his job.
4 Paul is quite capable .... doing the work himself.
5 There was an attack .... the small village by enemy soldiers.
6 Sarah was exempt .... taking the exam due to her recent illness.
7 Carol didn't get the job due to her lack .... experience.
8 Peter was irritated .... the noise in the library.
9 Mr Foster donated his collection of rare books .... the school library.
10 Max is hopeless .... cooking; he doesn't know how to make anything.

4 Choose the correct preposition.

1 The government promised a reduction **in/of** public spending.
2 Jerry couldn't part **with/from** his old bike so he decided to keep it.
3 Mary dreams **of/at** becoming a famous actress someday.
4 Mike's parents were ashamed **of/from** his behaviour during dinner.
5 The group's work concentrates mainly **on/at** stopping deforestation.
6 The boys are obsessed **over/with** playing computer games.
7 The stranger mistook me **for/with** a friend and started talking to me.
8 Can I exchange this blouse **to/for** one in a larger size?
9 The waste from the factory has a terrible impact **over/on** the environment.
10 More money is necessary **for/to** the shelter, otherwise it will have to close.

5 Fill in the correct preposition.

1 They were stranded .... the road after their car had broken down.
2 Paul is terrified .... spiders.
3 I am responsible .... booking our flights.
4 Barry couldn't distinguish .... the original painting and the copy.
5 A poor diet contributes .... heart disease.
6 The dog sat next to the table and begged .... food.
7 Kyle feels uneasy .... flying.
8 The tsunami swept .... the coastal village.
9 We decided .... buying a car until we have more money.
10 James insisted .... paying for our dinner.

6 Choose the correct preposition.

1 I completely agree **on/to/with** Jack about the changes at work.
2 Joel is an expert **with/at/of** fixing computer problems.
3 You will get a better price if you pay **by/in/for** cash.
4 What was his reason **over/with/for** being late?
5 The boy threw a rock **at/to/in** the window trying to break it.
6 Ian blamed Fred **on/for/with** the mistakes in the report.
7 She died **in/by/from** a heart attack.
8 Sheila felt guilty **about/of/to** taking the money.
9 The boy looked familiar **with/to/for** David; he knew he had seen him somewhere before.
10 This coupon is valid only **in/on/to** certain supermarkets.
11 Alex survived only **from/with/on** water for three days.
12 Phillip takes pleasure **at/in/of** helping others.
13 We are all confused **about/for/with** the time of the meeting.
14 The customer complained to the manager **of/for/about** the poor service.
15 Have you heard **of/from/about** Mina recently?
16 There is a huge demand **for/from/against** the software program; everyone is buying it.
17 Fortunately, Daniel's part-time job doesn't interfere **on/with/ at** his studies.

7 Fill in the correct preposition.

1 Terry is angry with Jan .... using her laptop.
2 The shelter provides homeless people .... food.
3 The judge sentenced the thief .... ten years in prison.
4 There has been no contact .... the two brothers since they were children.
5 Tracy is optimistic .... being accepted at the university.
6 Gary is a specialist .... cosmetic surgery.
7 Carla didn't get the job; she wasn't qualified .... the position.
8 Kyle bumped .... an old classmate at the supermarket.
9 My friends are jealous .... my new car.
10 I was wrong .... Kay; she is actually a very good person.
11 Do you know the solution .... the problem?
12 Her books are popular .... teenagers.
13 Tony can rely .... his friends for help anytime.
14 They succeeded .... collecting enough clothes for the homeless shelter.
15 The students were prohibited .... demonstrating on the university campus.
16 The lawyer refused to comment .... the case and quickly left the courthouse.
17 Nobody laughed .... any of Bob's jokes.
18 The children have grown accustomed .... going to bed late at night.
19 When Stacy was sick, her mother arranged .... her to see a doctor.
20 Jason is confident .... his ability to ski and hopes to win the competition tomorrow.
21 After Rosie recovered from surgery, she was discharged .... the hospital.
22 Darren dislikes reading and gets bored .... it very easily.
23 Instead of dieting, Jenny prefers to indulge .... eating chocolate!
24 James is not very keen .... going shopping.
25 Sally suspects Tom .... lying.
26 Harry is enthusiastic .... his new job.
27 Ken disagreed .... Tom's statement.
28 Janet isn't fond .... doing housework.

Further Matura
Practice

Further Matura Practice

Rozumienie ze słuchu

Part 1

🎧 Usłyszysz dwukrotnie wiadomości radiowe. Na podstawie informacji zawartych w nagraniu zdecyduj, które zdania (1–5) są zgodne z treścią tekstu (TRUE), a które nie (FALSE). Zaznacz znakiem X odpowiednią rubrykę w tabeli.

	TRUE	FALSE
1		
2		
3		
4		
5		

1 Some people were seriously injured by the avalanche.
2 Skiers and snowboarders rescued the trapped skiers.
3 The injured were transported by chairlift down the mountain.
4 The cause of the avalanche is unknown.
5 The ski resort is currently closed.

Part 2

🎧 Usłyszysz rozmowę pięciu osób na temat pewnych osiągnięć. Do każdej osoby (1–5) dopasuj zdanie (A–F). W każdą kratkę wpisz odpowiednią literę. Jedno zdanie zostało podane dodatkowo i nie pasuje do żadnej osoby.

Speaker 1	
Speaker 2	
Speaker 3	
Speaker 4	
Speaker 5	

A A scholarship for people in developing countries.
B A motorist who obtained a license.
C An event to raise money for charity.
D An invention that provides aid to the third world.
E Someone who placed first in a sports competition.
F A successful business tycoon.

Part 3

🎧 Usłyszysz dwukrotnie nagranie dotyczące wypadku w kopalni. Z podanych odpowiedzi wybierz właściwą, zgodną z treścią tekstu. Zakreśl literę A, B, C lub D.

1 Which is true about Dan?
  A He lacked experience in mining.
  B He knew his job could be unsafe.
  C He was never prepared for work.
  D He was late for work.

2 The miners made a mistake drilling because
  A it was too dark to see.
  B they had read the map incorrectly.
  C the map was wrong.
  D the map had been damaged by water.

3 The rescuers finally agreed to
  A pump the water out.
  B feed a long pipe into the mine.
  C send divers into the mine.
  D use a giant drill.

4 What was the biggest problem for the miners?
  A The temperature in the mine.
  B Feeling depressed.
  C The rising of the water.
  D Lack of nourishment.

5 What delayed the rescue mission?
  A It was too dark to drill.
  B An electrical problem.
  C The drill broke.
  D The rock was very dense.

Rozumienie tekstów pisanych
Part 1

Przeczytaj tekst. Z podanych odpowiedzi wybierz właściwą, zgodną z treścią tekstu. Zakreśl literę A, B, C lub D.

1 It's a special evening at the opera house because
- A it is the last performance for La Sorelli.
- B a ghost had been seen for the first time.
- C it was the last performance at the opera house.
- D the management was leaving.

2 La Sorelli was annoyed because
- A she was interrupted by the other dancers.
- B she was having difficulties learning her speech.
- C she didn't like Jammes in her dressing room.
- D she didn't want the managers to resign.

3 The text describes La Sorelli's dressing room as
- A crowded with many things.
- B considerably better than the other dancers'.
- C similar to her mother's.
- D a place where the dancers socialised.

4 La Sorelli inquired about the ghost because
- A she wanted to prove that ghosts didn't exist.
- B she was very curious about the ghost.
- C she wanted to make fun of Jammes.
- D she thought Jammes was lying.

5 It was common knowledge at the opera house that the ghost
- A was an undertaker.
- B was trying to frighten people.
- C was a joke and not real.
- D moved quietly around the opera house.

IS IT THE GHOST?

It was the evening on which the managers of the Opera, were giving a last gala performance to mark their retirement. Suddenly the dressing-room of La Sorelli, one of the principal dancers, was invaded by half-a-dozen young ladies of the ballet, who had come up from the stage. They rushed in with great confusion, some forcing laughter and others crying in terror. Sorelli, who wished to be alone for a moment to "run through" the speech which she was to make to the resigning managers, looked around angrily at the mad crowd. It was little Jammes—the girl with the turned-up nose, the forget-me-not eyes, the rosy cheeks and the lily-white skin—who explained in a trembling voice:

"It's the ghost!" And she locked the door.

Sorelli's dressing-room was decorated with elegance. A mirror, a sofa, a dressing-table and a cupboard provided the necessary furniture. On the walls hung a few engravings belonging to her mother who had known the glories of the old Opera in the Rue le Peletieri. But the room seemed a palace to the brats of the ballet, who were lodged in common dressing-rooms where they spent their time singing, quarreling, smacking the dressers and hair-dressers and buying one another drinks, until the stage bell rang.

Sorelli was very suspicious. She shivered when she heard little Jammes speak of the ghost, called her a "silly little fool" and then, as she was the first to believe in ghosts in general, and the Opera ghost in particular, at once asked for details:

"Have you seen him?"

"As plainly as I see you now!" said little Jammes, whose legs were giving way beneath her, and she dropped with a moan into a chair.

Thereupon little Giry—the girl with eyes black as plums, hair black as ink, a dark complexion and a poor little skin stretched over poor little bones— added:

"If that's the ghost, he's very ugly!"

"Oh, yes!" cried the chorus of ballet-girls.

And they all began to talk together. The ghost had appeared to them in the shape of a gentleman in dress-clothes, who had suddenly stood before them in the passage, without their knowing where he came from. He seemed to have come straight through the wall.

"Rubbish" said a calmer one of them. "You see the ghost everywhere!"

And it was true. For several months, there had been nothing discussed at the Opera but this ghost in dress-clothes who stalked from top to bottom the building, like a shadow, who spoke to nobody, to whom nobody dared speak and who vanished as soon as he was seen, no one knowing how or where. Like a real ghost, he made no noise while walking. At first people laughed and made fun of the disturbing idea of a ghost dressed like a man of fashion or an undertaker; but the ghost legend soon grew to enormous proportions among the ballet dancers.

Adapted from The Phantom of the Opera by Gaston Leroux

Part 2

Przeczytaj tekst, z którego usunięto pięć zdań. Uzupełnij luki (1–5) brakującymi zdaniami (A–F), tak aby powstał spójny i logiczny tekst. Wpisz odpowiednie litery obok numerów luk. Jedno zdanie zostało podane dodatkowo i nie pasuje do żadnej luki.

The Power of a Suit

Austin Whitney has been unable to use his legs since a car accident left him paralysed several years ago. At the time, doctors told him that he would never be able to walk again. **1** However, this difficult change didn't stop Austin from fulfilling his dreams of going to university. After many difficult years, today is his graduation ceremony. He sits and listens as the list of students' names are read out. He watches as his classmates walk across the auditorium to receive their diplomas. Then he hears his name called. **2** The audience cheers and claps loudly!

A miraculous recovery? Actually, Austin is able to walk today with the aid of a special device designed by a team of engineers. **3** The team refers to their invention as "eLegs". This device has a computer program that can recognise and read the arm movements of a patient who is using a set of crutches. So as the patient puts one crutch forward, eLegs moves the opposite leg! While eLegs are a great invention, they are just the first stage of a much bigger plan. Scientists in Japan are currently developing a full-body cyber suit to combat almost all physical disabilities. In fact, a prototype already exists and has been built to help those who have suffered spinal cord injuries and are undergoing rehabilitation. It is called HAL (Hybrid Assistive Limb). **4** Its robotic limbs are controlled by the power of thought! Tiny electronic sensors on the suit pick up brain signals intended for muscle control. These electronic sensors then signal HAL's mechanical limbs to move. This enables a disabled person to perform tasks they would otherwise find difficult, like standing and climbing stairs.

An invention such as HAL, which enables people to recover from crippling disabilities, could soon be a common sight in hospital wards. **5** It could also be helpful to people working in factories or at disaster sites where the labour is physically demanding. The military are testing a robotic suit system of their own, one that will let a soldier carry heavy equipment with little effort and give them the strength of 10 men! With so many advantages a cyber suit might soon be the most popular thing to wear to work. They certainly bring a whole new meaning to power dressing!

A However, HAL may have other uses too.

B They have developed computerised leg braces that can help disabled people walk.

C He had to adjust to a new life in a wheelchair.

D A great deal of research is still needed.

E The way it works is very unique.

F But instead of using his wheelchair, Austin stands up and strides across the stage.

Part 3

Przeczytaj tekst. Z podanych możliwości odpowiedzi wybierz właściwą, tak aby otrzymać logiczny i gramatycznie poprawny tekst. Zakreśl literę A, B, C lub D.

The Race for Safe Driving

At the age of 15, Zach Veach is no ordinary teenager. Although he is too young to even own a driver's license, Zach is an auto racing driver! The talented teen **1)** ..... since he was twelve years old, when he launched his career in go-karts. While this may seem very young, most hopefuls begin at a much earlier age – some as young as four! **2)** ..... his inexperience, Zach's talent was soon spotted by IndyCar driver Sarah Fisher. Under Sarah's supervision, Zach won a series of races and was even named Rookie of the Year by the Mid-state Ohio Karting Club.

Over the next two years, Zach quickly **3)** ..... from an amateur go-karting driver to a junior racing professional. In his first year as a professional driver, he placed fifth in the U.S. F2000 National Championship, even though he had missed the first race of the season! Now, the gifted teenager has even been recruited by a world-renowned racing team, and is being prepared for the highest level of IndyCar racing!

As well as being a talented young star, Zach also works to **4)** ..... safe driving to teenagers. Moved by a tragic car accident in his local area, Zach established a safe driving campaign, which works to inform teenagers of the dangers of texting while driving. Indeed, statistics show that motor vehicle crashes are the leading cause of death among American teenagers, and that 16-20 year olds are more likely than any other age group to become distracted while driving. As Zach travels around the country, he holds

seminars **5)** ..... teenagers not to use their phones while driving. He tells them that by doing so, they may be putting themselves and others at risk.

In support of his cause, Zach has even created his own mobile phone application. When a driver receives a text, Zach's application texts back automatically, informing them that the person is currently driving, and they will **6)** ..... later. Amazingly, Zach developed this ingenious application by himself! He spent several weeks reading internet forums and learned how to programme it. This potentially life-saving application can be downloaded online free of charge. "Every text and phone call can wait" says Zach, "It's not worth risking a life!"

1.
 A has raced
 B had been racing
 C had raced
 D has been racing

2.
 A Although
 B Despite
 C However
 D Since

3.
 A converted
 B developed
 C generated
 D progressed

4.
 A assert
 B spread
 C promote
 D alert

5.
 A alerting
 B warning
 C notifying
 D alarming

6.
 A hang out
 B check in
 C get across
 D call back

Revision
Modules 1-6

Vocabulary

A Choose the correct item.

1 Islanders ..... to cope after the earthquake.
   A fought   C pushed
   B struggled   D forced

2 The massive wave ..... away an entire village.
   A swept   B hurled   C tipped   D rolled

3 The volcanic ..... was caught on film.
   A explosion   C eruption
   B epicentre   D meltdown

4 The earthquake ..... off the coast of Thailand.
   A struck   C hit
   B slammed   D flew

5 The movie was so ....., I had guessed what would happen from the very beginning!
   A educational   C exciting
   B relaxing   D predictable

6 The roof of the town hall ..... during the earthquake.
   A smashed   C crumbled
   B collapsed   D crashed

7 Officials ..... a state of emergency after the earthquake.
   A notified   C declared
   B administered   D admitted

8 The girl ..... and broke her arm.
   A twisted   B sprained   C gashed   D slipped

9 The ..... services rushed to the car accident.
   A recovery   C survival
   B emergency   D relief

10 Always ..... precautions when going climbing.
   A take   B make   C have   D get

B Circle the correct item.

1 A tsunami can travel at the **speed / impact** of an aeroplane!

2 The landslide fell into the sea, creating **pebbles / ripples** on the water.

3 There was a **shaking / deafening** roar when the volcano shot out hot lava.

4 Natural disasters can sometimes result in a massive **loss / damage** of life.

5 After losing a limb in the car accident, Peter now uses a **prosthetic / tectonic** arm.

Grammar

C Choose the correct item.

1 Chris ..... volcano surfing every weekend.
   A goes   B is going   C has gone

2 The group ..... down the slope when the avalanche occurred.
   A skied   B was skiing   C had skied

3 Have you ..... the breaking news yet?
   A see   B seen   C seeing

4 Richard ..... to Chile next Monday.
   A travels   B is traveling   C travelled

5 Kate ..... a documentary last night.
   A had watched   B watched   C was watching

6 The news ..... by the time she turned on the TV.
   A has already started
   B already started
   C had already started

7 The plane ..... during the severe storm yesterday.
   A has crashed   B had crashed   C crashed

8 The rescuers are tired. They ..... through the rubble all afternoon.
   A have been searching
   B had been searching
   C had searched

9 What time ..... the earthquake happen?
   A does   B do   C did

10 The rescuers ..... for ten hours before they took a break.
   A have been working   B have worked
   C were working

D Choose the correct word.

1 Reports confirm that there are **a little/a few** miners still trapped in the mineshaft.

2 **Most/Much** people had to evacuate their homes due to the hurricane.

3 There haven't been **some/any** casualties as a result of the landslide.

4 **Either/Neither** Jeff nor Emma had experienced an earthquake before.

5 There was **several/a great deal of** rubble in the area after the tornado hit.

Reading

E Read the text. For questions 1-15 choose from the people (A-D).

Which person...

1	does not have a formal education in their work?
2	measures for the existence of a natural phenomenon?
3	is afraid when dealing with their work?
4	is involved in a variety of natural disasters?
5	is occasionally consulted during rescue operations?
6	believes their interest is often misunderstood by the public?
7	educates the public about their work?
8	warns others of when a natural phenomenon will strike?
9	experienced a natural disaster as a child?
10	discovered their interest as a child?
11	turned their interest into a successful business?
12	was inspired by a relative to get involved in their work?
13	moved to be closer to their interest?
14	rescues people from disaster situations?
15	found a creative way to express their experiences?

Masters of Disasters

A Mona Wilson began her fascination with snow and ice when she was 6 years old, building snowmen in her back yard. When she was older, she headed north to the mountains of Alaska with her husband to study and learn all about snow and avalanches. After years of study and hands on experiences with avalanches, Mona has become a leading authority on the subject. Mona spent years advising and lending her expertise to rescue operations. But nowadays, she focuses her energy on avalanche prediction and danger areas. She often puts her own life at risk working in these dangerous areas. "It's the danger and fear that keep me cautious and enable me to do my work well. I never let go of the fear", explains Mona. Mona is now writing about her fascinating experiences. Avalanche prediction and writing may occupy most of her days, but sometimes Mona will still find a rescue team and their helicopter in her driveway ready to take her to the latest avalanche disaster site.

B According to Stan Moore, most people know very little about tsunamis and how they occur. "They think it's a giant wave like in surfing, but it's actually more like a coastal flood or series of waves." And Stan knows what he is talking about. As a leading researcher and professor in Oceanography, Stan works at a top Tsunami centre where he monitors oceans, using high tech equipment placed on the ocean's floor to measure actual tsunamis passing over head. This equipment not only identifies a tsunami but calculates how fast it is moving, allowing Stan and his co-workers to predict estimated arrival times at coastal areas and thus inform coastal populations to evacuate the area. Due to the unpredictable nature of tsunamis, Stan's work helps to save thousands of lives by keeping a watchful eye on the oceans' floor.

C Roger Mills will never forget his 11th birthday. It was the day a devastating tornado ripped through a field near his Kansas farm as he and his brother watched in complete awe. "It was incredible: the debris was flying around everywhere and of course the destruction it left behind was unbelievable" recalls Roger. It wasn't until years later, when Roger came face to face with another tornado driving down a highway, that he realised he actually wanted to learn more about this amazing weather phenomenon. Roger invested in a good video camera and set out in search of storms and tornados. At the time he was a financial analyst and knew little about tornados. Roger soon met up with some serious professional storm chasers and learned everything he knows today from them. The thrill of getting so close to such a force of nature keeps Roger chasing and he now offers that thrill to others with his tornado tour company which is fully booked throughout the storm season.

D Ever since Vince Carson saw his dad, a firefighter, pulling people from burning buildings, he knew he wanted to save lives. Vince trained and began working at the Red Cross disaster relief unit. Vince has since been sent out to some of the biggest natural disasters with the goal of saving as many lives as possible. After years of experience in disaster response, Vince now shares his valuable knowledge with others through seminars and courses. For Vince, what's important is not the kind of disaster, but beating the odds and saving lives.

Listening

F 🎧 You will hear an interview with a woman called Brenda Philips who is a hurricane survivor. For questions 1-10, complete the sentences.

Brenda's family heard the news on the

[1] .

In the wardrobe, they used

[2] to

protect themselves.

When the hurricane hit, it sounded similar to a

[3] .

Brenda recalls packing food, drink and a(n)

[4] .

The hurricane had damaged everything and the

[5] was missing.

Outside, Brenda compares the road to a

[6] .

In the debris, Brenda uncovered a(n)

[7] that

belonged to her mother.

The neighbour's husband survived with a

[8] .

At the moment, the [9]
is being repaired.

Brenda suggests that people should

[10] and

work as a team.

Everyday English

G Read the dialogue and fill in the missing phrases.

- What's on later?
- As long as we can change the channel at 7 o'clock.
- Sports programmes are boring!
- Why don't you check the TV guide?
- I don't like either of those.
- What is it?

A: What are you watching this for?
  1)...
B: I happen to find it interesting. Anyway, it's nearly finished.
A: 2)...
B: I'm not sure. 3) ....
A: OK. After this there's a game show on Channel 1 or a police drama on Channel 4.
B: 4) .... Is there anything else on?
A: Big Brother is on Channel 2. We can watch that.
B: 5) ....
A: It's a reality show.
B: I like the sound of that! 6) ....
  I want to see The Simpsons.
A: Sure. That's fine with me!

Writing

H Write a story about a scary holiday experience you had (200-250 words). Follow the plan below.

Plan

Para 1: who the main characters were
  when and where the story took place
  what the weather was like
Para 2/3: describe the events
Para 4: describe ending/feelings

Vocabulary

A Choose the correct item.

1 Supermarkets always have ..... displays to make you buy things.
   A tricky   C tempting
   B sneaky   D intentional

2 He ..... revenge on his enemy.
   A had   B took   C made   D did

3 Sweets are in the ..... next to the dairy products.
   A aisle   B booth   C line   D checkout

4 The computer will ..... you by name when you swipe your card.
   A expose   B access   C address   D convert

5 The sleeve on the dress is ..... .
   A scratched   C cracked
   B torn   D broken

6 Can you give me some dietary ..... to help me lose weight?
   A advice   C awareness
   B values   D strategy

7 Joanne's ..... appliances are from the 1980s.
   A designer   C consumer
   B fashion   D household

8 Jill uses her ..... card to get discounts at the supermarket.
   A bargain   B loyalty   C trade   D retail

9 Try and ..... an effort to be a responsible shopper.
   A make   B do   C have   D give

10 The material is made from cotton and acrylic ..... .
   A garments B textiles C fabrics D fibres

B Circle the correct item.

1 My mobile phone has instant internet **access** / **demand**.

2 His new job should help him get **ahead** / **across** as a salesman.

3 Be careful the **manual** / **sliding** doors don't hit you.

4 All mobile phones are **reduced** / **banned** in school buildings.

5 The **working** / **manufacture** conditions are terrible in the factory.

Grammar

C Choose the correct item.

1 Sarah ..... at the supermarket tomorrow.
   A is working   B going to work
   C works

2 I don't mind ..... second hand items.
   A to buy   B buy   C buying

3 That's a great blouse. I ..... it.
   A will take   B am going to take
   C am taking

4 By this time next month they will ..... building the new mall.
   A is finishing   B have finished
   C have been finishing

5 This computer screen isn't as ..... as that one.
   A bigger   B biggest   C big

6 Mary refuses ..... products that can't be recycled.
   A purchasing   B to purchase C purchase

7 Tracy ..... the CD player because it's damaged.
   A returns   B has been returning
   C is going to return

8 ..... the great sales, I didn't buy anything.
   A Even though B Despite   C Although

9 The ..... the computer, the more expensive it is.
   A faster   B more fast   C fastest

10 By this time next week I ..... into my new house.
   A will move   B will have moved
   C am moving

11 Jill avoids ..... on Saturdays because of the crowds.
   A shopping   B to shop   C shop

12 I promise I ..... the paperwork ready by 5.
   A am going to having   B am having
   C will have

13 This shop has by far ..... prices on the high street.
   A the highest B higher   C the higher

14 By the end of this year Joe will ..... computer games for ten years.
   A design   B be designing
   C have been designing

15 I'd prefer ..... and look around for the best price.
   A waiting   B wait   C to wait

167

The Sixth Sense

The age of technology is upon us, and very soon, we may all become cyborgs...

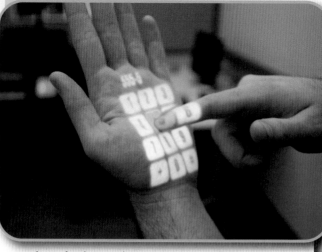

Chris Harrington needs to make a telephone call. Instead of reaching into his pocket for his mobile phone, Chris holds out his hand. Instantly, it becomes illuminated by a virtual screen. He punches in the numbers on the palm of his hand, and it dials!

It may sound like something from a science fiction film, but this device is real! Although the technology is still undergoing development, a virtual reality keypad has been unveiled by designers at Carnegie Mellon University. **1** [ ] Instead, the phone can be worn on the body!

OmniTouch is mounted on a user's shoulder. From here, it can project a screen onto just about anything. **2** [ ] It will also automatically adjust its virtual screen according to the angle, distance and shape of the object upon which it is projected!

By using a depth-sensing camera, the virtual screen of OmniTouch is fully interactive. It can detect a user's finger movements, just like a touchscreen. **3** [ ] It can respond to pointing, tapping, and even the use of multiple fingers. And it's not just a phone. Wearers can use the device to open, create and edit documents. It is a fully portable personal computer.

As if all this isn't enough, OmniTouch is also connected to the internet. Users can check their email or browse a search engine on their arm! It can also find product reviews while you are shopping. Imagine being in a bookstore. **4** [ ] It could even compare prices with other bookstores on your behalf.

Unfortunately, Omnitouch has one massive disadvantage. It is distinctly lacking in privacy. Since it is projected onto a surface, it is impossible to cover your screen. This would mean everyone around you would be able to see your display. **5** [ ] That's why other developers are working on displays that aren't even noticeable at all.

One team of researchers in America is currently experimenting with computer displays in contact lenses. This means your own eyes would be transformed into a screen! **6** [ ] No-one else would be able to read your emails or social networking pages!

Just imagine the possibilities when these technologies become available on the high street! We will have hidden displays which we will control using our own bodies. The next generation of technology will merge humans and machines together. **7** [ ] The only question is; are you ready to be a cyborg?

Reading

D Read the text. Seven sentences have been removed from the article. Choose from the sentences (A-H) the one which fits each gap (1-7). There is one extra sentence.

A Since this display would be personal, users would have complete privacy.

B The surface could be a wall, a notepad or even your own hand.

C We ourselves will become computers.

D Their amazing invention eliminates the need for a handset entirely.

E The display can only produce a limited range of shapes and colours.

F OmniTouch could automatically scan the novel you are holding and tell you what other people think of it!

G The device is programmed to recognise dozens of finger and hand gestures.

H Most people don't want the world to see their emails!

Listening

E 🎧 **You'll hear people talking in eight different situations. For questions 1-8, choose the best answer** *A, B* **or** *C.*

1 You hear a man talking about a recent trip to a supermarket. Why did he leave the supermarket?
   A He couldn't find what he needed.
   B He thought it was too expensive.
   C The queue was too long.

2 You hear a woman talking about her job. What is she?
   A a shop assistant   B a cashier
   C a designer

3 You hear a young man talking about a computer he just bought. How does he feel about the computer?
   A He is anxious about learning how to use it.
   B He is proud to own it.
   C He is worried that he paid too much for it.

4 You hear a woman talking to a man. Why is she talking to him?
   A to make a suggestion
   B to request action
   C to ask for help

5 You hear two shoppers talking. Where are they?
   A at a florist   B at a post office
   C at a book shop

6 You hear a lecturer talking about responsible shopping. What is the lecturer describing?
   A common mistakes shoppers make
   B shopping trends of the future
   C poor quality products

7 You hear two people talking in a clothing shop. Why doesn't the man buy the jacket?
   A It's too small.   B It's too trendy.
   C It's the wrong colour.

8 You hear a professional shopper talking on the radio. What does she recommend?
   A always shop with a friend
   B never pay with a credit card
   C take a look at second hand shops

Everyday English

F **Choose the correct response.**

1 A: Do you need any help?
   B: a What size are you?
      b I'm looking for a jacket.

2 A: Can I try this shirt on?
   B: a We've almost sold out.
      b The fitting rooms are over there.

3 A: How do they fit?
   B: a Really well.
      b Any good?

4 A: Can I have your ID, please?
   B: a Can I pay by credit card?
      b Here you are.

5 A: I'll take them.
   B: a That's £24.99, please.
      b Your receipt is in the bag.

6 A: These are the last pair in your size.
   B: a Can I try them on?
      b I'm a size 10.

7 A: Here's your credit card back.
   B: a No problem.
      b Thank you very much.

Writing

G **Read the rubric and write an email of complaint to the head office of the shop (200-250) words. Include:**

• opening remarks & reason for writing
• your complaint(s)
• what action you want the shop to take
• closing remarks

> You recently bought an electrical item from a shop. When you took it home and opened the box, you realised that it didn't work. When you took it back to exchange it, the manager wasn't very helpful.

Vocabulary

A Choose the correct item.

1 The homeless man was dressed in ..... clothes.
A puffy   B scruffy   C messy   D frizzy

2 Greenpeace tries to ..... awareness of environmental issues.
A promote   B lift   C expand   D raise

3 The campaign we are planning will surely ..... people's attention!
A catch   B draw   C hold   D reach

4 Andy is ready to ..... the challenge of climbing Mt. Everest.
A face   B have   C set   D get

5 Urban developers are often ..... by ecologists for damaging the environment.
A accused   C criticised
B abused   D charged

6 Wilma is very generous and regularly ..... money to charity.
A presents   C gathers
B donates   D supplies

7 We can use power from the sun to ..... electricity.
A construct   C generate
B conserve   D build

8 You can ..... your local charity by volunteering.
A encourage   C sustain
B adopt   D support

9 You should try bungee jumping for a(n) ..... adventure.
A eye-opening   C hair-raising
B nerve-wracking   D sharp-toothed

10 Joey always sticks to his ..... and does what he thinks is right.
A traditions   C judgement
B principles   D reputation

B Circle the correct item.

1 Ann **wandered / wondered** around the market.
2 Jim was attacked by a **school / swarm** of bees!
3 The homeless man found shelter in an old building with a **leaking / dripping** roof.
4 Jason shivered in the **chilling / biting** cold.
5 Scientists are concerned that a meteorite may **extract / wipe out** life on Earth.

Grammar

C Choose the correct item.

1 We .... help out at the homeless shelter; it's a good idea.
A have to   B must   C should

2 If I won a lot of money, I .... donate some to charity.
A will   B would have   C would

3 This is the cabin .... we stayed last winter.
A which   B when   C where

4 I wish I .... in the charity race, but I was busy.
A ran   B had run   C would run

5 If Joe had left earlier, he .... the bus.
A won't miss   B wouldn't miss
C wouldn't have missed

6 He .... come to the clean up day, he is working.
A mustn't   B doesn't have to   C can't

7 Max , ... work has helped many street children, was given an award.
A whose   B who   C which

8 I wish I .... on holiday, but I don't have enough money.
A had gone   B would go   C was going

9 That's Mr Rogers .... works at the wildlife reserve.
A whose   B which   C who

10 You .... enter the building; it's forbidden.
A shouldn't   B don't have to   C mustn't

11 If I .... you, I'd do some volunteer work.
A am   B had been   C were

12 We'll go to the outdoor festival .... it rains.
A if   B unless   C since

13 If John .... education, he would be a teacher now.
A had studied   B will study   C studies

14 People .... start forest fires should be put in prison.
A that   B whose   C which

15 Mike .... find a job; he's still unemployed.
A mustn't   B couldn't   C can't

Reading

D Read the text. For questions 1-15, choose from the places (A-D). Which place ...

1		recently had a special event?
2		held rallies to support their cause?
3		was initially built for seasonal use?
4		is open to the general public?
5		has more than one location?
6		provides education for their guests?
7		was established by someone with experience in the industry?
8		does not receive any donations?
9		has given advice to the government?
10		closed down and re-opened?

11		requires some form of payment?
12		has only one person living there?
13		was given as a gift to the charity?
14		once occupied a former public space?
15		wants their residents to find somewhere else to live?

DogsTrust

Take Shelter!

A Boulder Shelter in Colorado was established in 1982 to protect homeless people during the area's harsh winters. At first, the shelter took the form of an abandoned bus terminal and was only open until spring. After that, the local council reclaimed the land, forcing the charity to relocate. Dr. Barbara Farhar, the charity's founder, managed to find a suitable building, but unfortunately could not afford the $250,000 required to purchase it. 'Luckily,' smiles Barbara, 'some investors decided to donate the building to us!' This building was then renovated in time for the following winter. During that season alone, Boulder provided shelter for over 225 homeless people. Since then, many donations have been received to keep the shelter open all year round!

C The Dogs Trust is a charity-run organisation which cares for around 16,000 dogs every year. Founded in 1891 by novelist Lady Gertrude Stock, Dogs Trust has led many campaigns against animal cruelty. The charity voiced concerns about the cruel treatment of dogs by railway companies, and also campaigned against the use of animals in space flight. The Dogs Trust is even consulted by the government about matters concerning pet ownership, and has helped to implement laws that protect animal welfare. With 17 nationwide shelters, Dogs Trust workers are always kept busy! However, saving an animal is just the first step – the ultimate goal is to find them a new home. In order for their work to continue, funding is essential, which is why the charity invites those who cannot adopt a pet to sponsor one instead.

Wildlife Reserve

B Handa Island Sanctuary is a wildlife reserve that is home to over 100,000 birds! The area is protected by the Scottish Wildlife Trust, a government-funded organisation that preserves all wild animals and plant life in Scotland. Since Handa is a protected area, no-one is allowed to live there, except for the warden whose job is to oversee the people that visit the island each year. Tourists can spend up to eight hours a day on Handa, but then they must leave. They are also warned not to disturb any of the animals or their habitats.

The Pepper Pot Centre

D After being a community worker for many years, Pansy Jeffery decided to open her own centre for the elderly. 'It was clear to me that there was an increasing number of senior citizens who were suffering from isolation, loneliness and depression. I had to do something,' recalls Pansy. The Pepper Pot Centre, which has just celebrated its 25th birthday, encourages elderly people to socialise with each other. This involves taking field trips, organising functions and simply having fun! While the centre runs mostly on donations, it does charge a small fee to cover the cost of its many services. Services include physical therapy sessions and also a range of classes. Members can take part in literature classes, art lessons and plenty more!

Listening

E **You will hear an interview with a conservationist. For questions 1-7, choose the best answer *A*, *B* or *C*.**

1 Why was the national park established?
   A To conserve the rainforest.
   B To help endangered species.
   C To save the jaguar.

2 What is currently endangering the wildlife?
   A The mining industry.
   B Continued deforestation.
   C Illegal hunters.

3 What are the future plans for the project?
   A Hiring wardens to protect the forest.
   B Educating local people.
   C Restoring the rainforest.

4 Why did Andrew relocate to Costa Rica?
   A To study ecology at university.
   B To examine the effects of climate change.
   C To become a member of a conservation group.

5 Why does the reserve need more money?
   A To pay the staff that work there.
   B To plant more trees.
   C To raise jaguars in captivity.

6 What material are the lodges in the reserve made from?
   A Straw.   B Bamboo.
   C Rosewood.

7 If you adopt an animal, what will you receive?
   A Photographs of the animal.
   B A certificate.
   C A gift from the website.

Everyday English

F **Read the dialogue and fill in the missing phrases.**

- I'd like to make a single donation of £25, please.
- Could you give me your credit card details?
- I'd like to make a donation. • Thank you for your donation.
- And your telephone number? • It's May next year.

A: Hello, Blue Cross. How can I help you?
B: **1)** ....
A: Would you like to make a single donation or a regular monthly donation?
B: **2)** ....
A: OK. Could you tell me your name and address, please?
B: Certainly. It's Mary Reid. My address is 16 Woodlands Grove, London.
A: **3)** ....
B: It's 020-856-9877.
A: **4)** ....
B: Sure. The number is 8596 4599 3782 3320.
A: And what is the expiration date?
B: **5)** ....
A: That's great! **6)** ....
B: My pleasure. Goodbye.

Writing

G **Read the rubric, match the viewpoints to the reasons/examples and write an essay (200-250 words). Remember to include:**

- the topic & your opinion. • viewpoints & examples
- opposite viewpoints & examples
- your summary/restatement of your opinion

You have had a class discussion about the following statement: "Should the government spend money on space exploration?" Now your teacher has asked you to write an essay giving your opinion.

Viewpoints

1		Money could be better spent.
2		It allows human beings to discover new things.
3		It risks human life.

Reasons/Examples

a Due to its harsh conditions, living in space can be dangerous for astronauts.
b The funds could be used to reduce poverty and improve society.
c We may find new materials or more natural resources.

Vocabulary

A Choose the correct word.

1 This is such a ..... novel; I can't put it down.
   A gripping   C life-changing
   B fast-paced   D surprising

2 A large crowd ..... to watch the firework display.
   A unfolded   C roamed
   B wandered   D gathered

3 The horror film was so .....; I had guessed the ending.
   A original   C realistic
   B mysterious   D predictable

4 He has been ..... that song all day.
   A buzzing   C whistling
   B screeching   D rustling

5 The injured man was rushed to the hospital but doctors could not ..... him.
   A reactivate   C reverse
   B revive   D preserve

6 Scientists are ..... experiments to bring dinosaurs back to life.
   A making   C conducting
   B trying   D causing

7 Her heart ..... when she heard the bad news.
   A sank   B dropped   C fell   D lowered

8 Jack ..... angrily at her and then left the room.
   A glared   B glimpsed   C peered   D peeped

9 They recovered a piece of ..... from the plane crash.
   A debris   B findings   C ruins   D remains

10 He managed to ..... a path through the forest.
   A smack   B slap   C whip   D hack

B Circle the correct item.

1 The journalist was asked to **report / witness** on the UFO sighting.

2 The cryptologist is **sceptical / reluctant** to talk about his discovery.

3 The UFO was actually a balloon **hovering / floating** in the wind.

4 The youngsters were **splashing / smacking** about in the lake.

5 Eric **gazed / glanced** at his watch for a second.

Grammar

C Choose the correct item.

1 The dinosaur is ..... extinct species that died out over 60 million years ago.
   A the   B –   C an

2 Roswell ..... by thousands of tourists each year.
   A was visited   B has been visited
   C is visited

3 Tom and Larry really enjoyed ..... at the music festival last week.
   A ourselves   B themselves   C yourselves

4 David made the skeleton sculpture by ..... .
   A myself   B itself   C himself

5 The alien photographs ..... examined by experts now.
   A are   B were   C are being

6 Why don't we visit ..... Tower of London?
   A –   B a   C the

7 The new museum will be opened ..... the Mayor.
   A from   B with   C by

8 John works as an usher at ..... Theatre Royal in London.
   A a   B the   C –

9 A new space centre ..... built soon.
   A is   B was   C will be

10 Don't forget to book the tickets, ...?
   A do you   B will you   C could you

11 Let me introduce .....; I'm Bill Evans.
   A yourself   B himself   C myself

12 Let's go on a ghost tour, ...?
   A shall we   B are we   C will we

13 The strange creature ..... caught yet.
   A isn't   B hasn't been   C wasn't

14 There are many haunted buildings in ..... London, England.
   A the   B a   C –

15 You don't believe in ghosts, ...?
   A do you   B aren't you   C don't you

Making Contact

When at last Cavor and I had made an end of eating, the Selenites linked our hands closely together again, and then untwisted the chains about our feet and rebound them, so as to give us a limited freedom of movement. Then they unfastened the chains about our waist. To do all this they had to handle us freely, and every now and then one of their odd heads came down close to my face, or a soft tentacle-hand touched my head or neck. I don't remember that I was afraid then or offended by their proximity. I think that our natural instincts to want creatures to be like humans led us to imagine that there were human heads inside their masks. The skin, like everything else, looked bluish, but that was on account of the light; and it was hard and shiny, in a rather insect-like fashion, not soft, or moist, or hairy, as an animal's would be. The Selenite who untied me used his mouth to help his hands.

'They seem to be releasing us,' said Cavor. 'Remember we are on the moon! Make no sudden movements!'

We remained passive, and the Selenites, having finished their arrangements, stood back from us, and seemed to be looking at us. I say seemed to be, because as their eyes were at the side and not in the front, it was difficult to determine the direction in which they were looking, such as in the case of a hen or a fish. They conversed with one another in high pitched sounds that seemed to me impossible to imitate or describe. The door behind us opened wider, and, glancing over my shoulder, I saw a large space beyond, in which a little crowd of Selenites were standing. They seemed a curiously diverse group.

'Do they want us to imitate those sounds?' I asked Cavor.

'I don't think so,' he said.

'It seems to me that they are trying to make us understand something.'

'I can't make anything of their gestures. Do you notice this one, who is moving his head like a man with an uncomfortable collar?'

'Let us shake our heads at him.'

We did that, and finding it ineffective, attempted an imitation of the Selenites' movements. That seemed to interest them. At any rate they all set up the same movement. But as that seemed to lead to nothing, we stopped at last and so did they, and fell into an argument amongst themselves. Then one of them, shorter and very much thicker than the others, and with a particularly wide mouth, bent down suddenly beside Cavor, and put his hands and feet in the same stance as Cavor's were bound, and then skilfully stood up.

'Cavor,' I shouted, 'they want us to get up!'

He stared open-mouthed.

'That's it!' he said.

And with much difficulty, because our hands were tied together, we struggled to our feet.

Adapted from The First Men In The Moon by H.G.Wells

Reading

D **Read the excerpt from a novel. For questions 1-8, choose the answer** *A, B, C* **or** *D.*

1 How did the Selenites treat the men overall?
   A They twisted their ankles.
   B They threatened to tie them up.
   C They were quite gentle.
   D They let them go hungry.

2 What was the writer's impression of the Selenites?
   A He feared them.
   B He was disgusted by them.
   C He believed them to be human.
   D He was undisturbed by their closeness.

3 How does the writer describe the Selenites?
   A They had blue skin.
   B They had human-like heads.
   C They were hairy animals.
   D They looked like insects.

4 The writer uses the word 'us' (line 17) to refer to
   A Cavor and himself.   C the Selenites that untied him.
   B the Selenites in general.   D the Selenite and himself.

5 What does the writer say about the Selenites?
   A They had poor vision.
   B They had difficulty determining direction.
   C They were overly curious.
   D They communicated in an odd manner.

6 What did the writer find unusual about the Selenites?
   A They wore uncomfortable clothing.
   B They had strange looking heads.
   C They all moved in the same direction.
   D Their actions were difficult to understand.

7 The men tried to imitate the Selenites' because they wanted
   A to make them angry.   C to communicate with them.
   B to get their attention.   D them to fight with each other.

8 The writer uses the phrase 'That's it' (line 52) to show that they
   A had made contact with the Selenites.
   B understood what the Selenites wanted.
   C knew how to communicate with the Selenites.
   D found a way to confuse the Selenites.

Listening

E 🎧 **You are going to hear five different people talking about a strange experience they encountered. Match the speakers (1-5) to the statements (A-F).**

A found an explanation for what happened.

B isn't sure what they saw.

C had their property damaged by the phenomenon.

D saw something strange at night.

E experienced the phenomenon many times.

F did not actually witness the event.

Speaker 1	
Speaker 2	
Speaker 3	
Speaker 4	
Speaker 5	

F 🎧 **You will hear a monologue about Glamis Castle. For each question (1-5) choose the correct answer** *A*, *B*, *C* **or** *D*.

1 What is true about Glamis Castle?

A It sits at the peak of a mountain.

B Its residents are very secretive.

C The Queen was born there.

D A well-known play was set there.

2 The castle is unusual because

A of the shape of the towers.

B it has few windows for its size.

C it contains a hidden chamber.

D the tower at the top cannot be reached.

3 Who possibly knows the secret of Glamis Castle?

A A few of the local people.

B A nobleman's son.

C Some of the castle servants.

D Members of the Royal Family.

4 Which ghost is said to appear while you are lying in bed?

A The Monster of Glamis Castle.

B A lady in a grey dress.

C A gentleman with a beard.

D A frightened female servant.

5 Tourists are attracted to the castle because

A it is easy to get to.

B the setting is full of natural beauty.

C the Queen is often there.

D it hosts dances and dinners.

Everyday English

G **Choose the correct response.**

1 A: Can I buy tickets for the tour here?
  B: **a** That sounds good.
  b Yes, certainly.

2 A: When would you like to go?
  B: **a** It's valid for 7 days.
  b This evening if possible.

3 A: That's £42.50 then.
  B: **a** Here you are.
  b Enjoy your visit.

4 A: How many tickets would you like?
  B: **a** One adult please.
  b It's £20 then.

5 A: What does the ticket price include?
  B: **a** You can choose your own time.
  b A tour of the haunted castle.

6 A: Where does the tour start from?
  B: **a** At the entrance.
  b Every half hour.

7 A: Thank you for your help.
  B: **a** That's right.
  b My pleasure.

8 A: I'd like to book a ticket, please.
  B: **a** Could you tell me the price?
  b When do you want to go?

9 A: How can I help you?
  B: **a** Does it include a guided tour?
  b This is where I buy tickets, isn't it?

Writing

H **Your teacher has asked you to write a review of a book you've read in school (200-250 words). Include:**

- background information (title, type, author)
- main points of the plot
- general comments (plot, characters, beginning/ending)
- recommendation & reasons

Vocabulary

A **Choose the correct word.**

1 The misbehaving student was ..... from school.
  A dropped   C released
  B suspended   D kicked

2 Brian's determination comes from his ..... strength.
  A mental   B physical C inner   D body

3 Tuition ..... for university can be expensive.
  A resources B wages C donations D fees

4 The teacher ..... her students by offering a prize for the best story.
  A motivated   C disciplined
  B committed   D focused

5 Helen doesn't have the ..... to try extreme sports.
  A courage   C patience
  B determination D pride

6 He often leaves notes on his fridge to ..... himself to do things!
  A recall   C remember
  B remind   D memorise

7 The flexible gymnast can ..... the splits easily.
  A create   B make   C do   D cause

8 The advertisement was brightly coloured in order to ..... attention.
  A approach   C claim
  B process   D attract

9 George managed to ..... through the exercise and finish it.
  A land   B stumble   C trip   D fall

10 Tom is a real ..... to the team.
  A asset   C requirement
  B resource   D service

B **Circle the correct item.**

1 Malcolm is such a great student, he is a **shining / bright** example for the others!

2 Before she visits Paris, Jane plans to take a **crash / smash** course in French.

3 To my **relief / comfort**, nobody was hurt during the accident.

4 Jackie **gasped / breathed** in amazement when she saw the acrobats perform!

5 You must work hard to achieve your **goals / aims**.

Grammar

C **Circle the correct item.**

1 Jack ..... him to turn off the computer when he had finished using it.
  A suggested   B complained   C reminded

2 I ..... him if he was a martial arts expert.
  A said   B asked   C told

3 Jeff ..... that we could do the course online.
  A offered   B told   C explained

4 ..... I pass my driving test; I plan to buy a car.
  A Until   B By the time
  C As soon as

5 Ann ..... to text me every day while she was on holiday in France.
  A promised   B apologised   C denied

6 Tracy ..... us that the lecture was boring.
  A said   B told   C asked

7 Tony said he would go to the gym ..... .
  A tomorrow   B the following day
  C next week

8 Jill told Fiona that she ..... the video clip.
  A has seen   B had seen   C was seeing

9 She suggested ..... the university books online.
  A to purchase   B purchasing   C purchase

10 He will go on holiday in the summer ..... he graduates from university.
  A after   B since   C until

D **Rewrite the sentences in reported speech.**

1 'I won a scholarship last year,' Bob said.
  ....
2 'I have passed the exam,' said Joe.
  ....
3 'We will go to the performance tomorrow,' they said.
  ....
4 'I was studying in the library,' Ann said.
  ....
5 'Jake is training to be a Kung Fu master,' Mary said.
  ....

Reading

E   **Read the text. In each question 1-5, choose the correct answer** *A, B, C* **or** *D*.

1   While travelling to the Husky farm Martin felt
   A   he would have a relaxing holiday.
   B   he was ready for an adventure.
   C   unsure about what would happen.
   D   regret about deciding to go so far away.

2   Owners of the farm expect volunteers to
   A   remain at least one year.
   B   have previous experience with dogs.
   C   be confident around dogs.
   D   to know survival skills.

3   From his experience Martin didn't like
   A   feeding the dogs in the morning.
   B   training the dogs for the safaris.
   C   travelling to work in the morning.
   D   working in severe weather.

4   Martin didn't go ice fishing because
   A   he preferred to go snowmobiling.
   B   he was afraid of the ice breaking.
   C   he's too impatient for such an activity.
   D   he wanted to relax instead.

5   Just before his departure Martin felt
   A   sad about leaving the dogs.
   B   proud of what he learned on the farm.
   C   exhausted and ready to leave.
   D   anxious about returning home.

Gone to the dogs!

Martin Webber could hardly believe where he was going as he sat in his aeroplane seat. It was a 28 hour journey into the Arctic Circle, so he had plenty of time to think. "I had no idea about what to expect, but going to Finland to drive and care for sled dogs was sure to be exciting stuff as opposed to an easygoing holiday. I just hoped I was up to the challenge." Just out of secondary school, Martin was determined to get out of England and go somewhere completely off the map. His destination was a husky farm in Lapland, Finland. As the gap-year brochure had described, volunteers had to be prepared to face some physically demanding days in almost unbearable freezing temperatures for a minimum stay of 3 months. Although knowledge of training dogs was not necessary, it was emphasised that a certain degree of ease and self-assurance with the dogs was needed to do the job. Martin was certainly happy he had spent a summer at a survival camp learning valuable skills that he was sure would help make his experience a lot easier. After Martin's long journey and a brief adjustment period, he soon got in to the routine of starting each day at 5am to feed and care for 93 Siberian husky dogs. This involved preparing huge buckets of food the night before and sharing it equally among all the hungry barking huskies. Feeding so many dogs did take a while, even with several other volunteers helping out. Once this was done, the next task was to prepare the sleighs for the client's safari excursions and pick the teams of dogs that would pull them. Deciding which dogs to put together was harder than it sounded, but fortunately for Martin, he was only tasked with fetching the chosen dogs.

Martin's accommodation was a small log cabin that he shared with 6 other people, but at least it was warm inside and located close to where he worked. However, the hardest part of the job certainly had to be enduring the extreme outdoor weather conditions and temperatures that were routinely 20-30 degrees below freezing!

During his free time Martin had the chance to take part in many different activities such as canoeing, hiking, skiing and even driving snowmobiles. Yet, there was one activity that he never got round to trying and that was ice-fishing on the frozen lake nearby. It wasn't that he was afraid the ice would break or that it often took a great deal of patience to catch a fish, it was just that he would rather spend his time unwinding in the hot thermal springs that existed in the area.

Martin's time volunteering on the husky farm passed quicker than he ever imagined it would. The skills that he had learned during the summer survival camp had certainly come in handy. It had been an exhausting several months but Martin didn't want to leave. He had formed a close bond with the huskies and was definitely going to miss them. However, he knew he could look forward to telling his friends back home about all the amazing experiences he'd had. It had definitely been a holiday to remember!

Listing

F 🎧 You will hear an interview with a stuntman. For questions 1-10, complete the sentences.

Johnny enjoys his job because it is very [1].

The most important thing for stunt performers is [2].

Johnny had an accident when a [3] broke.

When Johnny woke up, he had a [4].

Before he worked as a stunt performer, Johnny took part in many [5].

When a person finishes a stunt programme, they will obtain a [6].

Applicants are divided into groups based upon their [7].

Johnny says that the [8] is both enjoyable and helps to boost fitness.

Children can attend the camp in the month of [9].

In order to become a stunt performer, its vital to maintain a [10].

Everyday English

G Read the dialogue and fill in the missing phrases.

- Can I see your library card, please?
- I'm afraid that book is out right now.
- The books are due back in one week.
- What's the title of the book and the author?
- It should be brought back in two days.

A: Hi, I wonder if you could help me.
B: What seems to be the problem?
A: I'm looking for a book.
B: **1)** ....
A: It's *Modern Art* by Joanne Campbell.
B: **2)** ....
   Would you like to reserve it?
A: Yes, please. When will it be back in?
B: **3)** .... I can call you when I have it.
A: That would be great. My phone number is 8537866. Also, can I take these books out just now, please?
B: Sure. **4)** ....
A: Here it is.
B: OK. **5)** ....
A: Thank you very much.
B: My pleasure. Goodbye.

Writing

H Read the rubric, match the viewpoints to the reasons/examples and write an essay (200-250 words). Remember to include:

- a short introduction   • viewpoints & examples
- a summary that expresses your opinion

A student website is asking for opinions about this issue: *"Should it be compulsory for students to wear school uniforms?"* Write a for-and-against essay discussing this proposal (200-250 words).

Viewpoints

1		It reduces peer pressure.
2		It limits self-expression.
3		It saves parents' money.

Reasons/Examples

a School uniforms are cheaper than popular designer clothes.
b Children are unable to be creative with what they wear.
c Since everyone looks the same, there is no difference among students.

Vocabulary

A Choose the correct item.

1 Jane is not a very ..... person because she can't keep a secret.
   A eager   C efficient
   B trustworthy   D organised

2 Jill is a total drama queen. She ..... everything!
   A processes   C contributes
   B overcompensates D exaggerates

3 The police officer was ..... the suspect was lying.
   A convinced   C dominated
   B intimidated   D handled

4 The student felt restless and kept ..... in his chair.
   A scratching   C frowning
   B fidgeting   D twitching

5 Carol is often complaining. She's a bit of a ....!
   A chatterbox   C whiner
   B scatterbrain D steamroller

6 Daniel is too timid. He should be more ..... with his opinions.
   A assertive   C ferocious
   B hostile   D aggressive

7 Certain animals can ..... each other with sounds and gestures.
   A signal   B declare   C release   D notify

8 In the Arctic, a ..... of dogs is used to pull sledges.
   A flock   B herd   C pack   D swarm

9 'You cannot use my computer,' she said ..... .
   A intensely   C firmly
   B instinctively D confidently

10 A know-it-all takes great ..... in proving other people wrong.
   A interest   C care
   B triumph   D delight

B Circle the correct item.

1 The rugby **opponent / supporter** wore his team's colours.

2 After having **cosmetic / implant** surgery, Lydia feels more confident.

3 During the traditional dance, the tribesmen **stamped / slapped** their feet.

4 Phillip **widened / raised** an eyebrow in disbelief.

5 The politicians worked together in order to **resolve / conclude** the conflict.

Grammar

C Choose the correct item.

1 Paula behaves ...... she's better than everyone else.
   A so that   B as if   C since

2 You ...... feed the animals in the zoo! It's forbidden.
   A mustn't   B shouldn't   C couldn't

3 Jenny ...... her eyebrows plucked right now.
   A has   B has had   C is having

4 Gavin is always telling others what to do! He's ...... a bossy-boots!
   A so   B such   C because

5 Martin is having his beard ...... by the barber.
   A trims   B trim   C trimmed

6 Mark ...... his hair cut yesterday.
   A had   B has   C was

7 Laura's been sick in bed all day. She ...... have been to the gym.
   A might   B needn't   C couldn't

8 Some animals change colour ...... disguise themselves from predators.
   A so that   B so as to   C so

9 Tim was studying all night. He ...... be tired.
   A could   B should   C must

10 Mary ...... her hair dyed tomorrow.
   A will have   B has   C had

D Use the words/phrases to rewrite the sentences.

1 Eve didn't feel confident until she lost weight.
   Only after ....

2 I don't often get tongue-tied.
   Rarely ....

3 If you talk to Emma, ask her to call me.
   Should ....

4 I didn't know he was lying.
   Little ....

5 You will be on time for your appointment if you leave now.
   Only if ....

179

Reading

E Read the text. Seven sentences have been removed from the article. Choose from the sentences (A-H) the one that fits each gap (1-7). There is one extra sentence.

A They feel pressure to conform to a certain image.

B Teens often hope plastic surgery will fix their difficulties with peer groups.

C Such surgeries are on the rise because they are increasingly being seen as acceptable ways of improving one's image.

D They are aware of the limitations of plastic surgery.

E Thus, they are more willing to give consent and pay for their teenager's surgery.

F Here, a dangerous problem is developing with teenagers thinking surgery is the answer to whatever they don't like.

G There is also the added danger of a surgery going wrong and the results being worse than before.

H Unfortunately, many teenagers are unhappy with their reflections.

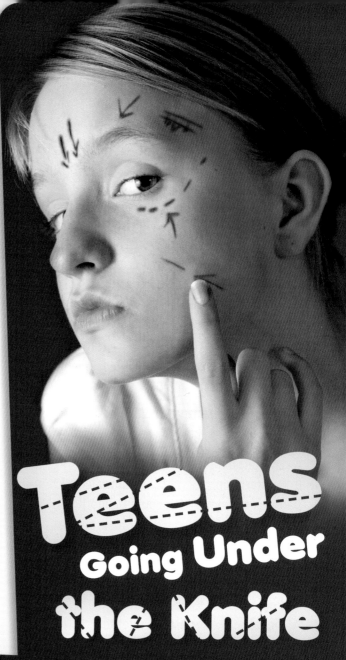

Teens Going Under the Knife

Most teens love mirrors and spend hours in front them experimenting with hairstyles, makeup and fashion. **1▮**. An increasing number of them each year are trying to change the image they see through plastic surgery. In the United States alone, the number of teenagers undergoing plastic surgery has doubled since 2002 with the most popular procedures being rhinoplasty, also know as a "nose job", and breast enlargements. **2▮**. Celebrities openly discuss what procedures they have done and are even proud of it. There are actually celebrities famous just for how good they look or for their number of plastic surgeries. Parents are more accepting of such procedures as many of them or their friends have undergone cosmetic improvements. **3▮**. For those parents and teenagers who can't afford it, many go into debt to finance the surgery by taking a loan.

While most adults have plastic surgery to improve their looks, young people tend to have surgery to fit in with their peers. **4▮**. When they don't and have a body part that is different such as a large or unusual shaped nose, they are often teased and even bullied for being different. "It can make a difference in how others treat you and how you feel about yourself, but it doesn't make you popular." Explains 17 year old Ken who had his ears operated on because they were sticking out. **5▮**. But usually the social problems come from their low self-esteem and how they feel about themselves than how they look. In the pursuit of happiness many young people are prepared to go under the knife and put up with often terrible pain, not to mention the risks associated with surgery. **6▮**. The cosmetic surgery industry is not regulated in most countries and there are many incompetent surgeons operating today.

In some cases teenagers are very pleased with a result of one plastic surgery and will opt for another surgery to improve another body part. **7▮**. It's often the beginning of addiction to plastic surgery that continues into adulthood. The true problem lies in poor self-image which can only be resolved by counseling. So when is it appropriate for a teenager to have plastic surgery? When they are emotionally and physically mature enough to undergo a procedure which in most cases is not until adulthood.

Listening

F 🎧 **You will hear eight people talking in eight different situations. For questions 1 to 8, choose the best answer A, B or C.**

1 You hear a young girl talking. Why did she decide to lose weight?
   A Her parents suggested it.
   B Her doctor recommended it.
   C She was motivated by a book.

2 You hear a man talking on the radio. What does he work as?
   A a sculptor.   B a body piercer.
   C a tattoo artist.

3 You hear a presenter talking about a woman who is about to have a make-over. How does the presenter feel about the woman?
   A She does not dress to suit her age.
   B Her clothes fit her well.
   C Her hair is a beautiful colour.

4 You hear a woman talking to a hairdresser. Why is she talking to her?
   A to discuss different hair styles.
   B to reschedule a booking.
   C to make an apology.

5 You hear a plastic surgeon being interviewed on the radio. Why did he decide to become a plastic surgeon?
   A to follow a family tradition.
   B to develop a natural talent.
   C to help other people.

6 You hear part of an entertainment show about fashion. What is the narrator describing?
   A The history of fashion.
   B The latest trends.
   C Buying used clothing.

7 You hear a man talking about his appearance. How does he feel about the way he looks?
   A awkward   B embarrassed
   C indifferent

8 You hear a woman talking about attending a fitness camp. During which activity did the woman get injured?
   A running   B doing yoga
   C playing hockey

Everyday English

G **Choose the correct response.**

1 A: Hello, Ann's Salon. How can I help?
   B: a I had to work late at short notice.
      b I'd like to rearrange my appointment.

2 A: When would you like to rearrange it for?
   B: a How about Friday the 2nd at 11am?
      b See you on the 11th.

3 A: I'm stuck in traffic and can't get there in time.
   B: a What time was your appointment?
      b I'm sorry that time is booked.

4 A: What time was your lesson?
   B: a It was supposed to be at 3pm today.
      b Next Monday at 1pm, if possible?

5 A: Could you come in on Tuesday at 9am?
   B: a That time is unavailable.
      b That should be fine.

6 A: There's been a family emergency.
   B: a I hope things get better soon.
      b I'm not feeling well.

7 A: How about next Thursday at the same time?
   B: a I'm sorry to hear that.
      b I'm afraid that time isn't available.

8 A: OK. So see you on the 18th!
   B: a Great. Thank you very much.
      b You're welcome.

9 A: Can I rearrange my lesson?
   B: a I got stuck in traffic.
      b When was it scheduled for?

Writing

H **Write an article about a famous person from your country (200-250 words). Mention:**

- who they are and what they are famous for
- what they are like (appearance, character, achievements, etc)
- why you admire them

Matura Oral Exams

Zestaw egzaminacyjny 1

- Świat przyrody
- Życie rodzinne i towarzyskie
- Turystyka i podróżowanie

Rozmowa wstępna (2 min)

Środki masowego przekazu

- What are the different types of mass media?
- Which ones do you use to get your news and information? Why?
- How much trust do you place in the media?
- How has the Internet influenced the mass media?
- Why is the Internet so popular?

Kultura

- Who are some of your favourite writers? Why?
- What type of books do you like to read? Why?
- Do people still go to libraries in your country? Why?/Why not?
- Do you think people will still be reading books fifty years from now?
- Do you read books online? Why?/Why not?

Praca

- What are popular professions in your country nowadays? Why?
- How does a university degree help you in the workplace?
- What's more important: job satisfaction or a high salary?
- What qualities make a good employee?
- Where do you see yourself working ten years from now?

Zadanie 1
Rozmowa z odgrywaniem roli (3 min)

Dyrektor szkoły poprosił uczniów, aby przedstawili propozycje prac, które chcą wykonać w trakcie obchodów Dnia Ziemi. Twoja klasa wytypowała Cię, abyś je zaprezentował/-a. W rozmowie z dyrektorem uwzględnij cztery poniższe kwestie.

- korzyści dla środowiska
- opis prac
- miejsce wykonywania prac
- korzyści edukacyjne dla uczniów

Zadanie 2
Opis ilustracji i odpowiedzi na pytania (4 min)
Opisz ilustrację.

Odpowiedz na pytania.

1 How do the people in the picture feel?
2 What kind of activities do you do with your family?
3 How much time do people spend with their families these days?

Zadanie 3
Wypowiedź na podstawie materiału stymulującego (5 min)

Przeczytaj zadanie i przygotuj swoją wypowiedź. Masz na to około minuty.

Popatrz na Zdjęcie 1, Zdjęcie 2 i Zdjęcie 3.

Wybierasz się z weekendową wizytą do przyjaciela mieszkającego w Londynie. Przyjaciel zapytał Cię, co chciałbyś/ chciałabyś robić podczas pobytu w stolicy.

- Z przedstawionych niżej sposobów spędzania wolnego czasu wybierz jeden, który najbardziej Ci odpowiada. Uzasadnij swój wybór.
- Wyjaśnij, dlaczego odrzucasz pozostałe możliwości.

Zdjęcie 1

Zdjęcie 2

Zdjęcie 3

Odpowiedz na pytania.

1 What kind of sights do people visit on holiday?
2 Is it better to visit places on your own or as part of a tour?
3 What are some popular tourist destinations in the world?
4 What is the most memorable holiday you have ever had?

Zestaw egzaminacyjny 2

- Zakupy i usługi
- Żywienie
- Nauka i technika

Rozmowa wstępna (2 min)

Człowiek

- What does your best friend look like?
- What is he/she like?
- What would you say is his/her best quality? Why?
- Have you got the same interests? What are they?
- What makes a friend trustworthy?

Szkoła

- What is your favourite subject in school? Why?
- Do you take part in any after-school activities? Which ones?
- What are some of the benefits of after-school activities?
- What happens if you break the rules at school?
- What are some of the qualities that make a good teacher?

Sport

- Do you play any kind of sport?
- Are there many sports facilities in your area? What kind?
- Do you support a particular sports team? How?
- What are the most popular sports in your country?
- What type of sport do you not enjoy watching? Why?

Zadanie 1
Rozmowa z odgrywaniem roli (3 min)

Kupiłeś/-aś aparat cyfrowy, który okazał się być wadliwy.
W rozmowie ze sprzedawcą uwzględnij cztery poniższe kwestie.

- data zakupu aparatu
- określenie problemu
- przedstawienie żądania
- niedogodności związane z problemem

Zadanie 2
Opis ilustracji i odpowiedzi na pytania (4 min)

Opisz ilustrację.

Odpowiedz na pytania.

1. How do the people in the picture feel?
2. What is your favourite meal or recipe?
3. Which appliances help people save time in the kitchen?

Zadanie 3
Wypowiedź na podstawie materiału stymulującego (5 min)

Przeczytaj zadanie i przygotuj swoją wypowiedź. Masz na to około minuty.

Popatrz na Zdjęcie 1, Zdjęcie 2 i Zdjęcie 3.

Twoja szkoła otrzymała dotację, którą zamierza wydać na sprzęt wspomagający naukę.

- Z przedstawionych poniżej rodzajów sprzętu wybierz jeden, który wydaje Ci się najbardziej odpowiedni. Uzasadnij swój wybór.
- Wyjaśnij, dlaczego odrzucasz pozostałe możliwości.

Zdjęcie 1

Zdjęcie 2

Zdjęcie 3

Odpowiedz na pytania.

1 How important is technology in education?
2 Has technology made our lives easier over the years? Why?/Why not?
3 What invention in history, in your opinion, affected people's lives the most? Why?
3 What kinds of gadgets are popular at the moment?

Irregular Verbs

Left columns

Infinitive	Past	Past Participle
be /biː/	was /wɒz/	been /bɪn/
bear /beər/	bore /bɔːʳ/	born(e) /bɔːʳn/
beat /biːt/	beat /biːt/	beaten /biːtᵊn/
become /bɪkʌm/	became /bɪkeɪm/	become /bɪkʌm/
begin /bɪgɪn/	began /bɪgæn/	begun /bɪgʌn/
bite /baɪt/	bit /bɪt/	bitten /bɪtᵊn/
blow /bloʊ/	blew /bluː/	blown /bloʊn/
break /breɪk/	broke /broʊk/	broken /broʊkən/
bring /brɪŋ/	brought /brɔːt/	brought /brɔːt/
build /bɪld/	built /bɪlt/	built /bɪlt/
burn /bɜːrn/	burnt (burned) /bɜːʳnt (bɜːʳnd)/	burnt (burned) /bɜːʳnt (bɜːʳnd)/
burst /bɜːrst/	burst /bɜːʳst/	burst /bɜːʳst/
buy /baɪ/	bought /bɔːt/	bought /bɔːt/
can /kæn/	could /kʊd/	(been able to) /bɪn eɪbᵊl tə/
catch /kætʃ/	caught /kɔːt/	caught /kɔːt/
choose /tʃuːz/	chose /tʃoʊz/	chosen /tʃoʊzᵊn/
come /kʌm/	came /keɪm/	come /kʌm/
cost /kɒst/	cost /kɒst/	cost /kɒst/
cut /kʌt/	cut /kʌt/	cut /kʌt/
deal /diːl/	dealt /delt/	dealt /delt/
dig /dɪg/	dug /dʌg/	dug /dʌg/
do /duː/	did /dɪd/	done /dʌn/
draw /drɔː/	drew /druː/	drawn /drɔːn/
dream /driːm/	dreamt (dreamed) /dremt (driːmd)/	dreamt (dreamed) /dremt (driːmd)/
drink /drɪŋk/	drank /dræŋk/	drunk /drʌŋk/
drive /draɪv/	drove /droʊv/	driven /drɪvᵊn/
eat /iːt/	ate /eɪt/	eaten /iːtᵊn/
fall /fɔːl/	fell /fel/	fallen /fɔːlən/
feed /fiːd/	fed /fed/	fed /fed/
feel /fiːl/	felt /felt/	felt /felt/
fight /faɪt/	fought /fɔːt/	fought /fɔːt/
find /faɪnd/	found /faʊnd/	found /faʊnd/
fly /flaɪ/	flew /fluː/	flown /floʊn/
forbid /fərbɪd/	forbade /fəʳbæd/	forbidden /fəʳbɪdᵊn/
forget /fərget/	forgot /fəʳgɒt/	forgotten /fəʳgɒtᵊn/
forgive /fərgɪv/	forgave /fəʳgeɪv/	forgiven /fəʳgɪvᵊn/
freeze /friːz/	froze /froʊz/	frozen /froʊzᵊn/
get /get/	got /gɒt/	got /gɒt/
give /gɪv/	gave /geɪv/	given /gɪvᵊn/
go /goʊ/	went /went/	gone /gɒn/
grow /groʊ/	grew /gruː/	grown /groʊn/
hang /hæŋ/	hung (hanged) /hʌŋ (hæŋd)/	hung (hanged) /hʌŋ (hæŋd)/
have /hæv/	had /hæd/	had /hæd/
hear /hɪər/	heard /hɜːʳd/	heard /hɜːʳd/
hide /haɪd/	hid /hɪd/	hidden /hɪdᵊn/
hit /hɪt/	hit /hɪt/	hit /hɪt/
hold /hoʊld/	held /held/	held /held/
hurt /hɜːrt/	hurt /hɜːʳt/	hurt /hɜːʳt/
keep /kiːp/	kept /kept/	kept /kept/
know /noʊ/	knew /njuː/	known /noʊn/

Right columns

Infinitive	Past	Past Participle
lead /liːd/	led /led/	led /led/
learn /lɜːrn/	learnt (learned) /lɜːʳnt (lɜːʳnd)/	learnt (learned) /lɜːʳnt (lɜːʳnd)/
leave /liːv/	left /left/	left /left/
lend /lend/	lent /lent/	lent /lent/
let /let/	let /let/	let /let/
light /laɪt/	lit /lɪt/	lit /lɪt/
lose /luːz/	lost /lɒst/	lost /lɒst/
make /meɪk/	made /meɪd/	made /meɪd/
mean /miːn/	meant /ment/	meant /ment/
meet /miːt/	met /met/	met /met/
pay /peɪ/	paid /peɪd/	paid /peɪd/
put /pʊt/	put /pʊt/	put /pʊt/
read /riːd/	read /red/	read /red/
ride /raɪd/	rode /roʊd/	ridden /rɪdᵊn/
ring /rɪŋ/	rang /ræŋ/	rung /rʌŋ/
rise /raɪz/	rose /roʊz/	risen /rɪzᵊn/
run /rʌn/	ran /ræn/	run /rʌn/
say /seɪ/	said /sed/	said /sed/
see /siː/	saw /sɔː/	seen /siːn/
sell /sel/	sold /soʊld/	sold /soʊld/
send /send/	sent /sent/	sent /sent/
set /set/	set /set/	set /set/
sew /soʊ/	sewed /soʊd/	sewn /soʊn/
shake /ʃeɪk/	shook /ʃʊk/	shaken /ʃeɪkən/
shine /ʃaɪn/	shone /ʃɒn/	shone /ʃɒn/
shoot /ʃuːt/	shot /ʃɒt/	shot /ʃɒt/
show /ʃoʊ/	showed /ʃoʊd/	shown /ʃoʊn/
shut /ʃʌt/	shut /ʃʌt/	shut /ʃʌt/
sing /sɪŋ/	sang /sæŋ/	sung /sʌŋ/
sit /sɪt/	sat /sæt/	sat /sæt/
sleep /sliːp/	slept /slept/	slept /slept/
smell /smel/	smelt (smelled) /smelt (smeld)/	smelt (smelled) /smelt (smeld)/
speak /spiːk/	spoke /spoʊk/	spoken /spoʊkən/
spell /spel/	spelt (spelled) /spelt (speld)/	spelt (spelled) /spelt (speld)/
spend /spend/	spent /spent/	spent /spent/
stand /stænd/	stood /stʊd/	stood /stʊd/
steal /stiːl/	stole /stoʊl/	stolen /stoʊlᵊn/
stick /stɪk/	stuck /stʌk/	stuck /stʌk/
sting /stɪŋ/	stung /stʌŋ/	stung /stʌŋ/
swear /sweər/	swore /swɔːʳ/	sworn /swɔːʳn/
sweep /swiːp/	swept /swept/	swept /swept/
swim /swɪm/	swam /swæm/	swum /swʌm/
take /teɪk/	took /tʊk/	taken /teɪkən/
teach /tiːtʃ/	taught /tɔːt/	taught /tɔːt/
tear /teər/	tore /tɔːʳ/	torn /tɔːʳn/
tell /tel/	told /toʊld/	told /toʊld/
think /θɪŋk/	thought /θɔːt/	thought /θɔːt/
throw /θroʊ/	threw /θruː/	thrown /θroʊn/
understand /ʌndərstænd/	understood /ʌndəʳstʊd/	understood /ʌndəʳstʊd/
wake /weɪk/	woke /woʊk/	woken /woʊkən/
wear /weər/	wore /wɔːʳ/	worn /wɔːʳn/
win /wɪn/	won /wʌn/	won /wʌn/
write /raɪt/	wrote /roʊt/	written /rɪtᵊn/